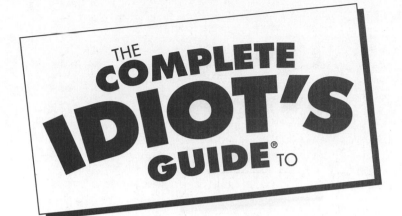

THE

COMPLETE IDIOT'S GUIDE® TO

Boosting Your Financial IQ

by Ken Clark, CFP®

D0250892

ALPHA

A member of Penguin Group (USA) Inc.

To the honest and knowledgeable advisors out there—may everyone recognize how priceless your wisdom is.

ALPHA BOOKS

Published by the Penguin Group

Penguin Group (USA) Inc., 375 Hudson Street, New York, New York 10014, USA

Penguin Group (Canada), 90 Eglinton Avenue East, Suite 700, Toronto, Ontario M4P 2Y3, Canada (a division of Pearson Penguin Canada Inc.)

Penguin Books Ltd., 80 Strand, London WC2R 0RL, England

Penguin Ireland, 25 St. Stephen's Green, Dublin 2, Ireland (a division of Penguin Books Ltd.)

Penguin Group (Australia), 250 Camberwell Road, Camberwell, Victoria 3124, Australia (a division of Pearson Australia Group Pty. Ltd.)

Penguin Books India Pvt. Ltd., 11 Community Centre, Panchsheel Park, New Delhi—110 017, India

Penguin Group (NZ), 67 Apollo Drive, Rosedale, North Shore, Auckland 1311, New Zealand (a division of Pearson New Zealand Ltd.)

Penguin Books (South Africa) (Pty.) Ltd., 24 Sturdee Avenue, Rosebank, Johannesburg 2196, South Africa

Penguin Books Ltd., Registered Offices: 80 Strand, London WC2R 0RL, England

Copyright © 2009 by Ken Clark, CFP®

International Standard Book Number: 978-1-59257-941-9
Library of Congress Catalog Card Number: 2009928399

11   10   09   8   7   6   5   4   3   2   1

Interpretation of the printing code: The rightmost number of the first series of numbers is the year of the book's printing; the rightmost number of the second series of numbers is the number of the book's printing. For example, a printing code of 09-1 shows that the first printing occurred in 2009.

Printed in the United States of America

Note: This publication contains the opinions and ideas of its author. It is intended to provide helpful and informative material on the subject matter covered. It is sold with the understanding that the author and publisher are not engaged in rendering professional services in the book. If the reader requires personal assistance or advice, a competent professional should be consulted.

The author and publisher specifically disclaim any responsibility for any liability, loss, or risk, personal or otherwise, which is incurred as a consequence, directly or indirectly, of the use and application of any of the contents of this book.

Most Alpha books are available at special quantity discounts for bulk purchases for sales promotions, premiums, fund-raising, or educational use. Special books, or book excerpts, can also be created to fit specific needs.

For details, write: Special Markets, Alpha Books, 375 Hudson Street, New York, NY 10014.

Publisher: *Marie Butler-Knight*
Editorial Director: *Mike Sanders*
Senior Managing Editor: *Billy Fields*
Executive Editor: *Randy Ladenheim-Gil*
Development Editor: *Lynn Northrup*
Production Editor: *Kayla Dugger*
Copy Editor: *Amy Borrelli*

Cartoonist: *Steve Barr*
Book Designer: *Trina Wurst*
Cover Designer: *Kurt Owens*
Indexer: *Tonya Heard*
Layout: *Brian Massey*
Proofreader: *Laura Caddell*

Contents at a Glance

Contents

6 Your Mutual Funds · 75

7 Your 401(k) and Retirement Plans · 89

Introduction

As a kid, one of my favorite Saturday morning rituals was watching that Looney Tunes cartoon featuring the Road Runner and Wile E. Coyote. I used to love watching that poor coyote fail miserably in his quest to nab the Road Runner. It was a seemingly simple task that always ended with the coyote being blown up, falling off a cliff, or being run over by a semi truck—usually with a look of exhausted resignation on his face.

Well, my guess is that if you're picking up this book, you're probably feeling a little bit like that coyote. But instead of chasing after the Road Runner, you're chasing after financial stability, the growth of your net worth, and even financial freedom. But no matter how hard you try to accomplish your goals, you may feel like you just can't seem to catch a break. In fact, just like that ACME company in the old cartoon, the only people who seem to be getting ahead are the people who sell you the supposed "solutions" to your financial problems.

That brings me to what this book is meant to be. It's an insider's guide to catching your financial Road Runner. More than that, it's a manual to helping you understand what the ACMEs of your world are trying to sell you. It's a behind-the-scenes look at what works, what doesn't work, and how others are trying to maximize their profits off your quest for financial freedom. It's about boosting your financial IQ so you feel more in control of your financial future.

By the time you've finished this book, you'll be able to walk down the street with your head held a little higher. You'll feel smart enough to have a conversation with that fast-talking stockbroker, wise enough to say no to that new account you're offered at the bank, and informed enough to avoid some of the most common financial pitfalls that detour most people.

In this book, you'll learn:

- How banks, brokerages, and every other kind of financial service profession makes their money at your expense.

- How to spot and protect yourself against some of the nastiest tricks of the trade.

- How to read that dreaded fine print, as well as the rules they don't want you to notice.

◆ How to negotiate and save big on some of life's biggest expenses.

◆ Some little known shortcuts on the road to financial freedom and security.

Since we're on a mission to increase your financial IQ, I want you to view this book as your "textbook" of sorts. Except that you can write all over this one without your teacher getting mad at you (in fact, I'd like to encourage you to do just that).

How This Book Is Organized

The wisdom crammed into this book is divided into five parts grouped by common themes. That way, if you've got a pressing need in one of these areas, you'll know exactly where to skip to:

Part 1, "The Basics of Financial IQ," reviews the day-to-day topics you'll encounter as you manage the flow of money in and out of your household. Not only will we talk about how to protect yourself from your profit-hungry bank and credit card companies, we'll give you the opportunity to quiz your knowledge and see exactly what subjects you need the most help on.

Part 2, "Grow Your Investing IQ," takes the mystery out of some of the most confusing and frustrating financial relationships many of us have. We'll take a look at Wall Street's efforts to profit at your expense, your investment advisor's hidden agendas, and the fine print of mutual funds and 401(k)s.

Part 3, "Build Your Real Estate IQ," takes a hard look at an industry that has left many Americans feeling cheated, lied to, and taken advantage of. You'll learn how to cut through the sales pitches so that life after you move in doesn't turn into a living nightmare.

Part 4, "Life's Big Expenses," gives you the heads up on some of life's costs that are major setbacks for the unprepared and less than savvy. Whether it's understanding health care, buying a car, dealing with college costs, or getting life insurance, you'll be armed and ready to make an informed financial stand.

Part 5, "Dealing with Your Uncle Sam," helps you deal with that obnoxious member of your financial family that you wish would stop showing up and ruining all the fun. Whether it's taxes, Social Security, Medicare, or government assistance programs, you'll learn how to take charge and protect yourself.

Extras

One of the things that sticks out to me about those with a high IQ is how they are masters of the random factoid. They know all kinds of useful tidbits about all kinds of stuff. Well, when it comes to having a high financial IQ, I want you to be that person. Not just because I want you to be able to impress people at cocktail parties, but because there are a lot of little things that you just need to know. So throughout this book, I've added four types of sidebars to help fill you in:

def•i•ni•tion

No longer will you sit there with a glazed-over look when some professional starts in with the financial jargon. By the time you're done, you'll know exactly what they're talking about.

Watch Your Back

Increasing your financial IQ isn't just about book knowledge, but also about street smarts. As we go, I'll point out some of the dark alleys and shady figures you want to be sure to avoid.

In the Know

These short nuggets of knowledge are some of the best tips and tricks I've run across for getting your financial ducks in a row.

Your Bottom Line

Many of the topics in this book have a direct effect on your financial bottom line. Whether they change your credit score, save you some cold hard cash, or improve the way your money grows, you can look here to see how it'll affect you in real dollars.

Acknowledgements

As always, I'd like to thank my amazingly patient and wise editors at Penguin/Alpha Books, Randy Ladenheim-Gil and Lynn Northrup.

To my agent, Bob Diforio at D4EO Literary Agency, I'm continually thankful for your advice and guidance.

To the marketing and publicity gurus who have helped me make a career out of writing; Gardi Wilks and Patty Henek at Wilks PR and Dawn Werk at Penguin Books.

To the other talented authors and editors who've given me a chance to share my knowledge and hone my skills, especially Melissa Phipps at About.com, Sean Joyner at Investopedia.com, Rachel Humenny at Investopedia.com, and Tara Struyk at Investopedia.com.

To my dad, Ken Clark Sr., who wrote the book on caring for clients like they were family.

To my grandparents, Hu and Patty Clark, who filled my childhood with science, culture, politics, and travels. No discussion of IQ would be complete without mentioning the impact you two have had.

To Drew, Price, and Ryan, who are all so smart and unique in their own ways. I've learned as much watching you as I've ever been able to teach.

But most of all, to my wife, Michele. Marrying you was the smartest thing I've ever done. You sacrifice endlessly for our family and for me. Any success I enjoy is wholly attributable to you.

Trademarks

All terms mentioned in this book that are known to be or are suspected of being trademarks or service marks have been appropriately capitalized. Alpha Books and Penguin Group (USA) Inc. cannot attest to the accuracy of this information. Use of a term in this book should not be regarded as affecting the validity of any trademark or service mark.

Part 1

The Basics of Financial IQ

Legendary football coach Vince Lombardi once lamented that many people focus too much on the complexities of football without mastering the basics. Nothing could be truer when it comes to your financial IQ. People who try to master complex topics like investing without a thorough working knowledge of the basics of banking and credit often do no better than breaking even. In this part, we'll test your financial IQ and then go over some of the most common tricks, traps, and tips that you need to know to make the most out of your relationships with banks and credit card companies.

Chapter 1

What Is a Financial IQ?

In This Chapter

- Financial literacy vs. financial IQ
- How and why professionals keep you in the dark
- Why your low financial IQ equals big profits for others
- The best investment you'll ever make
- Take a quiz to gauge your financial IQ

If you're like most people, when you hear someone described as having a high financial "IQ," you immediately assume that they must know a lot of things about personal finances. You'd almost imagine them as a walking encyclopedia of facts and rules, or some type of walking calculator that can perform complex mathematical calculations. But that's not really what IQ is; that's more a description of financial literacy.

Financial literacy refers more to knowing facts and figures about personal finances, whereas financial IQ is the ability to use and learn from those facts and figures. Our highest goal should be to continually increase our financial IQs by making ourselves financially literate.

Understanding Financial IQ

Similar to the normal concept of IQ, *financial IQ* is as much a measure of someone's ability to think critically about a situation as it is a measure of his or her book knowledge. So just like younger children can demonstrate higher IQs than their college-educated parents, people with relatively little personal finance experience can demonstrate a stronger financial IQ than those who have been managing their own finances for 50 years.

def•i•ni•tion

Financial IQ refers to maintaining the knowledge and abilities necessary to reach your financial goals in a world filled with complicated topics, self-interested advisors, and constantly evolving options.

Having a high financial IQ isn't just about knowing every trick, tip, and pitfall that exists for managing your finances. That would require an immense amount of ongoing study, since the world of personal finance and the products are in a constant state of evolution. Rather, it's about understanding the "why" of personal finances so that as you're confronted with new opportunities or situations, you can begin to decipher the best course of action for yourself.

The People Who Prefer You Stay Uneducated

One of the things I figured out early on in my career as a financial planner is that no one goes to work on Wall Street out of the goodness of their hearts. That's not to say that Wall Street isn't filled with charitable people; it most definitely is. Rather, it's to say that the people who advise you on your financial decisions are also trying to earn a very good living doing it. This creates a natural conflict of interest between the best deal for you and the best deal for them.

The same holds true on Main Street, whether it's the people who sell you your insurance or help you finance your home or automobile. They're all in it to make a profit for themselves and their companies. Again, there's nothing wrong with that by itself, but it does put them in a position where your needs often come second to theirs.

Your Bottom Line

Do you know what the top 10 percent of commission-based financial professionals make annually? Look at this list and ask yourself if there's a temptation for them to serve their own best interests over yours:

- ◆ Personal financial advisors: $145,600
- ◆ Insurance sales agents: $115,090
- ◆ Real estate agents: $111,500
- ◆ Loan officers: $107,040

Source: Bureau of Labor Statistics, 2008–2009 Occupational Outlook

The Less You Know, the Better for Them

Having worked in the financial services industry, I can tell you that most professionals *do* work hard to find a balance between making a living and serving their clients' best interests. Yet, most of these professionals would also prefer that you take their word for their trust-worthiness. They'd prefer that you don't know too much about how things actually work. They'd prefer that you don't ask too many questions. They'd prefer that you just trust them and let them do their job.

Sadly, as the saying goes, it only takes one bad apple to ruin the bunch. Having just one advisor who fails to navigate that fine line between your future and theirs can undo much of the progress you've fought for. Therefore, to ensure that you achieve your long-term financial goals with minimal backtracking, you've got to increase your financial IQ to the point where you're your own best advisor. You may still delegate key tasks to different professionals, but you know enough to hold them accountable when something's not right.

How They Keep You in the Dark

Keeping you in a position of trusting dependence is at the heart of most marketing efforts by the folks on Wall Street and Main Street. Their goal is to paint themselves as indispensable guides who can help you navigate decisions you'd be unable to make without them. If they can do that, they've accomplished two things for themselves—they've greatly lowered the chance of your leaving them and they've created a situation where their recommendations and compensation go largely unquestioned.

There are three primary ways that those in the know work to keep you in your place:

- ◆ **Terminology.** If the financial world speaks a foreign language, then you're going to need an interpreter. By not using everyday language to explain relatively simple concepts, they drown you with industry lingo and technical terms, making themselves indispensable in the process.

- ◆ **Fine print.** The fine print has become so excessive in many industries that the professionals can't even tell you exactly what you're signing up for. Not to worry, though—their lawyers will in the event that you think you've got a legitimate claim against them!

- ◆ **Confusing compensation.** Unfortunately, the ways in which companies make money off of you is becoming less and less transparent. Many people in the midst of large financial transactions are completely unable to explain how their different advisors are getting paid. Of course, that leaves plenty of room for professional after professional to whittle away at your hard-earned net worth.

In the Know

Most people begin developing their financial IQ much too late in life, oftentimes only after they've gotten burned. Thankfully, there are a number of nonprofit organizations that are making it their mission to help educate children and young adults in the area of personal finance. For more information about getting a child involved or bringing a program to your local school or youth program, visit the National Endowment for Financial Education at www.nefe.org.

Life's Best Investment: Increasing Your Financial IQ

Many of the most important financial opportunities in life only come along once. If you or someone you're trusting to look out for your best interests fumbles the ball, there may be no recovering from it.

The single best investment you can make in your financial future is to increase your financial IQ. By expanding not just your financial knowledge, but also your perspective of how and why the financial world works, you'll be sure that the road to financial freedom is a one-way street.

Test Your Financial IQ

Any great wilderness guide would tell you that when you've lost your way, the first thing you need to do is figure out exactly where you are. In other words, it's virtually impossible to figure out which way you need to go when you don't know where you're starting from. Even more true is the idea that, if you don't realize you're lost, you've got a bigger problem than just figuring out the way home.

These same ideas hold true with increasing your financial IQ. If you can't identify the areas that you really need to work on, it'll be hard to make significant progress. Even worse, if you don't realize that you've got a problem with your financial IQ, then it's likely that you don't even realize the opportunities you're missing or the ways you're being taken advantage of.

To help you find yourselves on the map, I've put together the following quiz. The questions are pulled from the subjects covered in each chapter of the book and hopefully will help you to know where to focus your extra attention. Go ahead and circle the answers right here in your book. Ready?

In the Know

I've designed a companion website for this book, YourFinanceIQ.com, that contains more quizzes as well as links to other resources that will be of use to you in your journey.

Financial IQ Quiz

What areas of your personal financial situation could use more in-depth study? Answer true or false to each of the following questions:

1. The Federal Reserve requires banks to hold a deposited check of $5,000 or more for a minimum of three business days.

2. Your credit card companies can raise your interest rate without your permission.

3. One of the primary advantages of buying no-load mutual funds is the lack of fees associated with ownership.

4. U.S. Treasury bonds, which are backed by the full faith and credit of the U.S. Treasury, cannot decrease in value.

5. It is legal for your stockbroker or financial advisor to receive trips, golf outings, and gifts for steering you toward his or her favorite mutual fund.

6. In general, most clients of Wall Street stock brokerages cannot sue their brokers over errors, regardless of the magnitude or cost of the error.

7. As part of the 2008 financial bailout, Federal Deposit Insurance Corporation (FDIC) insurance was expanded to cover brokerage accounts.

8. One of the best types of mutual funds to choose for an investor seeking broad diversification is an S&P 500 Index Fund.

9. Taking a loan against your 401(k) can result in the amount being taxed as high as 40 to 50 percent.

10. Most short sales of homes result in a loss that is deductible to the owner.

11. You can receive a major discount on your mutual fund commissions simply by promising to invest more at a later date.

12. If your landlord refuses to repair a broken toilet, you can subtract the cost of repairs from your next rent check.

13. Car dealers cannot truly sell cars at or below their invoice price and make money over the long run.

14. Terminated employees have 60 days to elect continuation of their health plan benefits under COBRA.

15. You can keep your children on your health insurance as long as they are enrolled in college.

16. The average college increases its tuition at twice the rate of inflation.

17. The typical first-year commission on a whole life insurance policy is 90 percent of the total premium you pay.

18. The more tax deductions you claim, the more likely you are to get audited by the IRS.

19. A properly filed bankruptcy will eliminate balances owed to the credit card companies, auto and mortgage lenders, and the IRS.

20. Refinancing their homes every few years when rates drop ends up saving Americans a ton of money in the long run.

Score Your Financial IQ Quiz

So how did you do? Did you feel like you knew most of the answers? Or, did you feel like you were taking a test meant for rocket scientists?

Go ahead and take a few minutes to score yourself with the following answer key. Give yourself one point for each answer you got right (that's 20 possible points). Don't worry too much about the explanations now; I'll be touching on each area in depth throughout the book in the chapters referenced next.

1. **False.** The Federal Reserve doesn't place any requirements on banks to hold checks. While some banks do this to protect themselves and you, others do it to earn a little extra interest for themselves on your money (see Chapter 2).

2. **True.** Most credit card companies *can* raise your interest rates on purchases without your permission. You technically gave them this right when you signed up for the card. Further, even though new federal legislation will require notice of increases, it does not keep them from increasing your rate for a number of valid reasons (see Chapter 3).

3. **False.** While no-load mutual funds do not charge an up-front commission or surrender fee, they still charge an annual management fee, which can easily exceed 1 percent of your invested amount per year (see Chapter 5).

4. **False.** The U.S. Treasury only guarantees the value of its bonds at their maturity date. If they are sold prior to their maturity date, they may experience a gain or loss depending on the movement of interest rates (see Chapter 4).

5. **True.** Unfortunately, there are numerous legal and regulatory loopholes that allow mutual fund companies to reward brokers with noncash incentives on top of the commission or fees they earn (see Chapter 5).

6. **True.** Most new account forms for Wall Street brokerage firms contain an "arbitration clause" in which you agree to binding arbitration in place of filing a lawsuit (see Chapter 5).

7. **False.** The FDIC, which guarantees the safety of certain deposits at member banks, does not provide any coverage for securities firms (see Chapter 5).

8. **False.** Despite the term "S&P 500" seeming to imply that an investor owns 500 stocks in equal proportions, these funds (as well as the index) are affected primarily by the fortunes of just 10 to 20 companies (see Chapter 6).

9. **False.** While a 401(k) loan by itself is not taxable, it becomes a distribution in the eyes of the IRS the moment your employment is terminated. If it cannot be repaid within a short period of time, you will owe federal and state income taxes plus a 10 percent penalty (see Chapter 7).

10. **False.** Most short sales in fact result in the owner of a home being forgiven a portion of the mortgage, which may be includable as income for many taxpayers (see Chapter 8).

11. **True.** Most mutual funds allow investors to sign a "letter of intent" and receive a discounted commission now for promising to invest more within a reasonable period of time (see Chapter 6).

12. **True.** While there are certain rules about documenting the expenses, most states allow a tenant to subtract costs from their rent payment if a landlord will not provide necessary repairs (see Chapter 10).

13. **False.** It is not uncommon for car dealers to make larger profits off the resale of your trade-in or ongoing maintenance than on the initial sale of the car (see Chapter 12).

14. **True.** Generally, terminated employees have 60 days, subject to certain notice requirements, to elect continuation of their health plan benefits under COBRA (see Chapter 11).

15. **False.** Being in college does not guarantee that your child is permitted to stay on your health insurance. Different states and companies allow different cut-offs for inclusion, which often affect students who wait a few years before starting college (see Chapter 11).

16. **True.** The typical college in America increases its tuition at a rate of 5 to 6 percent annually, approximately twice the historical rate of inflation in the United States (see Chapter 13).

17. **True.** Most life insurance policies pay a commission to the agent that is approximately 90 percent of all the premiums you pay in your first year. This makes life insurance one of the highest-commission financial products anyone can sell you (see Chapter 14).

18. **False.** Claiming numerous deductions doesn't necessarily put you at risk of an audit compared to someone with few or no deductions. The audit trigger system at the IRS is much more complex (and accurate) than that and compares a variety of factors (such as income, line of work, type of deductions, etc.) against national averages (see Chapter 15).

19. **False.** Many types of bankruptcy do not eliminate balances owed, but create payment plans instead. Further, no form of bankruptcy discharges money you owe to the IRS (see Chapter 17).

20. **False.** Because most people continually refinance with 30-year mortgages, they end up paying far more in interest (even with their lower payment) than if they had kept their original loan and paid it off in 30 years (see Chapter 9).

If you got 18 or more answers correct, congratulations, you're at the top of your game! Hopefully, this book will fill in those last few holes for you.

If you got between 14 and 17 answers correct, you should still give yourself a pat on the back. You know more than most people, but it's still enough to leave you exposed to some major financial pitfalls. Instead of learning the answers the hard way, I'd suggest you put your feet up and spend some time reading.

If you got fewer than 14 answers correct, then you're like the vast majority of people who have taken this quiz. In fact, the average score for most people is somewhere around 10 answers correct. So even if you totally bombed, *that just means you're normal.* But at least for you, that's about to change. By the end of this book, you'll be well on your way to raising your financial IQ beyond that of the average Joe or Jane. In fact, don't be surprised if people begin turning to you for financial advice.

The Least You Need to Know

- Increasing your financial IQ isn't just about learning more facts; it's about building an awareness of how and why to look out for your own interests.

- Even the best professionals must wrestle with a conflict of interest between serving your needs and making a living off of you.

- To grow your financial IQ, you'll need to break the chains of terminology, fine print, and confusing compensation structures.

- Increasing your financial IQ will get you farther than picking the best mutual fund, buying the right real estate, or using your credit cards wisely ever will.

Chapter 2

Banking On Your Ignorance

In This Chapter

- ◆ The evolving nature of banking
- ◆ How banks take your money
- ◆ What they won't tell you
- ◆ Tips for lowering your banking costs

In the literary classic by Dante, *Inferno*, the deepest level of Hades was reserved for a really special group of folks. As punishment for their "cold" acts, they were frozen into a lake of ice, doomed to spend the rest of eternity wishing for a warm pair of socks.

What deeds could warrant such disdain and cruel punishment? The poor souls in Dante's tale were traitors—people who had betrayed a trusted relationship with someone else. My guess is that if Dante were to write an updated version of his book, he'd be sure to include a few bank executives in his "rink of regret."

Banks, which often play the most basic and central role in many people's finances, have evolved into one of the largest violators of consumer trust. Does your bank promise convenience and service, all the while picking your pocket through hidden fees? Does your bank promise you a juicy interest rate on a savings account, only to load it down with rules about minimum balances and transactions? When it comes to banks, the only hope for a sane co-existence comes from you knowing their agenda and their tricks. You've got to develop your financial IQ in a way that ensures that banks are serving you, not the other way around.

How Banks Profit Off of You

The banking industry has evolved immensely in the last 30 to 40 years. In the good old days, even the branches of the largest banks had a hometown feel to them. You were on a first-name basis with the tellers and often the bank manager. You'd get a telephone call if your account was overdrawn or a check was going to bounce. Some banks even gave out toasters for opening a new account. It was a simple, happy existence where banks made their living off of an $8 to $10 monthly account fee and lending money to other customers.

But then deregulation, ATMs, and online banking came along. Banks found themselves in an interesting position of having their fees squeezed by competitors, while simultaneously being able to serve their customers without ever having to see them face-to-face. What followed was an unprecedented era of banks scrambling to attract customers with big promises, while secretly decreasing customer service and increasing sources of hidden revenue.

Watch Your Back

While it might be tempting to overlook the significance of this chapter, don't. If you can protect just $15 a month of your money from banks trying to turn a profit, that's the equivalent of $22,355 in additional savings over a 30-year period (assuming 8 percent growth of savings). That's like winning a free car!

Unfortunately, no amount of financial IQ will change the lack of customer service that exists at most larger national banks. But developing your understanding of how banks try and use you to pad their bottom line is crucial in keeping hundreds of dollars from evaporating from your wallet every year.

Fees, Fees, and More Fees

Pirate jokes are all the rage with my elementary school–aged kids right now. The punch line to every joke has to do with the letter "Argh!"

Of course, I couldn't help but think of the treasure-plundering ways of pirates when someone recently asked me about the growing trend of banks offering "free" accounts. I responded by telling them, in a cheesy pirate accent, that the only difference between a "free" bank account and one charging a "fee" is the letter "ARGH!"

In all seriousness, though, the trend toward free bank accounts is nothing more than a marketing gimmick banks use to lure people in. The reality is, banks are happily waiving monthly fees because they're robbing you at every turn with other administrative and transaction-related fees.

Lending Activities

Aside from charging ridiculous fees for things that essentially cost a bank nothing, the next most profitable activity for banks is lending money. Whether it is loans for homes, cars, or businesses, every bank desperately wants you to borrow money, even if you don't need it. Of course, banks aren't made of money, so they're in fact actually lending out the money their customers deposit at the bank.

You'd be hard-pressed to find a process filled with more bitter ironies for consumers. Banks that typically pay low rates of interest on customer deposits turn around and lend it out at much higher rates, netting the difference. Even more insulting is the fact that many of the people whose deposits are lent out by their bank are not considered credit worthy enough to borrow those same funds!

The biggest single factor affecting your cost of borrowing is always going to be your credit history and credit score. Before you approach your bank or any other lender, you should have a good handle on your unique creditworthiness. You can receive your credit report for free at www.annualcreditreport.com and your credit score for a small fee at www.myfico.com.

If your FICO credit score is under 700, you need to begin doing some homework about how to raise your score. While there are no silver bullets (despite what you might hear on those debt reduction TV commercials), a little hard work, education, and time to heal can do a lot for your score. More than anything else, you need to begin paying your bills on time and trimming down your existing loan and credit card balances. Check out *The Complete Idiot's Guide to Getting Out of Debt* (see Appendix B) for a step-by-step guide.

Co-Branded Products

In recent years, one of the most alarming trends in American consumer finance has been the purchase of some of the largest nonbanking financial institutions by banks. Just like that horror movie *The Blob*, banks are slowly gobbling up Wall Street brokerage houses, mortgage lenders, insurance companies, etc. The result for consumers is more *co-branded product* being waved in their faces. Those with a high financial IQ know that this leads to increased sales pitches, sneaky cross marketing, and less competitive costs and features.

def•i•ni•tion

A **co-branded product** is one that looks like it is offered by a separate company, but in reality is owned by the same mammoth company that is already providing all your other financial services.

Tricks of the Trade

Virtually everyone has been through this scenario at least once, if not on a semiregular basis. You stop at the ATM on the way out for a fun night and your account is somehow overdrawn by some random amount like $227.50. Thinking it must be an error, you rush home, log on to your bank's online banking site, and discover that your paycheck hasn't been direct deposited yet. As a result, this morning's $4 latte, the gas you bought yesterday, and your newspaper subscription all caused you to be overdrawn. Instead of simply denying your debit card when you went to pay, your bank was kind enough to put the transactions through, knowing full well each one was worth a $30 NSF (nonsufficient funds) fee. Of course, when your paycheck comes, the money you need for bills is already partially consumed by these fees!

One of the most frustrating things about banks is that they seem to make up the rules as they go. It's almost as if they're looking for opportunities to charge you a fee, and change the rules just to make it happen. When you actually call and complain, they refer you to some obscure piece of fine print that you can almost swear wasn't there before.

Due to the almost impossible customer service process at most large banks, it's crucial that you steer clear of these revenue tricks. Once they find a reason to suck up some of your money, it's pretty much as good as gone.

In the Know

A growing number of class-action lawsuits are being filed against banks for their excessive fees and unethical business practices. To find out if one of your current or prior banks is being sued and how you might recoup some of your money, visit www.classactionworld.com, a free site that tracks lawsuits and provides claim instructions.

Overdraft/NSF Fees

You would think that banks would close the accounts of careless or accounting-challenged people who perpetually spend more money than they have. The truth is, they live for it. Thanks to overdraft fees and NSF fees, banks can now make more than they ever did on monthly account fees.

Think about it: a customer who bounces just five checks per year on their "free" bank account might incur $150 or more in NSF fees. That's more than the bank would've earned in the old days when it charged someone $10 a month for the privilege of just having an account.

What about the customer who bounces one check or makes one over-the-limit purchase *per month?* They're going to pay $360 per year in NSF fees. That makes them one of the best customers the bank has!

You'd think, with the absurd level of these fees, that consumers would have this figured out and banks would be under an extreme amount of pressure to change their practices. Just the opposite. In a recent study from Bankrate.com, the cost of NSF fees has increased 8 out of 10 years from 1998 to 2008. The most recent year's increase was 2½ percent, and there's no sign of a slowdown.

Watch Your Back

While many consumers never have to worry about a "currency fee," anyone planning international purchases or travel should pay close attention. This fee, which generally averages between 2 and 5 percent, is charged by banks when you use your card to make purchases denominated in another currency.

Required Minimum Balances

If you ever see an asterisk after the word "free," it doesn't mean that that this account is reserved just for the bank's favorite customers. That asterisk, like so many others, points those with high financial IQs toward the fine print. Here they discover the account is only free if they meet certain conditions. For example, that free account will cost you $12 per month unless you maintain an average daily balance of at least $5,000, use a live teller, stand on one foot while using the ATM, and put a sticker on your car saying that "Happiness is a XYZ Checking Account."

These minimum balance rules are one of the oldest tricks in banking, tied to both free checking accounts and interest-bearing savings accounts. The juicy perks you were promised are only given if the amount in your account, calculated each day or over the course of the month, stays above a certain amount. Fail to meet this requirement, and you're back at square one.

The required minimum balance version of this trick, which is the older of two versions, simply says that if your balance falls below a certain amount on even just one day during the month, you have to pay the monthly fee. As it turns out, consumers actually managed to follow that straightforward rule, so the banks made it more complex.

The *average daily balance* was the banking industry's answer, and is designed in a way that most consumers will never understand how it's calculated. Just the time alone that it would take to calculate often enough to make a required adjustment makes it not worth the effort to most consumers.

To calculate the average daily balance, a bank adds together the balances your account showed at the end of each day and then divides that total by the number of days that have elapsed in the month. For example, if your bank account had a $2,000 ending balance in it every day in the month of January, your average daily balance would be also $2,000 ($2,000 at the end of each day multiplied by 31 days, then divided by 31 days).

def•i•ni•tion

> **Average daily balance** refers to a mathematical formula that sums up the total of all the month's daily ending balances, then divides them by the total days in the month. Hence, with every day that passes, the average daily balance may actually change, even if there haven't been any recent transactions.

If, however, your account only had $2,000 in it for the first 15 days of January, then you paid all your bills, leaving a zero balance, your average daily balance would drop to $961.75. This number is the result of only 15 days having an ending balance of $2,000, with the remaining 16 days of January carrying no balance. So our average daily balance is calculated by dividing the sum of each days balances ($2,000 × 15 days + $0 × 16 days = $30,000) by the number of days in the month (31).

Of course, since most people have a large balance for only a few days right after they get paid, most people's average daily balance is much smaller than the large limits required to have their fees waived.

Posting Dates and Times

When it comes to how the bank adds your deposits and subtracts your expenditures, what's good for the goose is definitely not good for the gander. Perhaps you've noticed this: how banks subtract your spending immediately but often won't credit your deposits until a day, or maybe even four to five days later. Of course, it works out well for them, because money leaving your account faster than it goes in equals more NSF fees and lower average daily balances.

Here're some examples of what you need to watch out for:

◆ **Daily posting times.** In an effort to generate increased fees, many banks will only count deposits made before a certain time each day, such as 4 P.M. Any deposits made after that are credited to your account on the next business day. Not surprisingly, any checks or debit card purchases presented against your account up until 11:59 P.M. are still counted as that day's transactions, instead of being rolled over like your deposits. That leaves a large gap where NSF situations can occur.

♦ **Delays on transaction types.** As part of their campaign to encourage the use of debit cards, many of the banks have made them look and function like credit cards, right down to the brand-name logo. Unfortunately, when these debit cards are swiped by your local merchant as a credit card, it may delay posting to your account by two to three days. Naturally, this leads to confusion about how much money you've got left to spend in your account. This leads to—you guessed it—more overdraft and NSF fees.

♦ **Holding deposits.** One of the most heinous tricks of banks is "holding" certain deposits to make sure they clear. In the old days, there was some merit to this, since checks took a longer amount of time to be processed and banks did not want to cash a large check that may bounce. However, in today's high-speed information age, there is no valid reason that sizeable deposited checks need to be held three to five working days. No reason, except of course to allow the bank to earn interest off of your money as well as raise the chances that you'll bounce a check or transaction in your account.

 Watch Your Back

One of the most famous bank transaction tricks is known as "reordering." While it would seem logical for a bank to subtract charges and checks in the order they come in, transactions on the same day are often "reordered" so that the biggest transactions are subtracted first. This ensures that all subsequent smaller charges will have a greater chance of being hit with NSF fund fees.

Overdraft Protection

Are you sick of hearing me harp on NSF fees? Are you sick of getting NSF fees? Well, there's good news! The bank that is more than happy to charge them to you, is also more than happy to sell you a product that keeps you from having to pay them.

Aren't banks swell? Of course they are. They're happy to trade the unsure revenue stream that comes with hoping you'll bounce checks and replace it with the *guaranteed* revenue stream of you paying to not bounce checks. If that's not a scam, I'm not sure what is.

Not being one to miss out on an opportunity to make a buck off every aspect of the transaction, the banks make sure that overdraft protection is a fairly raw deal as well. In addition to often paying a monthly fee for the service, you typically pay a per transaction fee of $5 to $10. This sounds much better than $30 per NSF transaction.

Further, many banks set up their NSF feature to work as a loan, charging you double-digit interest rates on the overdrawn amount until you repay it. Some even deposit money to your account in $100 or $250 increments, to "make sure" you don't bounce any more checks. In reality, they're making sure that they get to charge you interest on a larger amount than you actually need until the end of the month, when you get your statement and discover that you've dug yourself into a hole.

The Fine (Almost Invisible) Print

Banks are required under the Truth in Lending and the Truth in Savings acts to fully disclose all the terms relating to their savings and loan accounts. Specifically, the acts require the standardized calculation of interest rates (called APR and APY, respectively) to help consumers fully understand what they're signing up for.

When it comes to the things the banks don't tell, calling it "fine print" does a disservice to how hard they've worked to hide the facts from you. While things like the NSF fees and the average daily balance rule are buried in the fine print for those with high financial IQs to discover, there are other things you'll only know because someone fills you in.

While none of these things are reasons for you to not use a specific bank, they do affect *how* you should use that bank. You need to do your homework in each one of these areas to make sure you're protecting your assets and minimizing your banking costs.

We Act Safe, But ...

With their tall buildings and reassuring commercials, banks would like you to believe that your cash is sitting in a vault on top of a mountain, surrounded by a moat, a pack of rabid attack dogs, and a team of ninja-trained bank guards. The scary reality though, is that for the most part, your bank exists on paper. Your money is not sitting somewhere, but has been loaned back out to other customers. In fact, most banks maintain reserves that are only a small fraction of their total assets.

The only reason most Americans aren't rounding up torches and pitch-forks to go demand their money is that these deposits are guaranteed by the Federal Deposit Insurance Corporation (FDIC), which is directly backed by the U.S. Treasury. Most consumers believe, correctly, that the government would step in to cover a bank's deposits should the bank go out of business.

In the Know

The FDIC offers the ability to check the status of your bank's federal protection through www.myfdicinsurance. gov. Additionally, consumers can sign up for free e-mail alerts when a bank is being taken over by FDIC by visiting the News and Events section of www.fdic.gov.

Unfortunately, as witnessed in the most recent banking crisis, people grew too comfortable with the safety of their banks and their idea of what FDIC covered. Thousands of consumers deposited amounts in excess of the FDIC coverage limits, only to lose them as seemingly top-tier banks folded like old lawn chairs. Further, many falsely assumed that investments bought through their banks, such as most money market accounts, were protected by the FDIC.

Our Tellers Are Salespeople

You know that sweet young lady or charming man who greets you with a smile when you come in to cash your paycheck? The truth is, they won't hesitate to use their relationship with you to make some extra money for themselves.

It's not uncommon for many banks to have sales contests for their tellers, offering lucrative bonuses for those who can open the most new revenue-producing accounts for the bank. In fact, as soon as tellers type in your account number, their screen flashes with an offer they should attempt to make you.

Our Rates Are Lousy

Over the years, I've known a lot of waiters and waitresses at high-end restaurants. They've often told me that dessert is a far easier sale than appetizers or drinks, in part because people often go elsewhere for those first. But once they plop down in that chair and order their big meal, tacking dessert on the end is, as they say, a piece of cake. Because it's such an easy sale, most restaurants don't bother making their own dessert, instead just buying something of lesser gourmet quality from their food supplier.

The same goes when it comes to the credit cards, savings accounts, and loans your bank offers their customers. They're the dessert to your financial main course (the basic checking you came in to do). They know that there's a great chance of getting you to try a piece, since you're already there. Because of that, the fact that you're a bit of a captive audience, they're often going to offer you a lower-quality product than what you deserve.

Even banks that offer the best checking accounts in town often offer some of the highest rate credit cards and loans, along with the lowest rates on savings accounts. They know that only those with a high financial IQ are going to shop around to ensure that every one of their financial transactions is maximized in their best interest instead of any one bank's.

Ways to Save

Throughout this book, you'll hear a lot of recommendations on how to negotiate with the different financial professionals you'll run across in your life. Banks are going to be the exception to that rule.

Since most branch managers are simply following company procedure when it comes to fees and other features, there are only two real ways to lower your banking costs. The first is to follow the rules in their own fine print. The second is to simply find a better bank. High financial IQ individuals typically do both.

Shop Around for Other Banking Options

Classic brick-and-mortar banks are now only one of the many options consumers have when it comes to their checking, borrowing, and saving needs. Finding a solution that works is often just a matter of thinking outside the box and developing a comfort level with other banking formats.

Here's a breakdown of other options to consider based on your unique situation:

♦ **The heavy banker.** If your banking routine (or sanity) depends on you visiting your favorite teller once a week, then you should look into using a federally insured credit union. Unlike banks, which are typically open to anyone, a credit union membership is often built around a unique demographic such as members of a community, employees of a company, or military affiliation. Since credit unions are actually owned by their members (which would include you), the profits of their operations are passed on to consumers in the form of dividends and lower cost services. The only drawback may be the lack of an ATM on every street corner, so you'll need to grab your cash when you have the chance.

The National Credit Union Administration maintains a searchable directory of all credit unions nationwide, as well as information on credit union safety, at www.ncua.gov.

In the Know

If you're shopping for the best CD or money market rates, many larger newspapers publish the best rates from around the country in their Sunday editions. You can also visit websites like Bankrate.com to do some comparison shopping.

♦ **The tech-savvy banker.** If you are already leading a virtual life, you might as well make the jump into online banking. More and more FDIC-insured banks are popping up around the Internet. Even better, since they maintain very few brick-and-mortar locations, they're able to pass the savings on to consumers in the form of lower fees and higher earning accounts.

♦ **The investor.** More and more brokerage firms (both full-service and discount) are offering cash management accounts that give you most of the features of traditional banks. While some of these accounts can come with high fees, they're often waived for investors who maintain larger balances.

Automate Your Accounts

Many of the banks' "free" checking and savings accounts, as well as some of their top-tier features, are offered for free to investors who automate their account functions. In other words, if you can save the bank from having to pay someone to process your transactions, they'll agree to save you some dough in the process.

Examples of features you can automate to receive waived fees or lower costs include:

♦ Setting up direct deposit with your employer

♦ Using the ATM for all deposits and withdrawals

♦ Auto-transfers from another institution

♦ Electronic statements

♦ Online bill pay

♦ Linking multiple accounts within that bank

Open a Business Account

In many consumers' experiences, business accounts are still treated with the same kind of respect that individual accounts were decades ago. For example, when you walk into many branches, there'll be a special (much shorter) line just for business customers, where they also let you do your personal banking. You'll also receive offers for better rates on savings and lending features, and often get the fees waived on your personal accounts! So if you own a small business, you should definitely consider doing your business banking and personal banking at the same institution.

The Least You Need to Know

◆ NSF and bounced check fees have become the number one source of profit for banks with most customers.

◆ Accounts with average daily balance rules are almost impossible for most consumers to succeed with.

◆ Banks apply different rules to the posting times and dates of transactions to generate NSF fees.

◆ The rates offered by your bank are often some of the least competitive available.

◆ More and more consumers are saving money by using credit unions and online banks.

Chapter 3

Credit Cards: Costing You an Arm and a Leg

In This Chapter

- ◆ It's all about the interest
- ◆ Tricks to trip you up
- ◆ Negotiating to save yourself thousands
- ◆ Protecting your credit card rights

In the Disney classic *Pinocchio*, our wooden friend and his pals were seduced into visiting a seemingly wonderful place called Pleasure Island. On Pleasure Island, rebellious boys could do as they pleased with no supervision or accountability. It was heaven on Earth, until the boys realized that they were turning into the "donkeys" that they'd been acting like. At that point, they became lifelong slaves to the people who originally invited them there and provided them with the means of their enjoyment.

I'm not sure I'd view the issuers of credit cards any differently. They invite you to experience life to the fullest by way of their credit cards, but seek to enslave you for their own purposes.

Only instead of pulling their wagons as in the movie, you're padding their company's bottom line.

According to CardWeb.com, the average American household is carrying close to $10,000 in credit card debt, with no path to freedom in sight. Many of these people will spend the next 10 to 20 years of their lives slowly paying down their balance. Instead of building a financial future, they remain enslaved to past purchases.

Increasing your financial IQ has everything to do with avoiding the quicksand of credit card debt, and knowing how to quickly extricate yourself if you do fall in. If you do everything else right financially, but fail at this, there's a good chance that you'll barely break even.

Your Pain, Their Gain

Interestingly enough, many people still have a semineutral view of credit card companies, even if they're drowning in debt. While they rightfully come to terms with their own role in digging themselves into debt, they fail to see the credit card companies as the financial vampires they are, intent on sucking every available dollar from a household.

In the Know

One of the single best things you can do to avoid falling prey to the marketing schemes of credit card companies, as well as to potential identity thieves, is get off the credit card company's mailing list. The quickest way to do this is to visit OptOutPrescreen.com, a free service that will remove you from all marketing lists for five years.

In protecting yourself, you've got to see how they deliberately set about trying to harm you. To not understand the source of their profits is to walk through one of life's largest financial minefields blindfolded.

Charging You Interest

The magic (or curse, depending on how you look at it) of credit cards is compound interest. It's what makes them so ridiculously profitable for their issuers, even after they offer you all those fancy perks like airline miles. It also makes them so ridiculously hard to escape even when you're diligently trying to pay them down.

The killer part of compound interest is that each month after it's calculated, it's added to the balance of the loan on which future interest will be calculated. So next month, you essentially end up paying interest on your interest. Because of this, debt subject to compound interest doesn't grow in a straight line, it grows exponentially, like a mountain that gets steeper with every step you take.

So just as the banks do everything they can to subject you to NSF and other fees (see Chapter 2), credit card companies do everything they can to subject your balances to as much interest as possible. The more excuses they can find to raise your rate or add to your balance, the more profit they generate. Your mission, as someone with a growing financial IQ, is to not let them get away with it.

Charging You Fees

While fees aren't the bread and butter of greedy credit card companies, they're still a potent weapon in their battle to keep you paying interest. Whether it is adding money to your balance or decreasing the amount of your payment that is applied toward it, they accomplish the same goal of slowing your payoff process.

Here are some of the most common fees you need to watch for:

♦ **Late payment fees.** These fees usually range from $20 to $50, and often have a cutoff time, as well as a date. It is not uncommon to see credit card companies require that a payment be received by 11 A.M. Eastern Standard Time, which means that even if your check is delivered on the right day, it still may incur a fee.

In the Know

How do your credit cards measure up? According to a study performed by the nonprofit group Consumer Action, here are the averages for some key credit card costs:

♦ Annual fee: $44.74
♦ Interest rate: 14.53%
♦ Late fee: $28

♦ **Over-the-limit fees.** While most people associate this fee with actually spending above their limit, it's also commonly applied simply if the current month's interest or other fees added to your account push you over your limit.

◆ **Cash advance fees.** While some credit card companies like to advertise the fact that you can use their card to get cash at millions of locations, they fail to mention that they charge you heftily for the privilege. While usually stated as an unintimidating percentage (2 to 4 percent of the withdrawn amount), most cash advance fees also have a hard dollar minimum, such as $5 per transaction. When you do the math, you quickly see that a $20 withdrawal with a $5 fee really amounts to a 25 percent fee!

◆ **Annual fees.** One of the worst things about annual fees is that when you're carrying a balance, you're stuck paying them. Credit cards know this, and commonly raise their annual fee on consumers who are married to a company because of their balance.

◆ **Pay by phone fees.** Want to avoid the $35 late charge? It'll cost you $14.99 …. Virtually all of the credit card companies now offer some type of online or phone payment system for people running short on time. Of course, using this system (something some people do every month) throws one more straw on your financial camel's back.

Selling Other Services

Throughout the book, I talk about the growing trend of financial companies to try and cross sell their co-branded products to you. Of all the companies, credit card issuers have the highest success rate at this, something you should be very aware of.

They're not successful because their products or ability to promote them is that good. Rather, they're successful at cross selling you junky products and services because they have something the others do not … your credit card number!

Because of this, credit card companies are notorious for adding services to your monthly bill that you never requested. The most famous of these is credit insurance, which is also labeled in such a way that most consumers have a tough time even recognizing it on their statement, if you notice it at all.

Credit Card Sucker Punches

Do you remember watching *The Three Stooges?* Often, when Moe would wallop on the other Stooges, he'd hold out his hand and tell the others to look at it. Once they were focused on that hand, he'd use the other to clobber them. That's a sucker punch, and it's something that credit cards have turned into an art form—sticking it to you in ways you never saw coming.

Bait and Switch Rates

One of the most popular tricks is the teaser interest rate. The credit card companies lure you into submitting an application for a new credit card with a great rate. Of course, there's an asterisk attached to that rate that says something like, "rates vary depending on applicant's credit score and credit history."

So big surprise, two weeks later when you get your new credit card in the mail, the rate is 24.99 percent instead of the 11.99 percent that was advertised. Of course, the credit card company knows that between the time you receive the card and when you actually get around to calling to complain, you'll have probably settled into using it.

If this happens to you, you've got to be sure to call immediately. If you can't, cut up the card to make sure you're not tempted to use it.

Watch Your Back

Before you try to find a credit card with a better rate, stop to consider whether you'll be getting a loan in the next 6 to 12 months. The simple process of opening one credit card, transferring a balance, and closing the other can have a noticeable effect on your credit score and ability to qualify for a favorable loan rate.

Ensuring Your Payments Are Late

Just like many banks have subtle policies that put you in a position of bouncing more checks, many credit card companies do everything they can to ensure your payment is late. While that may seem counterintuitive, it's actually a highly profitable practice for them. Every late payment results in a fee and even a possible increase in your interest rate.

How do they pull off this devious act? They've got all kinds of sly tricks you need to be on guard for, for example:

◆ **Due dates near pay dates.** Ever notice how many credit cards have due dates around the first or the fifteenth of the month? By placing the due date near people's paycheck dates, the likelihood of a late payment skyrockets due to payroll problems, banks clearing paychecks, lack of time, etc. Sadly, most consumers subjected to this perpetual bad timing don't realize that they can usually call and simply request a different due date.

One of the easiest ways to avoid due date drama is to sign up for your credit card company's autopay service, not to be confused with online bill pay available through your bank. Under autopay, your credit card company is authorized to subtract the minimum payment directly from your account on its due date.

◆ **Delaying statements.** A few years ago, I used a credit card company that would mail my statement about 10 days before the payment was due. By the time it was in my hands, there were only seven to eight days left to pay on time, which didn't leave much room to adjust for surprises on my bill, post office holidays, etc.

◆ **Sending payments across country.** Many credit card companies have multiple processing locations around the country. In an attempt to give your payment every chance possible to be late, some companies have been known to provide you with a payment mailing address on the other side of the country, instead of their processing center in the next state over.

◆ **Frequently changing the payment address.** Over the years, I've witnessed a number of credit card companies that change their payment address every 6 to 12 months. Of course, their statement and enclosed envelope reflect the change, but that doesn't help out most people who use online bill payment services.

Payment Allocation

Yet more proof that credit card companies have no interest in helping you get out of debt, many use a procedure called "payment allocation." In this practice, credit card companies apply any extra money you send toward reducing the lowest interest rate portion of your balance. For example, if your credit card is half comprised of a balance transfer growing at 6.99 percent and half of new purchases at 29.99 percent, all excess payments above the minimum are applied to the lowest rate until it's paid off.

In the Know

The process of payment allocation can completely wipe out the benefits of a debt reduction strategy that sends your excess funds to the card with the highest interest rate. To ensure that you're not wasting your time, check with each of your credit card companies regarding their policies on how payments are applied to the different interest rate portions of your balance.

Period Calculation Tricks

As discussed in the beginning of this chapter, the profit engine for credit card companies is the calculation of compound interest on your balance. Therefore, the financially astute know that credit card companies will often do anything they can to beef up how this rate is calculated.

One of the most popular tricks, buried in the fine print of your account agreement, involves what is called "double-cycle billing," in which the interest rate calculated is computed on your average daily balance over the *last two* billing cycles (approximately 60 days) instead of over just a single billing cycle. The effect is to raise the amount on which interest is calculated for people successfully decreasing their balance. Consumers carrying a balance on a card using double-cycle billing should make a beeline for a new card.

Follow the Bouncing Rate

I'd be surprised if most consumers still have their initial credit card interest rate after 12 months of using a card. Like a cat watching a mouse, credit card companies are waiting for the smallest excuse to pounce on you and change your rate. Aside from the classic teaser rate, which goes away as expected after the introductory period ends, here are some of the other excuses companies find to raise your rate:

def·i·ni·tion

> Annual percentage rate, or APR, is a federally required method of calculating the interest rate you're being charged on an account. It enables you to make a side-by-side comparison of rates that are often quoted over other time periods such as monthly, quarterly, etc.

♦ **Late payments.** If you look at your credit card's fine print, you'll notice an interest rate called the "default rate." This rate is one the credit card company holds in reserve in the event that you fail to live up to your end of the relationship, which may be as simple as being late on a payment just once. This rate is often double the advertised *annual percentage rate* of the card.

♦ **Cash advance and balance transfer rates.** While they advertise it like they're doing you a huge favor, the ability to draw cash from your credit card or transfer a balance is a windfall for your credit card company. Almost always, these transactions are immediately or eventually billed at a much higher rate than your rate for purchases.

♦ **Changes in your credit score.** More and more credit card companies are changing your interest rates simply because your credit score changes. Even though you haven't applied for a new line of credit with them, they still reserve the right (in the fine print, of course) to raise your rate if your creditworthiness changes.

♦ **Economic conditions.** Credit card companies also reserve the right to change interest rates in response to changing economic conditions. Ironically, when the Federal Reserve makes numerous successive rate cuts, most credit card companies hold their rates steady. But as soon as rates begin to creep back up to where they were, the credit cards will use this as an excuse to increase the rate on your card. Unfortunately, you have no say in the matter, since you signed the application containing this fine print.

If you're notified that your rate is being raised, you've got to strike while the iron is hot if you hope to get them to reverse it. You should immediately call your credit card company, demand to know why they raised your rate, and threaten to move your account if they don't budge. Don't hesitate to follow through if they won't cut you a break. More on this at the end of the chapter.

The Truth Credit Card Companies Hide

There are a number of things the credit card companies work hard to hide from consumers. For good reason, too, since these things would hurt both their signup numbers, as well as their collection procedures. By adding these to your financial IQ, you'll save yourself some nasty surprises and give the credit card company a couple of your own.

They Can Demand Full Payoff

Many consumers struggling to pay off a large credit card balance are surprised to find out that their company can demand they pay more than the minimum monthly payment. In fact, they can demand that the entire balance be paid off within one billing cycle!

This is what is known as the "acceleration clause," a little piece of fine print that the credit card companies include to beef up their collection muscle. It usually states something along the lines of, "if the borrower fails to make the calculated minimum payment, the lender *may* exercise their right to demand full payment of the entire balance within 30 days." Yikes!

What this does is give credit card companies the ability to pursue collections actions against enough of your assets to sufficiently pay off the balance that you owe them. In order to keep them from exercising that muscle, it's crucial that you communicate with your credit card company in a timely manner. This way, they remain hopeful about your willingness to repay them without having to resort to more drastic measures.

Inactivity Fees

As much as they'd like America to believe that they encourage responsible use of their credit cards, issuers actually hate it. In fact, if you don't use their credit card enough, they'll charge you an "inactivity fee" on top of your annual fee.

This fee, which may be charged monthly, quarterly, or semiannually, can range from as low as $5 to as high as $50 or more! While I generally advise against the regular use of credit cards, allowing your credit card to be charged monthly for something such as a newspaper subscription is an easy way to avoid this fee.

You're Protected Under the Law

One of my favorite scenes in a movie is from the holiday classic, *A Christmas Story*. In the movie, the main character Ralphie and his friends are continually harassed by an older and larger bully named Scut Farkus. Every day, on the way home from school, Scut twists the kids' arms and makes them say "uncle." That is, until one day, when Ralphie snaps. In a moment of rage, he charges Scut, knocks him to the ground, and starts swinging his arms like a crazed windmill. Within a matter of seconds, Scut is the one screaming "uncle."

In the Know

For more information on the laws protecting consumers from unfair borrowing and lending practices, visit the Federal Reserve Board's website at www.federalreserve.gov.

When it comes to the financial bullying and arm twisting that many people experience at the hands of their credit card company, there's a few things that will leave them screaming "uncle" themselves. By letting them know that you know what your rights are, and then using them, many companies will back off and give you the respect you deserve.

Here are some things you'll never hear them mention, because you knowing them means they lose significant leverage over you. You can find sample versions of these letters in my last book, *The Complete Idiot's Guide to Getting Out of Debt* (see Appendix B):

◆ **Billing dispute letter.** Thanks to the Fair Credit Billing Act (FCBA), you can withhold payment on disputed amounts without any negative effects on your credit report. Asserting this right requires you to file a formal letter and follow certain procedures to guarantee protection.

◆ **Cease and desist letter.** Under the Fair Debt Collection Practices Act (FDCPA), if your credit card account has been turned over to a collection agency, you can file a simple "cease and desist" letter, which greatly limits their ability to hound you.

Ways to Save on Your Credit Cards

Unlike your relative inability to negotiate your banking costs, as I talked about in Chapter 2, there are all kinds of tips and tricks that those with high financial IQs can use to lower their credit card costs. Most of these don't require anything more than some guts and a phone call, and can save you thousands of dollars over the course of a few years.

Negotiate Your Rate

One of the easiest things to do, and something I'd recommend everyone try at least once every 12 months, is getting your credit cards' interest rates lowered. Based on my experience, roughly 50 percent of all attempts to get your rate lowered result in some type of positive result.

At the heart of this technique is the threat to take your business elsewhere, namely their competitor, who keeps sending you balance transfer offers.

"Why would they care?" you might ask.

You've got to realize that if you are paying 10 percent, 20 percent, or even 30 percent on your balances, you may be the single best-performing investment in the American economy! Where else can your credit card company find such extraordinary rates of return on their money?

With that in mind, I can almost guarantee you that they don't want to lose your business to someone else, even if it means cutting your rate from 30 percent to 20 percent to keep you. For them, they're still earning a fairly incredible rate, but you'd be paying $1,000 less in annual interest for every $10,000 in balance you're carrying.

Put Your Balance Out for Bid

If your company says no, call their bluff and look around for a balance transfer. Collect all the credit card offers you receive over a couple of weeks or go on the Internet and find a website that compares credit card rates, and begin making phone calls.

Tell the other companies that you've got a balance you're carrying elsewhere and that you'd be interested in switching to their company if they can provide you with a better rate. Chances are it'll only take three to four phone calls before you find a substantially better deal.

Just be sure you take note of a couple of key numbers before you say yes. Make sure that drop in interest rates you receive is more than your new company's one-time balance transfer fee (usually 1 to 5 percent). Second, make sure that the rates you'll receive after the teaser period is over are still better than what you were receiving at your old credit card company.

Negotiate Your Balance

While I generally recommend this technique as one of last resort, it's a great way for someone with some extra cash to knock out a large amount of credit card debt, especially if you're already behind on your payments.

In this technique, you approach your credit card company and tell them that you've recently come into some cash, and are looking at applying it toward one of your debts. Propose to them that you settle all or a portion of your outstanding balance for a fraction of its value. A company that is either hurting for funds or worried that you're not going to repay what you owe may jump at the chance to get its hands on anything.

For example, if you've come into $2,500, you might call and offer your credit card company $2,000 of that to pay off your $5,000 balance once and for all. If they're interested, they'll usually come back to you and ask for a little more, which is why you offered $500 less than you had. When the smoke clears, you've managed to save not just half of the amount you owed, but also the interest that would have accumulated on that until you eventually paid it off.

Monitor Your Credit Score

As mentioned earlier in the chapter, credit card companies will often change your interest rate simply because your *credit score* drops slightly. Not surprisingly, they don't roll out the red carpet and lower your rates when it changes for the better.

That doesn't mean they won't, it just means they don't do it on their own. By monitoring your *credit report* and credit score for any positive significant changes, you'll have some ammo to demand that the street run both ways.

def•i•ni•tion

Credit report and credit score are often used interchangeably by consumers and even some experts, but they're very different things. A **credit report** is the factual history of how you've used and repaid credit. A **credit score** is a company's opinion, expressed as a ranking on a numerical scale, of whether or not that history means you're a risky borrower or not.

Reform: Coming to a Credit Card Near You

In mid-2008, the U.S. Federal Reserve put new regulations in place to protect consumers from many of the deceptive and unfair practices outlined in this chapter. Following this, the U.S. Congress also passed the Credit Cardholders' Bill of Rights, which was signed into law by President Obama in May 2009.

Here are some key highlights of things to come:

◆ **Statement mailing dates.** Credit card companies must send statements at least 21 days before the payment due date to ensure consumers have a reasonable amount of time to respond.

- **Allocation of payments.** Credit card companies must either apply excess payments above the minimum to the highest interest rate balances, or spread them proportionately across your different interest rate balances.

- **Increases in interest rates.** Credit card companies must notify consumers at least 45 days prior to raising their interest rate. Rate changes based on an increase in the underlying index used by the credit card company are not included in this rule.

- **Double-cycle billing.** In most instances, this practice will be eliminated.

- **Credit cards and college students.** The new regulations put a number of rules into place that limit the amount of credit that college students can get.

While these regulations will go a long way toward protecting consumers, there's no guarantee that companies will comply immediately or uniformly when it goes into effect in mid-2010. Consumers with high financial IQs will continue to scour the details to make sure they're not being taken advantage of. To stay on top of the new changes as they're instituted, visit www.creditcardrights.net and sign up for the free newsletter.

The Least You Need to Know

- Since credit card companies make the bulk of their money by charging you interest, you need to watch for anything that helps them increase your rate or balance.

- Credit cards are notorious for adding services and products to your bill that you didn't clearly consent to.

- Stay on top of your company's changing payment procedures to avoid late charges.

- Know the rules that will cause your rates to change so that you'll avoid falling into their traps.

- Don't be shy about trying to negotiate your interest rates or balance, even shopping around for a better deal if need be.

- Keep your eyes peeled for the new Credit Cardholders' Bill of Rights and don't hesitate to put your new rights to use.

Part 2

Grow Your Investing IQ

While many people consider investing a goal, it's really a tool. But just like an electric saw can be dangerous in the hands of someone who doesn't know how to use it, so can investing in the hands of the careless or uneducated. To complicate matters, there's a mob of people competing to tell you how to use this tool. Unfortunately, most of them are more interested in building their own financial futures than yours. In this part, you'll hear straight talk on everything from mutual funds to stockbrokers to the people you see on the financial news channels.

Chapter 4

The Investment Markets

In This Chapter

- ◆ The media's agenda
- ◆ Investing rules of thumb that often backfire
- ◆ Not everyone should "do it themselves"
- ◆ Advice from investing geniuses

Before you tackle the tricks used by investment professionals or examine the fine print of your investments, you'd do yourself well to stop and examine your underlying beliefs about the investment markets. It's these faulty beliefs, in fact, that are often used to market us products and service we don't need, or to justify costs we can't afford.

As you read through this chapter, keep this classic phrase in mind: take everything with a grain of salt. In other words, I want you to begin to think critically about everything, from what you believe to what people tell you to believe. When you can do that, you'll be well on your way to developing the investment portion of your financial IQ.

A Bull Market for the Media

These kids nowadays ... they don't know how easy they have it. They've got multiple 24-hour financial news networks, investing chat rooms, stock quotes on their phones, and dozens of personal finance magazines to choose from. When I was a kid ....

Really, though, when I was a kid, we pretty much had *The Wall Street Journal* and one *weekly* financial TV show—*Wall $treet Week* with Louis Rukeyser. If you wanted to know more than that, you had to pay big bucks for a specialized newsletter or cozy up to a stockbroker who could get you your information fix. But for all its prehistoric nature, I'm not sure these simpler times were a bad thing.

Now you've got so many people talking, so many pieces of conflicting advice, and so many options to choose from, that most people feel more overwhelmed than informed. It's like drinking from the proverbial fire hose, only worse. Now you can't escape the fire hose—it's everywhere.

Is the Investing Media Trustworthy?

My wife, like a lot of mothers, was addicted to parenting books when our children were first born. Actually, I'm not sure it was an addiction—it was more like a fear of not reading the right book. Of overlooking some key piece of information that would keep our kids from turning into the children that all the other parents warn their kids about.

I used to remind my wife, as she'd show me each new book with each new set of rules for parenting, that these books counted on two things to drive sales—a sense of fear and a unique opinion. In other words, if they could convince you that you didn't know how to parent without their help, or that your child would miss out if you didn't do it their way, there was a pretty good chance they'd make a sale.

When I stop and look at my own industry, the financial media, I'm afraid that we've evolved into something very similar. We've become an industry that fights for consumer attention by offering the secrets to wealth, touting boom or gloom, and using the word "now" with a vengeance.

All that to say that it is an important step in increasing your financial IQ to begin seeing the media for what it is, a business like anything else. Which means, of course, that you are their customer and you need to be a wise, savvy one at that.

Watch Your Back

One of the greatest resources for information available today, the Internet, has also become one of the greatest sources of misinformation for individuals seeking to increase their financial IQ. Type any financial topic into a search engine, and your results will be a mix of expert advice and foolish chatter. Before you use information found on a website or blog to make a financial decision, be sure to get a second opinion!

The Media's Weapons: Fear and Greed

Before we give the media too hard of a time, it's important to recognize that they are often just responding to our demands for certain types of news coverage. Another way to look at it: if we all got together and said that we thought bright red suits were what legitimate news anchors should wear, there's a good chance you'd probably start seeing red suits all over the news.

With that in mind, it's important to recognize our own investor psychology. Many people waiver back and forth between the extremes of thinking it's a matter of time before they hit it big, or thinking the financial world is about to come to an end. The financial media, knowing that most people are hyperfocused and sensitive on these two extremes, will constantly use these types of storylines to grab your attention.

Really, can you ever imagine hearing your favorite news channel saying something like, "We don't really have anything else exciting to tell you, so don't sweat it if you can't stick around to see what's after this word from our sponsor"? As you become more and more media savvy, as your financial intuition grows, you'll begin to see that most *attention-grabbing headlines* are nothing more than *headlines meant to grab attention.*

"The Best 10 Money Moves to Make, *Now!*"

Don't get your hopes up. This section isn't really going to be filled with the 10 best money moves. It's actually meant to call your attention to one of the most classic attention-grabbing headlines out there.

It seems that you can't stand in the checkout line at my grocery store or browse my local book store without seeing at least half a dozen magazines promising to share the "best" of something if you're just willing to give them a look. Of course, when you add up all the financial magazines sitting there with these types of headlines, there might be 50 to 100 money moves you should be making right now! That's not counting the brand-new "bests" they're going to throw at you next month.

The point is, don't be suckered in. If you were really to try and follow all the advice in even one of these magazines, you'd be like one of those shooting targets at the local carnival. You're going through your month, feeling good about your finances, then plink, time to change directions. Another month goes by, and plink, time to change strategies again.

In the end, you should take the time to create a good financial plan that you revisit every 6 to 12 months, unless something major happens in the economy or your life.

Experts in Title Only

Just like the rest of the investment and personal finance industry, the people feeding you your news and investment tips like to position themselves as experts. Unfortunately for the many who rely on the media to provide them with their advice, many of these people are experts in title only.

In the Know

Do you feel like you're drowning in the alphabet soup of credentials thrown at you by financial professionals? FINRA (Financial Industry Regulatory Authority), one of the service industry's largest regulatory bodies, has a detailed website (www.finra.org) providing a searchable directory of over 75 different professional designations, what they mean, and what is required to obtain them.

That's not to say most of what you hear is wrong. Rather, it's to say that some of the things that are communicated as facts may be less than concrete. In fact, much of the information you hear from the various "experts" is actually fed to them from other experts. And, just like in that old game of telephone, what was originally accurate can come out completely wrong.

Additionally, many of the folks that you hear financial wisdom from on TV or read about in other sources have never actually had on-the-ground experience. They may know the rules, the theories, or the numbers, but they're completely unaware of the obstacles that can pop up when trying to put their advice into action.

When it comes to increasing your financial IQ, this means that you need to do more than simply listen to news or read lots of financial magazines. You also need to begin doing homework for yourself. You need to read the fine print, ask the hard questions, and do your own research.

Advertisers and Your Favorite Media

One of the great measuring sticks used by those with high financial IQs is what conflicts of interest their advisors bring to the table. Is it in your stockbroker's favor to recommend a trade that generates a commission? Might your investment professional have something to gain from recommending the bells-and-whistles account her firm offers? Sure, most people acknowledge the possibility that they do.

But many people never stop to consider whether conflicts of interest exist for the financial media. Are there factors that affect which stocks get favorable media coverage? Do magazines avoid giving bad reviews to mutual funds companies that are also advertisers? Those with high financial IQs know that all these things are possible and are always on guard for red flags. They are vigilant in watching out for places where that fine line between journalism and advertising might get crossed.

The two primary warning signs you should be on guard for are favorable reviews of a media outlet's advertisers and "special advertising supplements" included in certain publications. Both can lead inattentive consumers to make decisions that are in someone else's best interests, at the expense of their own.

In the first instance, there's a natural conflict of interest between the sale of advertising space and reviewing products. For example, might it be harder for a magazine or news program to shoot down an online brokerage firm's service record when that same firm spends millions in advertising? You bet.

In the second instance, advertisers buy one or more complete pages and structure them to look like an article or review about their product. Of course, somewhere at the bottom, the fine print indicates that this is a "special advertising section." Unfortunately, most people, because they're staring at something that looks like an article, assume that it's part of the magazine.

In the Know

Even the most dedicated financial professionals don't have the time it takes to sort through the ever-growing mound of investment and personal finance publications. One of the best ways to stay up to date is by downloading free financial news podcasts available through services like iTunes. Instead of trying to find time to sit and read, you can continue to expand your financial IQ as you drive, work out, or stand in line at the store.

Six Investing Truths That Aren't Necessarily So

People love to give each other investment advice, even if they themselves haven't managed their portfolio in a way that wins any awards. Maybe it's just the American thing to do, like telling other people how to parent or how to cut their lawn.

In fact, there are certain phrases and pieces of water cooler wisdom that get thrown around so much that people have come to believe they're immutable laws. If you're going to raise your financial IQ, you need to understand when and why these things aren't necessarily true. With that intuition developed, you'll be able to stave off the waves of boilerplate financial advice that can lead you astray.

Myth #1: Stocks Are the Best Long-Term Investment

Don't fall for this overly simplistic statement, but don't get me wrong either. I do believe that stocks can provide superior returns to bonds, real estate, gold, and other assets over time. But *that is not what makes a good investment!*

What makes something a good investment is whether it sufficiently accomplishes your goals while keeping your risks at a minimum. In other words, if something less risky can accomplish your goals for growth, then why would you take the additional risk associated with stocks?

Further, most of the historical rates of returns you see quoted for stock investments do not account for investment management costs and taxes. The first two (management costs and taxes) can easily shave a 10 percent annual return down to 7 or 8 percent.

> **Your Bottom Line**
>
> High-cost and tax-inefficient investing can cost you hundreds of thousands, possibly millions of dollars, over the course of your investing lifetime. A $100,000 stock portfolio that earns 7 percent instead of 9 percent, due to higher fees and taxes, will grow by $565,542 less over 30 years!

In short, high IQ investors choose the investment that most efficiently moves them from their current financial position toward their goals, without taking any unnecessary risks. They are not seduced by possibilities for greater return than they need.

Myth #2: Bonds Aren't Risky

When the investment markets get ugly, the first thing everyone starts murmuring about is the safety of bonds. This is especially true of the people who owned bonds when the market went in the toilet—there's something about saying I told you so. There's no doubt that at that point, earning a single digit interest rate feels much better than watching your portfolio shrink by double digits. But that doesn't mean bonds are safe, *just safer.*

What many investors don't realize is that any bond, even U.S. Treasury–backed bonds, can put you in a situation where you may lose a significant amount of money. Own bonds in a mutual fund and the potential for loss becomes even more real.

The risk of bonds comes from the fact that a bond's issuer only agrees to pay you back the face amount of the bond on its maturity date. If you choose to (or life forces you to) sell that bond before its maturity date, you may get significantly more or less than what you'd receive if you held it to maturity.

The reason for this has to do with the fact that most bonds' interest rates are set for the life of the bond. If your bond was paying 5 percent per year when you bought it, it'll generally be paying that same 5 percent throughout its life. So if new bonds are issued paying higher rates, your bond will suddenly look less attractive to a prospective buyer. Thus, if you have to sell it before the maturity date, you may have to sell it at a discount (a nice way of saying *loss*). And no issuer, not even the U.S. government, guarantees against a loss on bonds sold before their maturity date.

In a mutual fund, this risk can be even more significant, even for a mutual fund that only buys U.S. government bonds. Since the mutual fund may have to sell a substantial portion of its portfolio before its maturity date in order to pay cash out to other investors, the remaining mutual fund owners can take a significant hit.

Myth #3: Blue-Chip Stocks Are Safer

When we first had kids, we really wanted to buy a Volvo. Supposedly, Volvos are the automobile version of airplane black boxes—completely impervious to destruction. You could drive one off a cliff, and your adorable family inside wouldn't even notice.

In researching Volvos, I began to run across numerous statistics about automobile accidents. The most fascinating one, which was also the one that made me okay with *not* owning a Volvo, was that speed was the single largest factor in automobile fatalities. The faster you were going, the less likely you were to survive. The vehicle itself had far less to do with it (unless it was a Ford Pinto) than we'd imagined. In truth, Volvo drivers may die a lot less, not because their cars are so amazing, but because they're obsessed with safety and drive much slower!

Well, *blue-chip stocks* are kind of the Volvos of the investment world. We assume they're safe, because they're America's biggest companies and offer the products and services that we all can't live without. But there's a fatal flaw in this line of thinking.

def•i•ni•tion

> **Blue-chip stocks** refer to the stocks of the biggest and strongest companies in an economy. Due to their dominance within their industries, these companies are the most likely to survive hard times, and thus are considered less risky by many investors. The term itself comes from the blue chips used in casinos, which are the highest value of all the chips.

Just like a Volvo becomes extremely unsafe once you decide to go 120 mph in it, a blue-chip stock can become extremely unsafe if it becomes too overvalued. Or as I often explain it to clients, just because the best car wash in town earns a million dollars per year, doesn't mean you're smart for paying $500 million to buy it. In short, you can overpay for a good thing!

When people with high financial IQs evaluate blue-chip stocks, like any other kind of stock, they keep an eye on the company's price-to-earnings (PE) ratio. This ratio, which measures how many times its annual earnings a stock is selling at, is crucial in deciding if that blue-chip stock has its foot on the gas. As a starting point, keep in mind that the historical PE ratio of the broad stock market has averaged between 10 and 20 times earnings.

Myth #4: Buy Mutual Funds to Diversify

Mutual funds, especially *index funds,* are often the go-to choice for investors and advisors looking to diversify their holdings. Often times, mutual funds will own hundreds of stocks across all kinds of economic sectors. But those with the highest financial IQs know that you have to look below the surface to see *how much* of each stock a fund actually owns. Despite their claims of diversification, many funds are still highly concentrated in just a few dozen positions.

An **index fund** is a mutual fund that attempts to replicate the performance of one of the most widely followed stock market indices. Since it attempts to replicate the performance as closely as possible, no attempt is made to limit potential losses in a down market.

Take an S&P 500 index fund, for example. It seems to have 500 stocks in it—what could be more diversified than that? In truth, just about any portfolio that holds 20 to 30 stocks is likely more diversified than the S&P 500, because of the way the index is calculated. Instead of the index actually being divided evenly between each stock it tracks, it's divided on a market capitalization–weighted basis. While that sounds very complex, it simply means that the largest stocks are held in a higher percentage than the smallest. But since there is such a gap in size between the largest stocks and the smallest, the fate of those indices (and the funds that try to mirror their movement) depends almost entirely on the movement of those largest stocks. In fact, if the other 470 to 480 stocks in the S&P 500 went up for the year, but the 20 to 30 largest went down, an S&P 500 index fund would probably still show a loss!

Myth #5: Ratings Are Everything

One of the most important things you need to do in raising your financial IQ and developing financial intuition is learning to think critically about everything. In the investing world, this is especially true of stock, bond, and mutual fund ratings.

Wall Street is awash in ratings that supposedly take the guesswork out of what to buy, when to buy it, and how safe it is. We've got everything from star systems to numerical rankings to phrases like "strong buy" or "short-term sell." Unfortunately, as many have learned in the most recent financial crisis, ratings are often not worth the paper they're written on. The problem with ratings is that they are based on the known past instead of the unforeseeable future. At best, they're best guesses. At worst, they're invitations to disaster.

In fact, when we look at the history of different asset classes, we see something interesting: more often than not, last year's top dogs tend to become next year's mutts, something that is often overlooked when average returns for an investment or asset class are calculated over long periods of time. As happens so often, investments tend to get their highest ratings and most public attention after a single year's performance has been above average. But history would tell us that that is probably the last time we'd want to be putting all our money there. There's a good chance that things may be headed south in a hurry, in part since there may be no one left to buy and keep driving the price up (they all jumped on board when it got five stars!).

Your Bottom Line

Two of the best known and trusted rating systems are the Morningstar Star System and the Standard & Poor's (S&P) Bond Rating system. Morningstar ranks mutual funds from one to five stars, based on their potential for return within their investment categories. S&P rates bonds for safety, ranging from AAA (the safest) down to C (junk bonds).

Those with high financial IQs never buy anything solely on its rankings. They might use the ratings as a place to begin their search, but they rely heavily on deeper research to see if the rating is sustainable.

Myth #6: Anyone Can Invest for Themselves

There's no doubt that this book takes its fair amount of potshots at the "full-service" financial services industry. While the largest of Wall Street firms is often at fault for milking and misleading their clients, the discount and Internet brokerages of Wall Street have their moments, too.

Many of these firms, touting $5 commissions and free accounts, wrongly encourage investors with the belief that they can easily make money in the markets for themselves. While this is more true with things like "buy-and-hold" investing in mutual funds, it is far from true when it comes to the daily trading of stocks for a profit. In truth, many full-time Wall Street brokers and traders cannot pull off such a feat!

One of the most heartbreaking times in my professional career was the late 1990s, at the peak of the dotcom boom. I watched teachers, police officers, and other gainfully employed people leaving their jobs to trade stocks from home. Of course, for a while, it was easy. You just had to buy an IPO, watch it go up 200 percent over a couple of days, then sell it and move on. I knew people who made $50,000 to $100,000 for a year or two when that market was at its peak. All of them, and I mean all of them, lost it all when the boom unraveled.

Don't get me wrong, I'm not discouraging you to become involved with your own portfolio management—just the opposite. However, I'm saying don't confuse cheap or lucky for capable, because both will come back to bite you in the end. Just because the stock market is doing well or because you can save hundreds of dollars trading at a discount firm, doesn't mean you should.

One of my favorite quotes, for both life and investing, comes from Shakespeare's *Henry IV*. The character Falstaff says, "The better part of valor is discretion." In other words, it's as important to know *when* to be brave as it is to actually be brave. Knowing that you may not be ready to handle complex financial tasks yourself doesn't mean you're incapable, but rather that you've developed a very high financial IQ!

Your Bottom Line

Numerous studies of individual investors who trade their own stocks (instead of using a broker or a professionally managed mutual fund) show that the majority of these investors substantially underperform the broad investment market. The largest identifiable reason for this is that individual investors "chase returns," always shifting to what was recently hot, and thus missing out on what is about to go up next.

Tips from True Investing Geniuses

When it comes to investing, if you want to sharpen your financial IQ you'd be a fool not to memorize some of the great quotes on investing from those who have wrestled the markets into submission. Most of these investors made billions by being smarter than the rest, avoiding the fads of their time, and always viewing themselves as perpetual students of investing.

As always, take what they have to say with a grain of salt. Each of them I'm sure, if you could pull them away from rolling around in piles of money, would tell you that the only constant thing is change. These are great rules, but there will always be exceptions. You'll have to rely on your ever-expanding financial IQ to tell the difference.

Sir John Templeton

There have been few more fascinating investors than Sir John Templeton, the founder of Templeton Mutual Funds. The man made billions as an investor, renounced his U.S. citizenship to avoid taxation, moved to the Bahamas, and eventually became a British knight! Like many of the billionaires we'll look at, he seemed to love to give away money as much as making it.

Sir John's quote that I'd like you to burn into your brain has to do with the right time to buy. As he once said, "Buy when there is blood in the streets." In other words, when everyone else is looking for a window to jump out of, that's a heck of a time to be a buyer. Of course, that takes some serious commitment and an avoidance of windows, but it can pay off big time.

So next time someone tries to pitch you on a hot stock or mutual fund that "just won't quit," remember Sir John. Consider opting for a great stock, mutual fund, or sector that has recently experienced a blood bath.

Warren Buffet

There's probably no more well-known investing billionaire than Warren Buffet, the "sage of Omaha." Warren grew his company, Berkshire-Hathaway, into a billion-dollar enterprise by buying other undervalued and underappreciated companies. Like most billionaires, Warren has his quirks that endear him to the rest of us. For example, even with all that money (most of which he has promised to give away), he still lives in the same middle-class house he bought in 1958.

Warren's words of wisdom for you are in the area of diversification. Warren was once quoted as saying, "Diversification is for people who don't understand what they're doing!"

What the heck is Warren talking about? Isn't diversification one of the core principles of a balanced portfolio?

It most definitely is, and I don't think anyone would ever try to claim that Warren has only invested in one or two companies at a time. But I think Warren is making a case against what I like to call "de-worsification."

The idea here is that it's actually possible to own so many different mutual funds that your portfolio loses its ability to outperform the market because it has *become the market*. For example, if between your 401(k)s, IRAs, and college accounts, you own 10 different well-diversified mutual funds, you may literally be exposed to 1,000 or more stocks! With that kind of broad exposure, it actually may become impossible to outperform the market. Subtract all the fees associated with managing these different funds and there's a good chance you'll actually underperform the market.

In the Know

One of the quickest ways to increase your financial IQ is to study the greatest minds on the various subjects. In addition to the investors mentioned, I'd strongly recommend studying other classic works on the subject of investing, including *Extraordinary Popular Delusions and the Madness of Crowds* by Charles MacKay, and *The Intelligent Investor* by Benjamin Graham. Check out Appendix B for these and other investing classics.

Peter Lynch

Did you know that for every home run baseball great Babe Ruth hit, he struck out roughly 1.86 times? It's true. In fact, most people who enjoy great success also enjoy a good amount of failure. There's no doubt this is what investing great Peter Lynch was referring to when he said, "If you're good [at investing], you'll be right 6 out of 10 times."

Wow. The man who turned Fidelity mutual funds into the powerhouse that it is just told you that the best investors will only pick the right thing slightly more than half of the time. Peter Lynch did an incredible job growing the net worth of Fidelity investors by being right just slightly more than he was wrong. If that doesn't take the pressure off, I don't know what does.

The application for you is simple. Don't go switching your whole investment strategy just because one or two of your picks is having a rough go of it—that's natural. Give your well-researched investment choices adequate time to do what they're supposed to. Changing them too early or too often may cost you the growth you've been hoping for.

John Bogle

Few people have succeeded at investing like John Bogle, founder of Vanguard Mutual Funds. In fact, John invented the idea of an index fund in the mid-1970s and convinced America that investing didn't have to be expensive. Perhaps the wisest thing John ever said regarding investing was a phrase lifted from an old tale about King Solomon: "This too shall pass." Many of us have heard this phrase uttered to help people through bad times, but in the story of King Solomon, it was also meant as a reminder that the good times will pass as well.

When it comes to investing IQ, the wisest know that everything seems to run in cycles and between extremes. Whether it is really good, really bad, or really boring, it's a matter of time before it changes. If things are taking off like gangbusters, it's a matter of time before the party comes to an end. If investors can't seem to catch a break, it's a matter of time before that changes as well.

While that seems like common sense, the dotcom and housing booms both serve as evidence that people are quick to forget this wisdom. To help ensure your success over the long run, let John's words ring in your ears as the rest of the country (including your advisors) gets too comfortable with the way things are. Wise investors prepare for both the coming storm and the coming rebound!

Will Rogers

Okay, I'll admit that cowboy and cultural icon Will Rogers was not an investing genius on the level with those previously mentioned. He didn't invent a mutual fund or a new style of investing. But he did have a phenomenal way with words, which landed him on my list of people you need to listen to and remember. In one of Will's most insightful moments of economic thinking he said, "Invest in inflation, it's the only thing that'll go up."

Now it's important to realize that Will was known for his tongue-in-cheek way of putting things, so I don't believe he really thought inflation is the only thing that goes up. But he hits the nail right on the head when it comes to what every intelligent investor needs to keep in mind: inflation will eat away at your wealth if you do not stay ahead of it.

Inflation, or the average annual increase in your cost of living, has run about 2 to 3 percent per year historically. That means that in 25 to 35 years a nest egg of $500,000 will only buy you half as much as it does today. If you don't find a way to grow your money faster than inflation, you need to be prepared to live at a lower standard of living than you're used to now.

def•i•ni•tion

Inflation, or the annual increase in the cost of goods and services, may be one of the most important definitions for you to internalize. By fully understanding the ability of inflation to erode your purchasing power, you can plan accordingly for the future. Ignore it, and you'll eventually find yourself living well below the lifestyle you currently maintain.

This means that a money market account, savings account, or bond that is only paying 1 to 2 percent will not get most people where they need to go. Likewise, it means your plans for the future (what your child will need for college, what you'll need for retirement, etc.) need to be adjusted to account for inflation.

The Least You Need to Know

- Use your critical thinking skills to decipher the mixed messages and the hidden agendas of the media.

- Stocks aren't necessarily the best long-term investment, bonds aren't necessarily risk-free, and ratings are often only worth the paper they're written on.

- Remember, everything tends to run in cycles—today's top dogs become tomorrow's mutts.

- Just because you *can* do everything yourself, doesn't mean you *should* do everything yourself.

- Study the investing geniuses and ignore the water cooler investment advice.

5

The Cons of Your Investment Pro

In This Chapter

- ◆ How advisors get paid
- ◆ Finding the hidden costs
- ◆ Reading the fine print
- ◆ Keeping your advisor on a short leash

If this book were written a decade ago, this chapter would have focused primarily on stockbrokers: those classic Wall Street types who sit at their desk with a phone in each hand, yelling "Buy! Buy!" and "Sell! Sell!" often at the same time to different people. But over the last 10 to 20 years, Wall Street has given itself a rather substantial makeover. No longer is the hot job to be a gun-slinging, hot-tip-whispering stockbroker. As it turns out, many of America's households had broader concerns than just trading stocks for profit. It turns out that John and Sally Q. Public had broader questions about what to do with all their money once they had made it (or inherited it). They had questions about the tax implications of different types of IRAs. They wanted to know which type of college account would best help them educate their children. And it turns out, "buy" and "sell" aren't great answers to those questions.

So naturally, the financial industry began to reposition its foot soldiers with attractive titles and duties like "financial planner," "wealth advisor," or "investment professional." Almost overnight, other financial-service industries, such as insurance sales, jumped on the bandwagon and also adopted those very wise-sounding titles.

Unfortunately, changing their title doesn't mean that they instantly increased their knowledge or dropped their old habits of looking out for themselves over your interests. This leaves many people, people like you, trying to decipher which professional can really serve your needs and what financial products they're going to try to sell you to do it.

In this chapter, we take a look at the people who actually provide your investment advice. For simplicity's sake, I'll simply refer to them as investment professionals or financial advisors. In later chapters, we'll also take a look at some of the other folks who have adopted these new titles.

How They Make Their Money

There's nothing more important in your relationship with your investment professional than understanding how they are charging you for their time. When you fail to understand that, especially if they perceive you fail to understand that, there is room for abuse. Many investment professionals are on the up and up, but that one who's not can set your financial goals back significantly.

In the Know _____

Can your financial advisor be *too* successful? If it means having more than a few hundred clients, the answer is probably yes. Many industry measures consider a full practice to be between 200 and 250 clients. So be sure to ask a potential advisor how many clients they have and what level of service they expect to maintain as they grow.

Commissions

Though they may call themselves all kinds of fancy and helpful-sounding things, many investment professionals are still nothing more than stockbrokers. That's not to say that there aren't fabulous stockbrokers, including those who understand broad financial planning. Rather, it's to say that at the end of the day, they only get paid for "brokering a trade."

Unfortunately for the stockbrokers, they only get to keep a portion of the commissions they generate, which is determined by something they call their "payout grid." In short, the more commission they generate, the more they get to keep. This grid usually runs from about 25 percent to as high as 50 percent, and often includes performance bonuses.

The main problem with commissions, if you haven't noticed already, is that the advice you receive can be heavily influenced by whether or not a broker feels the need to generate more commission. If their kid's college tuition bill is due, or they've decided to take an expensive vacation, you may all of a sudden be getting more "advice." This is especially common at the end of the month, when the broker realizes he or she hasn't generated enough commissions to meet certain quotas. This is known as "churning" and is something regulators take very seriously; a broker can be fined or lose his or her license for violations.

Again, many brokers are above such tactics, but the very fact that it is a temptation should be something you're watching and questioning closely.

Asset Management Fees

The investment industry has come under increasing scrutiny for the conflict of interest that exists with commission-based financial advice, and rightfully so. In one of its most shining moments, the financial media has turned the microscope on how advisors get compensated and called the public's attention to potential abuses. In addition to the incentive to change that comes with negative publicity, the growth of discount and Internet brokerages have pushed full-service firms to reexamine their hefty commissions. The result has been asset management fees, which arguably offer a much more unbiased way to receive investment advice. Under these arrangements, you essentially pay your investment professional an annual fee for investment advice, regardless of the advice they actually give. Many people view this as beneficial, since sometimes the best advice is to do nothing.

This fee is usually calculated as a percentage of your total investments under his or her care, such as 1 percent per year. Sometimes these fees are literally billed to the client, sometimes they are simply subtracted from the cash in their account, and sometimes they're subtracted by a mutual fund company and remitted to the brokerage firm.

While these arrangements seem to be much more apt to encourage balanced advice, they can also be far more expensive than is beneficial for a lot of customers. As a rule of thumb, I'd recommend that your total investment expenses be no more than 1 to 1½ percent per year (even if you're still using a commissioned broker). This should be even lower if you maintain a large portfolio. Yet it's not uncommon to see some firms charging as much as 2½ percent for these types of accounts. When you subtract that large of a fee from your annual return, especially in the poor-performing years, it begins to not make any financial sense.

In the Know

If you're looking for the best of both worlds, individualized advice and reasonable costs, consider an *independent* fee-based advisor. These advisors have set up their own shops, often allowing them to net the same amount of profit even while charging their clients lower fees. You'll need to be willing to forgo the name-brand comfort of using the largest Wall Street firms, though.

Financial Planning Fees

Since all these Wall Street professionals are positioning themselves as financial planners and wealth advisors, they must offer some type of comprehensive advice beyond just helping you pick investments, right? *Sort of.*

In an effort to rebrand legions of financial salespeople as personal finance gurus, most of the firms now offer some type of turn-key financial planning product. At the firms, they often refer to these programs as the "black box." In essence, a client fills out a long questionnaire that covers everything from your assets to your mortgage to your insurance needs, which then gets entered into a computer program. That program then spits out an official-looking report that appears to be written just for you.

Generally, most advisors can't begin to tell you how they came up with these results or how they would change if your unique situation changed. But that doesn't stop them from pretending like this makes them an expert on your financial situation. Unfortunately for them, more and more people are figuring out that there are identical applications available on the Internet for free.

 Watch Your Back

> One of the classic "asset-gathering" tricks used by financial advisors and brokers is to offer a free evaluation of your holdings that aren't already with them. Of course, if there's any shot at transferring the assets under their care, they're going to make the case for it. Be prepared to hear a laundry list of what's wrong with your other advisors and investment choices.

Aside from making their salespeople look like experts, these programs have two other major benefits for the firms. First, they're usually going to charge you $100 to $250 for a report. While this may be much cheaper than a truly personalized financial plan (often $500 to $1,000), you're also going to get what you pay for. Second, this is a great way for these firms to figure out what assets you have that are not under their care. There's no doubt that these programs are strategically used by firms to "gather" your other assets, by manipulatively marketing to your unique situation.

Wall Street's Revenue Tricks

You need to face a cold, hard reality. Even if you are buddy-buddy with your investment professional, to most of their firms, you are still simply a potential source of revenue. Or, to put it more accurately, you're a potential source of *more revenue*.

Just because the firms are already making commissions and fees off of you doesn't mean they're not actively searching for other ways to pad their pockets. In growing your financial IQ, you're going to want to be on the alert for these tricks of the trade and how they impact your bottom line.

> ### Your Bottom Line
>
> One of the most common money-saving techniques used by those with a high financial IQ is to let a full-service advisor manage a small portion of their money. They then use the advice they receive there to implement the same strategies at a discount broker at a significant savings. At an average savings of 1 percent per year, every $50,000 "mirrored" at a discount brokerage will save you $500.

Hidden Commissions

If you were to talk to most Wall Street professionals, they would be angry at the very insinuation that they're attempting to hide commissions on certain financial products. However, I can tell you from my experience on their side of the table, there has been a huge attempt to create financial products that look free or low cost, even though they're costing you an arm and a leg. Here are some examples:

- **Mutual fund B and C shares.** These mutual fund shares cost you nothing up-front to purchase them, just like those "no-load" shares your investment professional really doesn't want you to ever bring up again. Of course, when you look closely, the annual management fees subtracted from your account's value are double or triple many no-load mutual fund fees. Additionally, if you sell the shares in the first few years, you may be charged an "exit fee" called a contingent deferred sales charge, that ranges anywhere from 1 to 5 percent.

- **Bond credits.** One half-truth I hear over and over again from investment professionals is "there is no commission to buy or sell bonds through our firm." In reality, most Wall Street firms maintain a large inventory of different types of bonds that they make available to their advisors to sell. And, just like any one selling anything, there's a markup that is invisible to you the consumer. Typically, this markup is in the range of $20 per $1,000 bond you buy. So if you're buying a bond with "no commission" for $1,000, a full-service investment firm actually bought it for around $980. Unfortunately, this markup can have a significant impact on the rate of return you earn on your bond, since the interest rate received doesn't change even though the purchase price did.

Account Maintenance Fees

One of the most recent trends in the financial services industry, which is having its bottom line squeezed by demanding consumers and fierce competitors, is the re-emergence of account fees. These fees are being used more and more to help large firms create a stable, predictable revenue flow that insulates them from economic downturns.

I guess I really can't call these account maintenance fees a hidden fee, because they're typically right there in plain sight for anyone to see.

While a $25 to $50 fee for IRAs and trust accounts has been standard in the investment industry for years, there's a new trend that you need to be on the lookout for. It's the "premier" account offered by many of these firms. These accounts are supposedly the Cadillac of brokerage accounts, conveniently available now to all investors for a "very reasonable" annual fee of $100 to $250.

Reasonable? Are you serious?

Of course not—I think they are a huge rip-off. While the firms try and dress these accounts up as having advance banking features, top-notch tax reporting, and other bells and whistles, the math says that they're just not worth it.

The reason I mention this here, in the section on investment professional compensation, is that these accounts have now become an additional way for your advisor to make money. In the old days, banks might give tellers a small bonus for opening new accounts. Nowadays, many Wall Street firms include the fees charged on these accounts as a commission that your advisor can get paid on just like any other transaction. In other words, your investment professional, despite what they may say, has a strong incentive for talking you into upgrading from the standard brokerage account to these premier accounts.

Limiting Your Money Market Options

One of the tricks that can literally cost you thousands each year is an investment firm's limited money market offerings. Though they may offer a wide variety of stock and bond mutual funds from a wide variety of other companies, they typically only offer one type of money market fund—their own. And, no surprises here, the yield is generally lower and the expenses higher, especially for customers with smaller balances.

By forcing you to use their "proprietary" money market funds, a Wall Street firm can easily earn an additional .5 to 1 percent off your cash balances without you ever noticing. For investors carrying large cash balances, this can amount to hundreds, if not thousands of dollars less in interest each year. I'd strongly recommend maintaining a more competitive money market account elsewhere.

Cross Selling Other Financial Products

One of the other major trends on Wall Street over the last few decades is a series of mergers that put many firms in the position of trying to be your "one-stop shop" for all your financial needs. They'd love to manage your investments, get you your mortgage, sell you insurance, and even issue you a credit card (aren't they supposed to be helping you?).

The financially astute know that these pitches and up-sells are coming and shop around before they're bullied into making a decision. Chances are, your investment professional's firm is going to be significantly less competitive on both price and benefits compared to a company that specializes in those unique products. So before you succumb to the ease of having to "only talk to one person" when you have a question, remember: you're paying a lot for the privilege.

The Fine Print

One of the things that blew me away when I went to work on Wall Street was the number of lawyers that these firms had working for them. Apparently, these firms think that clients may actually get perturbed about some of their business practices once they're fully understood.

Of course, the great equalizer for the firms is the fine print. It doesn't matter how sad your story of getting ripped off is, if it was covered in the fine print and you signed on the dotted line, the firm's responsibility is greatly reduced.

Sadly, even some of the best-intentioned investment professionals can't tell their clients exactly what the fine print says. It's so intimidating and confusing that even the people who work in the industry can't make heads or tails of it. To help you do what they're not likely to, here are some things to look out for.

You Can't Sue Us

I bet you thought arbitration agreements were just for overpaid athletes. Well, lucky for you, Wall Street thinks they're also great for people just like you!

These agreements, tucked into the fine print of new account applications, essentially remove the ability of customers to sue their investment professional or their firm in a court of law. Instead, they force the client to engage in binding arbitration in which a third-party arbitrator decides what damages a firm is liable for. If the client disagrees with the arbitrator's decision, they really have no other legal option to pursue.

While some might argue that this helps cut down on the occurrence and cost of frivolous lawsuits, others would argue that it greatly limits a consumer's ability to recover damages. Critics also argue that it encourages firms and advisors to be less cautious since it is a process that tends to stay out of the newspaper headlines.

Watch Your Back

Between the trend toward more technology and less paper, it's easy to opt for an electronic version of your account statements, confirmations, and fine-print-containing paperwork. However, when it comes to your personal finances, it's highly recommended that you hold onto every piece of paper that comes your way. These may make the difference between an arbitrator taking your side or your advisor's.

Ultimately, there is not much you can do about the arbitration agreement that most firms make you sign. While it never hurts to tell them that you may not consider opening an account if you have to sign it, they usually won't budge. More practically, it means that you shouldn't overlook your duty to yourself to do your homework about a firm or an advisor, since you won't be able to sue if things don't work out.

Our Credentials Aren't Real

If you haven't caught on by now, I'm not a huge fan of the official-sounding titles Wall Street folks like to come up with. I really don't think they serve a legitimate purpose besides making you feel more comfortable doing business with them. In other words, they're a marketing gimmick. In fact, many important titles like retirement plans consultant, managed accounts specialist, and even vice president are simply doled out to help people generate more business.

For what it's worth, here are the primary titles that truly carry weight when it comes to demonstrating expertise:

- ◆ **Chartered financial analyst (CFA).** This is the granddaddy of investment management designations. Someone who has obtained this has likely put in three years of study, passed some grueling exams, and signed a very strict code of ethics.

- ◆ **CERTIFIED FINANCIAL PLANNER (CFP).** This is to broad financial planning what a CFA is to the analytical side of investing. People who have passed the CFP exam have studied for three years to show mastery of retirement planning, insurance, estate planning, and taxation.

- ◆ **Certified investment management analyst (CIMA).** While definitely less heard of than the CFP or CFA designation, the CIMA is a legitimate mark of investing expertise. CIMA certificate holders have passed a rigorous course of study that includes a weeklong intensive session at the famed Wharton School of Business.

SIPC Protection Isn't the Same as FDIC

I cannot count the times I've heard a financial advisor misstate to clients what SIPC protection is and what it means for their accounts. The term is often trotted out when clients express concern about the safety of an advisor's firm or even of specific investments. The clients are often assured that SIPC is just like FDIC, but maybe even better, because it protects their accounts to a much higher limit.

According to the Securities Investors Protections Corporation (SIPC), they protect each qualifying investor against the loss of assets due to a brokerage's bankruptcy, for up to $500,000 per institution. Further, individuals holding a joint account (such as a husband and wife) may combine their coverage to provide for a maximum possible coverage of $1,000,000.

The problem here is not that the SIPC is a bogus organization, but that the explanation provided (or not fully provided, as the case may be) is omitting a major detail. SIPC *is not* a Treasury-backed program like the FDIC. Rather, it's an association of Wall Street firms that have pooled their money to attempt to provide the same type of coverage. As such, SIPC's pockets are only as deep as the money pooled together by the firms that choose to participate. If SIPC runs out of money, the government *is not* required to step in and bail out your account.

Further, SIPC does not cover investors against poor investments, failed money market accounts, bad investment advice, fraud committed by their advisor, etc. It solely protects customers against a loss incurred because their firm goes out of business. Truly, it's a great program, but not what many in the industry would lead you to believe. For more information on the limits of SIPC coverage, visit www.sipc.org.

We Play Golf a Lot for Free!

On one of my first days at my original firm, one of the brokers came around and told me that we were all going to lunch down the street at a swanky restaurant. When I informed him that I was newly married and broke, his response was, "Are you joking? Jim from XYZ funds is buying. It's free."

It turns out there were a lot of guys from various mutual fund and insurance companies who liked to go out and have a good time. Best of all, they were more than happy to pick up the tab. Golf, NASCAR, the theater, deep sea fishing, you name it. Of course, they'd all be mighty appreciative if you direct your clients to consider their products for their investing needs.

Anyone see a problem here?

As it turns out, there is a pretty phenomenal "pay-to-play" environment on Wall Street. In fact, there are people whose only job is to travel around to each firm's office to "educate" the advisors about their products over lunch, golf, etc.

While Wall Street has been trying to crack down on these practices in recent years, mutual funds and insurance companies keep coming up with creative ways to get their products in front of advisors. So before you sign on for XYZ fund family, do yourself a favor and ask your advisor if they receive any perks for recommending a specific product.

Watch Your Back

If your investment professional is a fee-based advisor, they are required to file a Form ADV with the Securities and Exchange Commission (SEC) or the individual state. This form requires your advisor to list any potential conflicts of interest, including beneficial relationships with other financial institutions. You can search for your advisor's Form ADV at www.adviserinfo.sec.gov.

Our Mutual Funds Won't Transfer

As mentioned previously with in-house money market funds, Wall Street firms would love to see you use their name-brand products over someone else's. That way, they get to keep both the up-front commission as well as the ongoing management fees.

While many advisors are quick to put their firm's funds at the top of their short list of recommendations (there's usually some internal incentive for doing so), they fail to mention one important fact. If you ever plan on transferring to one of their competitors, there's a good chance that these assets won't be transferable. Call it territorial, but most Wall Street firms don't have any interest in holding another firm's proprietary funds. This means that you'll have to pay a surrender charge or a new commission, maybe both, if you want to move your money elsewhere. Of course, that works out well for the firm you're leaving—but don't expect to hear that at the time they're initially selling them to you.

Our Buy Ratings Might Be Comprised

Wall Street is home to more funny sayings than you can shake a stick at. One of my favorites is the "Chinese Wall," a reference to the substantial barrier that the Great Wall of China was to foreign invaders. On Wall Street, the Chinese Wall refers to an ethical barrier that's supposed to exist between the units of a Wall Street firm that help corporations with their needs (called investment banking) and those that provide advice to individual clients (through full-service *retail* or self-service *discount* brokerage firms).

This barrier is supposed to keep advisors and their clients from being influenced by the very profitable relationships firms maintain with large corporations. The key phrase here is "supposed to."

def•i•ni•tion

> **Retail** financial service firms refer to the large, full-service investment firms that dominate Wall Street and focus on individual client-professional relationships. **Discount** financial service firms refer to lower-cost investment firms that provide the tools for clients who wish to invest on their own, without paying the higher fees.

In recent years, there have been a number of high-profile scandals where Wall Street analysts who provide buy and sell recommendations for their firm's clients were being inappropriately influenced by the companies that also had an investment banking relationship with the firm. In other words, companies that were dropping millions of dollars on corporate services thought that the firms owed them the courtesy of pumping up the demand for their stock as well. So next time your advisor provides you with a buy recommendation that's out of the blue, don't be afraid to ask him or her if their firm maintains an investment banking relationship with that company. It's your money, and you deserve all the facts.

Save Yourself Some Money and Heartache

Despite all their flaws, investment professionals and brokerages are a necessary part of your journey toward your financial goals. Whether you're using a discount broker or a full-service investment professional, your goal is to know enough to protect yourself and keep your financial "train" on the tracks.

In reality, it's very easy to get financial professionals eating out of your hand. It's a very competitive business, something high financial IQ people use to their advantage. While I'd never advocate treating anyone in a disrespectful manner, you should not hesitate to play these cards when the time is right.

Every Fee Is Negotiable

Remember those commissions, asset management fees, account fees, and financial-planning fees you read about earlier in the chapter? Turns out that they're very open to negotiation, especially at the full-service investment firms. In fact, you can save yourself thousands of dollars by simply communicating that a firm's pricing is not competitive and that you're not afraid to look around.

Here are some tips on getting each fee knocked down or even eliminated in some cases:

 ◆ **Stock commissions.** Though they won't advertise this fact, all
    brokers have a commission calculator built right into their com-
    puter. This calculator allows them to tweak the commission you
    pay by applying a discount, usually ranging from 5 to 50 percent.
    Depending on the size of the trade you're executing, a broker can
    usually discount the trade 20 to 30 percent without their "payout
    grid" percentage being lowered. To start getting a discount, try
    saying something scary like, "I'd really like to keep working with
    you, but I don't think these commission rates are helping me reach
    my goals. Can you discount them so I don't have to go elsewhere?"

 ◆ **Asset management fees.** These fees, just like commissions, aren't
    set in stone. In fact, at most full-service firms, they range from
    around .75 to 2½ percent annually, and are determined by what the
    broker thinks he or she can get you to pay. Even if you've already
    committed to a rate plan, don't be afraid to ask your broker to
    change it, especially if there are mutual funds in the account.

 ◆ **Account maintenance fees.** Account maintenance fees, some-
    times called custodial fees, are one of the easiest things to get
    waived if you have a substantial account. This is especially true

with IRAs. At discount brokerages, this is usually the decision of the branch manager; at full-service firms it's usually the decision of your investment professional (who will absorb them him- or herself). Either way, the tactic used by those in the know is generally the same as above. You need to voice both a concern that you're being charged these fees and an awareness that there are plenty of other firms that will waive them for you. That's often enough to save you $50 to $100 per year!

Check Your Firm or Professional's Background

Most consumers have no idea that they can do a fairly in-depth background check on their investment professional and firm. I'm not just talking about calling your local Better Business Bureau, but being able to see their history of complaints, education, licensing, registration information, and even a behind-the-scenes breakdown of many of their fees and services.

This information is available for free from either the Financial Industry Regulatory Authority (FINRA) or the SEC, and is something every investor should look at before beginning a professional relationship. In the financial intuition department, most savvy investors are as interested in whether or not their advisor has communicated honestly about their past as they are the facts themselves.

In the Know

To look up a stockbroker or firms complaint history, visit www.finra.org/ brokercheck.

You should make it your habit when considering a new investment professional to ask about licenses, education, length of time in the business, and history of complaints. If what they tell you doesn't match up very well with their records, you've got to question whether they'll ever communicate honestly with you when it comes to your own financial matters.

The Power of a Complaint

If there is one thing that scares most Wall Streeters more than the market crashing, it's customer complaints. Unlike some industries where customer complaints are fed to a customer service rep who couldn't care less about resolving your problem, most legit Wall Street firms take customer complaints very seriously. This is in part because Wall Street operates on a self-regulatory basis, meaning that they are responsible to a large degree for monitoring their own activities and reporting their own violations. When they fail to do so, it can result in big-time penalties, career-ending losses of licensure, etc.

So if you find yourself being taken advantage of, poorly advised, or not having your best interests placed above an advisor's, you shouldn't hesitate to throw your weight around. The best way to do this is to wave the threat of an official written complaint in the face of the branch manager or compliance officer. Written complaints, even if resolved, stay on a professional's record for a long time. Simply walk into your investment professional or firm's branch and ask to talk to your broker's supervisor or compliance officer, because you have some concerns over the way your account is being handled. I'd frankly be surprised if you weren't sitting in front of someone within five minutes.

Here's the key to getting immediate action: Don't show up with a written letter in your hand, but express to the manager that you're not afraid to write one if the situation doesn't get resolved. By doing this, you're leaving your advisor's manager with hope that they can make the situation right, instead of being backed into a corner.

The Least You Need to Know

- Asset management fees can be preferable to commissions because they remove a significant conflict of interest.

- Just because you can't see a commission, doesn't mean you're not being charged one. Find it!

- Don't get suckered into the "bells and whistles" account your investment professional offers; it's usually a waste of money.

- Fees are always negotiable; let them know you're not afraid to shop around to find a better deal.

- The best leverage you have is their reputation. Don't be afraid to complain loudly if you're not taken care of properly.

6

Your Mutual Funds

In This Chapter

- ◆ Understanding mutual fund costs
- ◆ Hidden mutual fund risks
- ◆ Mutual fund fine print
- ◆ Get mutual funds discounts

It would be impossible to raise your financial IQ without increasing your understanding of mutual funds, because they've become the preferred investment for the majority of Americans. Whether it's in 401(k)s, IRAs, college accounts, or just for speculation, mutual funds officially dominate the investing landscape.

Understanding why is no mystery. They offer professional and specialized management, easy diversification, low initial investment requirements, and a potentially lower cost investing structure. In fact, these features have become so popular, nearly a trillion dollars in new money is invested in mutual funds every year.

But that doesn't mean mutual fund investing is without its pitfalls. In fact, thanks to the explosion in the popularity of mutual funds, more and more investors are winding up with their own mutual fund horror story. Whether it was style drift, phantom gains, or runaway costs, they ended up getting something they didn't bargain for. In turn, their financial goals and strategies had to be adjusted to help them pick up the pieces.

Mutual Fund Costs

I emphasize throughout this book that no one on Wall Street is there out of the goodness of their hearts. In other words, every company is interested in making a buck (or a few million of them).

Mutual funds, even "no-load" mutual funds, are no different. They manage your money in order to make money for themselves. How they charge you, and how much of it you see, is nothing more than marketing smoke and mirrors. As we often say in the industry, "no-load is very different than no cost."

def•i•ni•tion

A **mutual fund,** in its simplest definition, is a group of investors who pool their money together to buy stocks or bonds. Each investor's share of the growth (or loss) is determined by how much they've put into the pool. Most mutual funds are open-ended, meaning investors can keep adding new money as often as they like.

Advisor-Sold vs. Direct-Sales Mutual Funds

As much as people throw around the terms "load" and "no-load" mutual funds, it's actually more accurate to describe them as either advisor-sold or direct-sales mutual funds. In other words, a mutual fund is either sold to you by an investment professional or purchased directly from the mutual fund company.

If they're sold to you by an advisor, it adds a layer of cost, commonly referred to as the load. If they are purchased directly from the mutual fund company, then there is no load that needs to be collected and paid out. In both cases, the mutual fund company itself also collects money to fund its operations and turn a profit. This fee is known as the annual expense ratio, and is expressed as a percentage of your holdings. It can range from as low as .15 to .25 percent in the case of index funds, to over 2 percent in the case of highly specialized stock funds.

The Additional Costs of Advisor-Sold Shares

Advisor-sold shares fall into three general categories, all of which ensure that the advisor receives some type of compensation for their role in "helping you select" a particular fund. This compensation may be paid for through the collection of an up-front fee, a surrender charge, as well as an annual 12b-1 (marketing) fee.

The fact that advisors get compensated should not necessarily be viewed as a bad thing, since a good advisor can be worth their weight in gold. However, you need to clearly understand how they're getting paid and when their compensation becomes excessive at your expense.

> ### Your Bottom Line
>
> Academic studies have shown no-load funds outperform load funds by 1 to 2 percent per year over time. While this can amount to hundreds of thousands of dollars over decades of investing, it doesn't take into account the value of advice. Many clients of advisors would argue that they wouldn't have earned that 1 to 2 percent extra because they would have chickened out of the market at the wrong times, made poor decisions regarding asset allocation, or selected wrong types of accounts (such as IRAs or Section 529 plans).

If you pay a fee up front, the mutual fund is referred to as an A share. While these shares may cost as much as 5 to 6 percent of your initially invested amount, they actually charge the lowest annual fee of all the advisor-sold shares. In fact, they actually end up being nearly as cheap as many no-load funds when held for 10 to 20 years.

If there is no up-front sales charge, but some kind of surrender fee if sold too early, these advisor shares are known as B or C shares. Typically, B shares have a surrender charge that lasts five to six years, starting at 5 to 6 percent and dropping by 1 percent each year. This is often referred to as a sliding-scale contingent deferred sales charge. C shares usually have just a one-year, 1 percent surrender charge. In other words, if you sell the fund in the first year, you pay a 1 percent surrender fee. If you sell after one year, you pay no surrender fee.

While that might make C shares sound like a better deal than B shares, it is important to note that C shares cost much more over time than B shares, even with their more substantial exit fee. This is because the annual expense ratio on most B shares drops to that of the A shares after the surrender charge period ends. C shares do not have this feature, and their expense ratio remains at the same level throughout their life.

Wrap Accounts

As I mentioned in Chapter 5, due to growing criticism of load funds, many full-service advisors are moving toward annual asset management fees as their primary mode of compensation. When mutual funds are bought under asset management arrangements, they're called wrap accounts within the investing industry.

The name comes from the idea that your access to any mutual fund of your choosing is "wrapped" into that annual fee you pay your advisor. Typically, a client will pay their advisor anywhere from .5 to 1½ percent annually for access to a buffet of mutual funds. On top of this fee, the client is charged the annual expense ratio associated with that fund.

The main benefit of these wrap accounts is that it has given many advisors the ability to offer strong-performing no-load funds to their clients and still be compensated for their advice. But as you add up the fees listed above (the wrap fee and the annual expense ratio), this advantage can be quickly overshadowed by its cost.

Hidden Costs of ETFs and Closed-End Funds

One of the biggest investing trends of the last few years, in part a reaction to the management fees of all mutual funds (not just advisor-sold funds), has been the growth in popularity of exchange-traded funds (ETFs) and closed-end funds. These funds, which trade more like stocks than they do classic mutual funds, offer investors a lower cost structure as well as the ability to trade throughout the day. Classic load and no-load funds, on the other hand, are only traded once, at the end of each day.

Unfortunately, as many uneducated investors don't realize, the increased flexibility of ETFs and closed-end funds comes with a different kind of built-in cost. ETFs and closed-end funds are subject to a bid-ask spread and the possibility of selling at a premium to their *net asset value* (*NAV*).

While those both may sound like advanced concepts, don't worry, they're quite easy to understand:

def•i•ni•tion

Net asset value (NAV) refers to the raw value of a mutual fund share, before a sales load is added, or a premium or discount has an effect. It is calculated simply by adding up the total value of everything a mutual fund owns and dividing it by the total number of shares outstanding for that mutual fund.

◆ The *bid-ask spread* is the slight difference between what a buyer of a stock, ETF, or closed-end fund will pay, and what a seller would charge, at any given moment. For example, if right at this second, someone wanted to buy XYZ fund, they might pay $10 per share. If they wanted to sell it, they might only be able to receive $9.50. That slight difference, created through the dynamics of supply and demand, should not be overlooked as a potential cost to an investor of using closed-end or ETFs.

◆ *Selling at a premium to NAV* essentially means that shares of an ETF or closed-end fund are selling for more than the underlying assets are actually worth (the NAV). This can happen when investors are feeling very bullish and speculating on an ETF or closed-end fund, driving up the share price. The risk here is that at some point, investors will stop speculating, and that the premium in price will disappear, resulting in a drop in price for investors who bought the fund at its peak.

What the Mutual Fund Industry Doesn't Want You to Know

It goes without saying that mutual funds, like much of Wall Street, would prefer that you just let them do their job and not worry about the fine print. They'd prefer that you just trust them to look out for your best interests and not question their way of doing things. Unfortunately for them, you've left trust at the door in favor of increasing your financial IQ. You've recognized that the only person who truly looks after your own best interests is *you*.

Mutual funds, whether they're load, no-load, ETF, or closed-end, all have their fair share of fine print. If you don't read it and know the implications, you could find yourself with some major regret.

Your Best Mutual Fund Investment: The Prospectus

If there's an investor equivalent of high school math homework over the weekend, it's being told that you need to read a prospectus. In fact, I would say that 99 percent of prospectuses sent to investors end up in the recycling bin without ever being opened.

Don't get me wrong. I understand that 75 pages of 10-point legalese-laden fine print is not your idea of romantic fireside reading. And in fact, more and more mutual funds are beginning to offer what is called a "short prospectus" or a "summary prospectus." This format, approved by and filed with the SEC, contains many of the key facts investors need to know while greatly minimizing the number of pages they have to flip through. Whatever size it is, high financial IQ investors know that it's absolutely necessary to read the prospectus if they're going to steer clear of nasty surprises.

Here's a list of the top questions you want to be asking as you read the prospectus:

- **Expenses.** How expensive is the mutual fund? Do different share classes have different expenses, etc.?

- **Objective.** Many mutual funds have fancy-sounding names that don't really describe what their purpose is. What are the investment goals of this mutual fund? Is it meant to grow your net worth through the price appreciation of its positions or through earning interest, dividends, etc.?

- **Portfolio holdings.** What is this mutual fund permitted to invest in? Many investors are often caught off-guard by the risky investments their mutual funds end up holding. Yet, when you look at the prospectus, it was clearly stated that the fund may invest in those types of investments.

- **Redemption rules.** Are there surrender charges or a minimum holding period? How long does it take to get your money back? How do you redeem your shares?

◆ **Pricing and exchange privileges.** Does the mutual fund company let you switch into another one of their funds at no cost? Do you get a discount on your load or fees after you own a certain amount?

In the Know _____

One of the most popular ways to classify a stock mutual fund's style is along one of two spectrums: size and orientation. When it comes to size, mutual funds are classified by whether they buy small, medium, or large companies. From an orientation perspective, they're classified by whether they purchase undervalued companies (value), high-growth companies (growth), or a mix of both (blend). Hence, it's common to hear a mutual fund referred to as a large-growth or small-value fund.

Style Drift

This is one of the most frustrating no-no's in the mutual fund world. It occurs when a mutual fund that was designed to invest in one thing, such as blue-chip stocks, ends up investing in something completely different, such as small international stocks. Most of the time it occurs simply because managers of mutual funds don't pay enough attention to what they're buying or how things they already bought change categories, even though that's their job. But it can also occur when some of these guys get a little too big for their britches and try to pump up their returns by buying things that weren't described in the prospectus.

If you're a heavy mutual fund investor, even just in your 401(k), you need to start monitoring against this "style drift." Perhaps the best way to do it is by using one of the free or fee-based services that "x-ray" a mutual fund's holdings. My favorite has always been Morningstar's basic subscription service, but many of the major investing websites offer comparable free versions.

Once or twice per year, using one of these services, you'll want to see if your mutual funds' top holdings and sector breakdowns really match up with its objectives. If not, there's a good chance your boat has lost its rudder and it might be time to jump ship.

Phantom Gains

Can you imagine investing $10,000 in a mutual fund in August, watching it go down in value, and then receiving an IRS *Form 1099* in January saying that you have $500 in taxable income from the fund? Believe me, it happens. This is a phenomenon those with high financial IQ like to refer to as "phantom gains." Investors caught off guard by this situation clearly had no clue about the way mutual fund distributions work.

def•i•ni•tion

> **Form 1099** is an IRS form commonly encountered by mutual fund investors. These forms, distributed in the beginning of each year, show the amount of the previous year's capital gains, dividend, and interest income that must be reported on a taxpayer's return.

Throughout the year, as a mutual fund buys and sells, it (hopefully) cashes out some of its profits. At least once per year, these profits are distributed to investors in the form of a capital gains distribution. However, since most people correctly have their mutual fund distributions set to automatically reinvest, they're completely unaware this transaction ever takes place.

Unfortunately, whoever is holding the mutual fund at the time of a capital gains distribution has to report that amount on their tax return, even if they weren't around for the fun part when the fund went up in value. In fact, it's fully possible to purchase a mutual fund, watch it go down in value (after having a great year), and then receive a 1099 that primarily covers the portion of the year you were invested elsewhere.

Of course, this is only relevant to investors who are purchasing their mutual funds outside of a tax-sheltered vehicle like a 401(k), IRA, or Section 529 plan. But investors who do purchase them outside these tax-protected settings are always looking for a special number called embedded capital gains. This number serves as an estimate of how much un-cashed-out capital gains a mutual fund is carrying at any given point. The higher the number, the greater the risk you'll get a Form 1099 with phantom gains on it.

Many mutual fund companies make their embedded capitals gains estimates available to investors who call in and ask for it. Additionally, some services such as Morningstar attempt to track these amounts in their mutual fund reports.

Tax Inefficiency

Mutual fund investing has its own version of the "two steps forward, one step back" routine. It's called tax inefficiency, and it refers to mutual funds that don't actively seek to lower the potential capital gains exposure of their trading strategies. In fairness, some funds avoid it because they believe it hinders their returns, but there's no doubt it also cuts into the portion of their returns investors wind up keeping.

In the Know

In response to growing investor concern over tax efficiency, many mutual fund families have begun to offer mutual funds specifically geared toward keeping a low tax profile. However, every investor should always keep in mind that performance is their top concern. It's better to earn a good return and pay taxes on it than to earn nothing and remain tax-free!

High IQ investors are always looking closely at a mutual fund's stance on tax efficiency. Does the fund make it a priority? Does the fund have a high turnover rate in their portfolio (which can lead to tax inefficiency)? Do they avoid stocks that have high dividend rates, etc.?

Again, as with phantom gains, tax inefficiency is not a reason to avoid a mutual fund altogether. In fact, the subject is irrelevant when you're talking about money invested in tax-deferred accounts. But in a regular taxable account, tax inefficiency can greatly reduce the effects of compound growth, costing you thousands of dollars.

The Risks of Low-Risk Funds

Whether it is for diversification purposes or to park money in crazy times, investors are always keeping their eyes open for low-risk mutual funds with competitive yields. Yet, many investors don't understand that *all* mutual funds contain the risk of losing their original investment, even if they are money market or government bond funds.

As this book is being written, investors are watching an unprecedented wave of money market funds "breaking the buck." Shares of money market mutual funds, which had been stable at $1 for the entirety of some investor's lives, began to be worth 99¢ or less. Those without high financial IQs were perplexed, thinking that their money in "savings accounts" was disappearing or being stolen. But high financial IQ investors knew that these were mutual funds like any other, with no guarantee against loss.

The same thing has happened in government bond funds, which investors mistakenly assumed carried a Treasury guarantee against loss. They failed to realize that these mutual funds were actually repackaged pools of government-guaranteed securities. That means they could be subject to substantial loss if enough investors demanded their money back prior to the underlying bonds' maturity dates.

"Safe" is a word high financial IQ investors learn to laugh at. Not because it doesn't exist in a few circumstances, but because it is thrown around so much by people (even professionals) who don't understand the limitations of certain investments. Next time you hear someone say something is safe, you shouldn't hesitate to tell them to show you the fine print and prove it.

Annuities *Are Not* Just Like Mutual Funds

Variable annuities burst onto the scene in the late 1980s as an alternative to owning mutual funds in a taxable account. To some investors, the idea of being able to shelter unlimited amounts of investments from taxation for 20 to 30 years sounded like the best thing since sliced bread.

How did they pull off such a tax-defying feat, since IRAs and 401(k)s had limits on the amount of money you could stuff into them? Simple: they took advantage of an IRS rule that allows investment earnings inside an insurance contract to avoid taxation until they're withdrawn. And voilà, variable annuities were a hit!

At the time, virtually every mutual fund company rushed out and part-nered up with an insurance company in order to be able to sell their mutual funds to investors anxious for tax deferral. Things were going swimmingly, until investors (and regulators) started doing the math.

 Watch Your Back

> There may be no greater advisor sin than trying to sell someone a variable annuity within an IRA or other tax-deferred vehicle. The whole argument for using an annuity in the first place was to defer taxation on an investment's growth—something an IRA or 401(k) does already. If someone gives you this advice, you can consider them either truly crooked or truly clueless.

As it turns out, despite many financial advisors' claims to the contrary, variable annuities were not just as good as mutual funds. In fact, they were a heck of a lot more expensive. On top of the standard annual expense ratio associated with mutual funds, they also had a mortality expense to pay for the insurance portion of the annuity, annual policy fees, and surrender charges that often lasted up to a decade. When you added up all those costs, variable annuities often cost investors up to 2 percent more per year than they were already paying to own the same mutual funds outside of an annuity.

You'd think with numbers like that, the variable annuity industry would have all but dried up and blown away. Yet, financial advisors and insurance companies continue to push these on investors who lack the financial IQ to know what a bad deal they truly are.

Save Some Money on Your Mutual Funds

In many professionals' opinions, mutual funds are the single best way for investors to diversify small- to medium-sized portfolios for a reasonable level of cost. That's not to say, however, that most mutual fund investors are doing everything they can to minimize the actual cost of the funds they own. In fact, there are a number of options every investor should take advantage of if available. Some of them are not well advertised, since these discounts come right out of an investment professionals' bottom line.

◆ **Automatic reinvestment/DRIPs.** Every legitimate mutual fund offers the ability to reinvest your capital gain and dividend distributions on a no-load basis, even if sold to you by a broker. Many ETFs and closed-end funds also offer free dividend reinvestment programs, more commonly associated with stocks. It's not unheard of, however, for self-interested investment professionals to actually avoid setting up this feature when they buy your funds, with the intent of purchasing loaded shares with your dividends and capital gains distributions down the road.

◆ **Mutual fund breakpoints.** Just like those mammoth warehouse stores, many mutual fund companies are willing to give you a bulk discount on the load you pay if you buy a substantial amount of their mutual fund. Usually, there are 5 to 10 "breakpoints" at which your sales charge will get reduced, even down to zero! Even better, this discount is applied across all the mutual funds in their family, so even if you buy $50,000 of XYZ's Growth Fund and $50,000 of XYZ's Bond Fund, you still qualify for XYZ's $100,000 breakpoint. Of course, unethical advisors will often try and break larger purchases up across multiple fund companies to keep their commission at the highest rate.

Watch Your Back

One of the favorite tricks of unscrupulous advisors is to sell B shares to investors instead of A shares that would have received breakpoints, thereby increasing their commission. In doing this, they've committed what is known as a breakpoint violation, which can result in a large fine and loss of their securities license.

◆ **Rights of accumulation.** Mutual fund companies would love to turn you into a repeat customer. To encourage this, many offer retroactive breakpoints known as rights of accumulation. With rights of accumulation, any purchases made during a specified period of time after the initial purchase (sometimes indefinitely) will be treated as if they were all made at the same time. If your additional purchases, months or even years later, push you over a breakpoint, then the lower sales charge is retroactively applied. High financial IQ investors know that they should always consider the merits of continued investment in a mutual fund family in which they're right on the cusp of the next breakpoint, before they look elsewhere.

◆ **Letter of intent.** Some investors know they're going to be investing a large amount with a mutual fund family in the coming 6
to 12 months. In these cases, they're permitted to sign a letter of
intent and receive the better breakpoints now, even before all the
money is invested. If there is a change in the investor's plans, the
higher sales charge is retroactively applied to their account.

◆ **Family discount.** Yes, Virginia, there is such a thing as a family
discount when it comes to investment professionals and mutual
funds. In fact, many mutual funds let investment professionals
completely waive the sales charge for their own family members,
simply by checking a box on their order form. If your aunt,
brother, or crazy cousin is your investment professional, you
should consider hitting them up for the discount. And don't
worry, they still get paid a "trailer" every year from the mutual
fund company for helping you manage the money, even if they
don't get the up-front commission. A trailer refers to the ongoing
fee paid by a mutual fund to an investment professional whose
clients are invested with that fund. This fee usually averages about
.25 percent per year, and is meant to encourage the advisor to
continue to serve the account. Many would argue, however, that
it's simply a bribe to keep the advisor from moving the money to a
new mutual fund company.

The Least You Need to Know

◆ There are two main ways to buy mutual funds—advisor sold and
direct sold, each with their own merits.

◆ The most cost-effective shares are either no-load shares or A
shares held for 10 to 20 years.

◆ No matter what an advisor or mutual fund company tells you,
you should read the prospectus to verify the facts.

◆ Be on the lookout for phantom gains and tax inefficient funds, as
both can chip away at your returns.

◆ Breakpoints, rights of accumulation, and letters of intent can make
loaded funds nearly as cheap as no-loads.

Chapter 7

Your 401(k) and Retirement Plans

In This Chapter

- ◆ Navigating retirement plan potholes
- ◆ The fine print about your future
- ◆ Retirement tax traps
- ◆ Tips to turbocharge your 401(k)

For most Americans, an uncooperative stock market has resulted in a well-founded panic about people's future ability to retire. In fact, aside from their home, people's retirement plan balances are often the single largest asset they own. According to the Department of Labor (2005), 75 million working Americans arc covered by a defined contribution plan, representing over two thirds of a trillion dollars. In other words, there's a good reason people are a little freaked out!

Of course, just like many other things, the tumultuous markets of the last decade have also shown us that there is more than just investment performance to be worried about. More and more people are discovering that their company pension and 401(k) plans have been poorly designed, inadequately managed, and even embezzled from. Naturally, that leaves many people (perhaps you) feeling like they need to get educated and take charge of their retirement nest eggs.

Retirement Plan Potholes

On the road to retirement, a company-sponsored retirement plan is very often the best vehicle for reaching your goals. However, some plans come with built-in potholes that can make the journey more than a little bumpy. Knowing how to navigate these is part of increasing your financial IQ and will result in you getting to where you want to go, sooner and in one piece.

Higher Fees

Back when I first started in the financial industry, I worked helping companies set up 401(k) and other retirement plans. So one thing I can tell you for sure, regardless of what plan your employer uses, is that they are not free to set up, run, and administer. Many of these plans can cost thousands of dollars per year, even for a small company.

While many employers are happy to absorb this cost as part of running their business, other employers (aided by the 401(k) companies) are happy to pass a good portion of these costs on to employees. This usually occurs in the form of higher annual expense ratios on the underlying mutual funds that would normally be absorbed by the employer. One of the worst versions of this (something you shouldn't be shy about bringing up with your employer) is the use of annuities as the underlying investment for 401(k) and other retirement plans.

    In the Know

Looking for the nitty-gritty details of how your plan works, what the rules are, and who's running the show? Ask your plan sponsor for a copy of the summary plan description (SPD), a document that must legally be provided to employees when they enroll in the plan, as well as upon request.

Do you remember annuities from Chapter 6? They were those high-cost insurance contracts that unknowing and unscrupulous investment professionals would sell to individuals, despite the availability of the same mutual funds elsewhere for 1 to 2 percent less in annual cost. Turns out that they are "perfect" for small business retirement plans since most of the 401(k) plans cost is passed on to the consumer through those higher fees. Almost without exception, these types of plans end up costing employees substantially more than other types of 401(k)s, which naturally slows down the growth of their investments.

Single Mutual Fund Family 401(k) Providers

Not quite as bad as the use of annuities, but still damaging to the future retirement ability of employees, is the use of single *mutual fund family* 401(k) and retirement plans. In these plans, a mutual fund company helps the employer to set up a retirement plan that only contains investment options managed by that one fund family. In other words, the employer's retirement plan might only offer mutual funds from the XYZ family of funds, but not any other outside fund families. Of course, XYZ may have one or two great funds. But the chances of their funds being the best in each different class of assets (stocks, bonds, etc.) is virtually nil.

def•i•ni•tion

> **Mutual fund family** is the more commonly used term within the investment industry to refer to a mutual fund management company and the different funds it offers.

Ideally, your retirement plan should offer you some of the best options from each fund family—kind of like the all-star team in baseball, except instead of filling positions on the field, your 401(k) provider is filling positions in your asset allocation options. If your employer is using one of these plans, again, you should not feel shy about bringing it up. The lackluster performance that can go with only being able to choose from one fund family may well put your future retirement at risk.

Delayed Matching Contributions

One of my favorite employer 401(k) tricks is what I like to call the "delayed match." This occurs in retirement plans where employees receive a matching contribution for money they put into the plan, primarily as a way for an employer to win the appreciation of their employees and to aid employee retention.

While most employers are on the up and up, matching employee contributions immediately, some employers work the system and hold onto their matching contribution as long as possible. It's not unheard of for some employers to wait until after the end of each calendar year to make all matching contributions due to their employees for the entire previous year. In other words, if you contributed in February, you might not be seeing your matching contribution until the following January.

In doing this, the employer accomplishes a couple of things at your expense. First, it gets to hold onto your matching contribution all year, earning interest on it and denying you the ability to put it to work in your own nest egg. Second, by holding onto your contribution, a business in financial trouble can use it to help keep afloat, putting you at risk that you may never receive the money if it goes out of business.

Matching in Company Stock

If the last decade has taught us one thing about the management of publicly traded companies, it's that they are always looking out for themselves. Whether it's hundred-million-dollar compensation packages, private jets, or golden parachutes, they consistently use their decision-making authority to ensure their own opulent lifestyle. One place many employees are now discovering this playing out is with retirement plans that match the employee's contribution in company stock.

Think about it: what could be better for executives who hold hundreds of thousands, if not millions of shares of company stock? By matching employee retirement contributions in company stock instead of cash, they help ensure the continual purchase of the stock they already own so much of. Based on the general laws of supply and demand, we know that a constant demand for something keeps the price stable or even drives it up. Do you see a conflict of interest here?

Unfortunately for investors, this opens them up to two unique risks. First, being matched (and often forced to hold without selling) company stock destroys any attempt an employee makes at having a diversified retirement portfolio. Over the years, I can't count the number of employees I've met whose retirement plan is 75 percent or more invested in their company's stock.

Aside from the normal performance risks of such an undiversified portfolio, there's the unique risk that comes with their specific company going belly up. That's exactly what happened to the employees of Enron. They were as much hurt by their forced overconcentration in Enron stock that became worthless, as they were by any other mismanagement of their retirement plan.

Automatic 401(k) Enrollment

Can you imagine, starting your dream job at a new company, finally getting that bump in pay you've always deserved, only to get your first paycheck and realize that your company is "forcing" you to put money in a retirement plan? Believe me, it's already happening and will likely become standard procedure over the next decade. The reality is, the more participants an employer has enrolled in a plan, the lower their overall per participant costs.

The trend is what is called automatic enrollment and is being instituted by more and more companies. Under this feature, employees are automatically enrolled in the company's retirement plan, with preset contributions being sucked out of their paycheck, unless the employee makes a point of opting out. Of course, having the knowledge and the paperwork to opt out completely depends on the competence of the human resources department, which varies from company to company.

 Watch Your Back

Another automatic program put in place by companies offering retirement plans is a default investment option. If you are automatically enrolled, or enroll yourself and fail to select a portfolio allocation, most plans direct all your contributions toward the option viewed as least risky. Often, employees go months and even years not realizing their retirement assets have been languishing in a money market account earning 1 percent or less. Be sure to double-check your statements to see if your money is going where intended.

Now don't get me wrong: I'd love to see every employee saving for retirement, but I don't think anyone should be surprised or forced into doing it. Sadly, in tight financial times, many employees are finding their paychecks to be far less than expected because of an auto-enrollment.

This in turn is leading to late fees and damaged credit scores that add weight to an already overburdened budget.

The Fine Print

When it comes to fine print, 401(k)s and other retirement plans are in fierce competition for the title of most overwhelming. Heck, even the term "401(k)" refers to Section 401(k) of the Internal Revenue Code, the granddaddy of fine print.

In the Know

Virtually everything you need to know about retirement plan rules, especially the tax treatment of contributions and withdrawals, can be found in a number of IRS publications. IRS Publication 560 covers most small business retirement plans and Publication 590 covers IRAs.

However, unlike many other forms of financial fine print, the stuff that surrounds retirement plans is far less malicious than it is just downright confusing. But make no mistake about it, that confusion about the fine print and what it means consistently costs those with low financial IQs thousands of dollars.

Vesting Schedules

While I do blame employers for withholding matching contributions until the end of the year, I don't hold it against them to put vesting schedules on these contributions. Doing so helps to ensure that companies are not forced to reward short-term employees at the cost of long-term employees.

Watch Your Back

If you believe your employer or plan's custodian is breaking rules or harming participants, you can contact the Department of Labor's Employee Benefits Security Administration at 1-866-444-EBSA.

A vesting schedule is simply a timeline that indicates when contributions made by an employer to your retirement plan truly become yours. While ethical employers deposit their matching contributions right away, many also wisely have rules that state if an employee leaves before a certain amount of time is passed, that employer contribution reverts to the company. Keep in mind, you are always vested in your own contributions to a retirement plan.

The major implication of vesting schedules that high financial IQ individuals are aware of is a decision to leave a company might leave thousands of dollars in unvested money on the table. Unfortunately, many people do not figure this out until after they've already left a company, much to their regret.

Typically a vesting schedule functions in one of three ways:

♦ **Gradual vesting.** In a gradual vesting plan, you are entitled to 20 percent of your employer's contribution for each year after two years of employment. For example, after two years, you'd be entitled to 20 percent. After three years, it would rise to 40 percent, and so on.

♦ **Cliff vesting.** In a cliff vesting plan, employees are either 0 percent vested or 100 percent vested, with no in between. The maximum length of time that cliff vesting can be applied is three years. So after three years of employment, an employee goes from 0 percent to 100 percent vested in their employer's matching contributions.

♦ **100 percent immediate vesting.** If you work for an employer that offers 100 percent immediate vesting, I'll let you in on a little secret: *you probably work for a great company!* These companies place no restriction on the match employees receive. You can literally work there for a month, receive a matching contribution, then quit and keep the money.

Borrowing a Bunch of Trouble

Do you have any idea who lends the most money to individual Americans? Would you believe, Americans themselves? That's right, more Americans borrow money from their 401(k)s than any other one corporate lender or bank.

While a large part of the reason is the dangerously easy access (no credit check or qualification requirements), it's no doubt aided and abetted by a series of myths and misunderstandings about how these loans function. In your quest to grow your financial IQ, you definitely need to understand the true mechanics and risks of these loans, lest you end up borrowing a whole mess of trouble.

- **Fact #1: You don't earn interest on your loan.** Time and time again, I'll hear someone justify a 401(k) loan over other types of loans by saying, "It's better, because I pay interest to myself instead of a bank." While this is technically true, since the interest you pay on your loan gets deposited into your own account, you're not truly earning interest. Rather, you're just being forced to save more of your own money, without any ability to have it matched by your employer! Further, your underlying 401(k) assets generally become frozen (they're your collateral) and stop growing while your loan remains open. High financial IQ individuals opt for the bank loan, and in doing so keep their assets growing and ensure that additional savings potentially receive a match from their employer.

- **Fact #2: You may have to pay tax on your loan.** One of the favorite rationales of people borrowing from their 401(k) is that it is a tax-free way to access their retirement funds. While this is true when everything is going well, the borrowed amount actually becomes a taxable distribution in the eyes of the IRS the moment you quit or are fired from your job. If you can't repay the loan balance within a short period of time (usually 60 days), the entire outstanding balance is now subject to federal and state income taxes, plus a 10 percent IRS penalty if you're under age $59\frac{1}{2}$. As I write this, thousands of already cash-strapped employees are being laid off around the country and finding out that they now owe thousands of dollars in taxes on money that they've already spent elsewhere.

- **Fact #3: 401(k) loan fees can be excessive.** Most 401(k) plans charge a setup or origination fee for the loan, usually between $50 to $100. While that may not seem like a whole lot, it's quite expensive on a percentage basis when you consider a smaller loan, such as $500 to $1,000.

Automatic Distributions

Imagine: after a bitter breakup with your former employer, you one day get a check in the mail from them for a few thousand dollars. Could it be? Do they want you back? Is this their way of saying sorry?

Hardly. If anything, it's the equivalent of your ex throwing your clothes all over the lawn because he or she's tired of staring at them.

Thanks to some rather recent changes in the laws that govern retirement plans, employers now have the option of automatically distributing balances of less than $5,000 to former employees. Not all companies necessarily do it, but it's definitely a growing trend for companies looking to cut costs and ties associated with former employees.

While getting your money and parting ways may seem like an okay deal, it's not without some major surprises. Oftentimes, especially when you as the former employee are not involved in the process at all, the check is processed as a withdrawal from your retirement plan. And, just like the 401(k) loan, this becomes subject to federal and state income taxes, plus a possible 10 percent IRS penalty.

Thus, if you have left or will be leaving your employer and you have a balance under $5,000, you need to do some homework. You need to find out what their distribution policy is and what you need to do to make arrangements for a rollover.

 Watch Your Back

The number one marketing technique for investment professionals trying to find new clients is to target employees with potential rollover balances, most often those that have recently been laid off. If you find yourself in this situation, be aware that every investment professional you run across has their eyes on your plan balance, and the more unscrupulous ones will tell you just about anything to get it.

The 60-Day Rollover Rule

If you can keep this rule straight (which isn't really that hard), you'll be a step ahead of half the financial professionals I've met in my lifetime. It's a good one to know, too, since every person could very well find themselves face-to-face with this set of rules someday.

When you move money from a 401(k) or other retirement plan to another plan or an IRA, there are very specific rules that need to be followed to avoid it being considered a taxable transaction. Specifically, you need to request what is called a trustee-to-trustee transfer. This ensures that a check, made out to your new retirement plan's custodian, is sent directly to that organization. If by chance the check is sent directly to you, you've got two options to pursue if you wish to avoid taxation on the entire amount:

- **Raise a fuss.** Especially if you think you completed your transfer paperwork correctly, you'll want to go back and say so. I'd encourage you to first nicely request the transfer be straightened out, and if that doesn't work, start using words like "supervisor" and "lawsuit."

- **Come up with some money.** If you get nowhere with your former company's retirement plan custodian, you can still avoid getting taxed and penalized by coming up with some money. If within 60 days you can deposit the check you received plus an additional amount equal to any withholding done on the distributed amount, the IRS will reclassify it as a "rollover." Then any tax that was withheld (usually 20 percent) will be refunded when you file your taxes in the following year.

Turbocharge Your Retirement Plan

On top of making the right investment choices, something you obviously know you need to do, there are some less talked-about wrinkles you can take advantage of to make sure you're getting the most out of your plan. Not all of these options are available to all plan participants, but those with a high financial IQ are knowledgeable and ready to pounce when the opportunity comes along.

Utilize an Outside Account

More and more 401(k)s are offering their plan participants the ability to invest their money outside of the regular menu of mutual funds offered in the plan. This flexibility allows you to ditch the often higher-cost and poorly selected mutual funds the plan sticks you with. Then you can invest in virtually any type of security you like, including individual stocks and bonds.

Why have you never heard of this option? Most plans that have these programs, especially at smaller companies, have put this feature in place for the benefit of the owner and executives. However, due to the high administrative costs to the company that often comes with this option, rank-and-file employees are kept in the dark.

In the Know

The IRS now offers an additional tax credit for low- and middle-income investors who fund an employer-sponsored retirement plan or IRA. The credit, which directly offsets other taxes owed, ranges from 10 to 50 percent of the amount you contribute to a qualified plan. Check out IRS Form 8880 to see exactly how the credit is calculated.

Coordinate Contributions with a Roth IRA

One of the most common questions I get asked by people hungry to grow their financial IQ is whether they should contribute to a Roth IRA or their company's retirement plan. The answer is simple ... both.

The best move you can make, one most people have no clue how to accomplish, is coordinating their 401(k) and Roth IRA contributions to maximize both the company match in the 401(k) and the more favorable tax treatment of the Roth.

In short, there's a pecking order of where you should contribute your money, depending on how much money you actually have to contribute. Here's how it goes:

1. **Take the match.** Your first dollars that you contribute should always go toward your company match. Even if you're only getting matched 25¢ on the dollar, that's still like a 25 percent instant return on your money.

2. **After the match, feed the Roth.** Most 401(k)s have a limit on the amount of your contributions they'll match. After your contributions exceed that limit, you can still contribute, but your company stops kicking in on your behalf. At this point, it's likely that you should shift gears and begin funding your Roth IRA, since this money will probably go farther in retirement, thanks to the tax benefits of a Roth IRA, than unmatched 401(k) contributions.

3. **Once your Roth is maxed, go back to the 401(k).** Roth IRAs have rules limiting the amount of money that may be contributed in any given year. If you've hit this limit and still have money you want to save for retirement, you should shift it back over to the 401(k).

Now some of you may be saying to yourself, there's a problem with this strategy. Specifically, you can't just change your 401(k) contributions on a whim. Turns out, your financial IQ is higher than you think!

This strategy, which yields huge results over time, also takes a little bit of planning at the beginning of each year. First, you need to decide how much money you want to save for the year. If this is less than the cutoff for your 401(k) match, then you're all done. Sign up for the plan and get on with life.

If it's more than your 401(k) matching limit, but less than your Roth limit, then you just divide your 401(k) match limit by 12 months and set your 401(k) contributions at that level. Do the same with what you plan to save into your Roth IRA and deposit that amount each month as well.

Your Bottom Line

The Roth IRA, first introduced in 1997, offers a very different tax benefit than the traditional IRA. Instead of receiving an up-front deduction for contributions, individuals contribute to the account out of their after-tax income. However, unlike the traditional IRA, which is eventually taxed when withdrawn, the proceeds from a Roth IRA may be withdrawn completely tax-free in retirement.

If you've got the firepower to save more than your 401(k)'s matching limit and your (and possibly your partner's) Roth limits, then you've got to do a little more math. Simply subtract the total you're going to contribute to your Roth IRAs from the total amount you want to save for the year. Divide the answer by 12 and make this amount your monthly 401(k) deferral. Do the same with your Roth, and you'll be all set to go with a coordinated 401(k) and Roth IRA strategy.

In the Know

Many websites (both free and fee-based) offer portfolio management programs that will compute your combined asset allocation across all your various accounts. Simply enter the different positions you own, and the programs do the rest. It's a great way to make sure you're truly diversified. Visit finance.yahoo.com and www.morningstar.com to give them a try.

Coordinate Fund Usage with Outside Assets

One of the biggest asset-allocation mistakes many investors make is treating their 401(k) as a standalone asset. Since many 401(k)s offer a limited selection of investments, only some of which we'd label as top-notch, smart investors coordinate their 401(k)s with other investment accounts.

For example, if your goal is to own 50 percent stock and 50 percent bond mutual funds, you shouldn't necessarily try and accomplish this separately in both your 401(k) and your IRA. Rather, if the only strong performer in your company's 401(k) is a stock mutual fund, you should consider using that for the stock portion asset allocation. Then use your IRA, where you have a lot more investment options, to pick a top-notch bond fund.

Target Date Funds

If your only true investment is your 401(k), and you're feeling a little overwhelmed at the prospect of finding that perfect balance between the different options, you'll definitely want to take advantage of target date funds if they're offered. These funds preblend different options within your 401(k) for you, based on your expected retirement age and some time-tested asset allocation formulas.

For many people, whose lives are full of other financial battles they're fighting, the idea of selecting and closely monitoring the funds within their 401(k) is overwhelming. But by using these funds, which rebalance their holdings on a regular basis in response to market conditions, many find themselves freed up to worry about more pressing matters.

NUA and Company Stock

If your company matches employee contributions, or even if you've chosen to double down and buy a bunch of company stock in your retirement plan, you need to know about net unrealized appreciation. Commonly referred to as the NUA rules, this loophole can save you more tax dollars than just about anything else you'll encounter in your life.

Normally, when you withdraw your money from your 401(k) or other retirement plan, it will be taxed as ordinary income, just like the wages you receive now. This would include company stock that you sell and then withdraw the proceeds. However, under the NUA rules, you are permitted (only once) to distribute your shares of company stock from your plan. Then when you later sell these shares, you receive two major tax breaks: you are only taxed on the stock's gain and you're taxed at the much lower capital gains tax rates.

In short, the NUA rules can easily save $20,000 to $30,000 in tax dollars for every $100,000 in company stock you own. However, the rules for this unique exception are incredibly complex and require the expertise of a tax accountant experienced in NUA rules. High financial IQ individuals know enough to take advantage of these rules, but also know they need help to do it!

The Least You Need to Know

- Don't be afraid to voice your concern if your company's plan is too expensive or too limited in its investment options.

- You should consider diversifying large amounts of company stock to avoid the risk of a catastrophic loss.

- 401(k) loans should be considered a lender of last resort.

- Take a look at your company's plan to see if you are subject to either automatic enrollment or distributions.

- Coordinate the use of a Roth and outside mutual funds with your company's plan to ensure the most effective asset allocation.

3

Build Your Real Estate IQ

Few things embody the American dream as much as the idea of owning a home. As recent history has shown us, though, the dream of owning a home can quickly turn into a nightmare. Rough times in the real estate markets have once and for all exposed the fact that many real estate professionals either don't understand the products they're offering their clients, or just don't care. In this part, we'll take a hard look at real estate agents, mortgage brokers, and even your landlord, turning the microscope on how they get compensated and how you can save thousands in the home-buying process.

Chapter 8

Buying and Selling a Home

In This Chapter

- Does it make financial sense to buy a home?
- The people who are making the money
- Agents' favorite tricks
- The not-so-fine print of contracts
- Cutting a deal on commissions
- Money-saving tips for buyers and sellers

There are few things that embody the American (or Canadian) dream more than owning a home. There's something about the white picket fence, two cats in the yard, and the absence of landlords that makes home ownership the goal by which most others are measured. But just like all of the other financial dreams and goals that you reach for, the process of buying or selling a home is interwoven with folks who want to use you to reach *their* financial goals.

As always, I believe there is a place for fairly compensated and honest professionals in your journey toward financial freedom. But just as those with the highest financial IQs would attest to, the responsibility falls on you to make sure that the professionals you use are both fairly priced and always acting in your best interest. To trust that every professional will do this for you is to set yourself up for the inevitable raw deal.

The Financial Myth of Home Ownership

Have you ever wondered why diamonds are so expensive? Aside from their occasional use in drill bits, they have no real practical purposes. And yet we shell out thousands of dollars for fragments of these shiny rocks as a sign of love and prestige. Perhaps the incessant commercials reminding us that diamonds are forever have something to do with the inflated value of these gorgeous (but semiuseless) stones.

I truly believe that the idea of home ownership has become similarly inflated. Don't get me wrong, it's nice to own your home and not have to deal with things like landlords or rent increases. But I'm not sure it makes slam-dunk financial sense in every housing market, though the industry who relies on home sales would have you believe otherwise.

This first dawned on me about a decade ago when we were still living in Southern California and were about to start a family. At that time, you could rent an 1,800-square-foot home for about $2,000 per month. You could also buy the exact same home using a 30-year fixed mortgage for about $4,500 per month (not counting the property taxes, maintenance, or $80,000 down payment). In other words, for me to enjoy the bragging rights and investment potential of owning the exact same home we were renting, I had to come up with $80,000 out of pocket and an additional $2,500 per month.

That begged the question of whether or not I'd be better off just renting the home and investing both my $80,000 down payment and the additional $2,500 per month it'd cost to own the home. I'll spare you the extended math here (which incorporated the tax benefits of ownership), but based on the historical rates of return on both real estate and a conservatively balanced stock and bond portfolio, I estimated that it'd take me 27.5 half years to accumulate more net worth by owning a home versus renting and investing the difference.

Does that mean we shouldn't have bought a home? Absolutely not. Rather, it means that I could ignore the pressure that everyone was putting on me to buy a home for fear of missing out on this great opportunity to accumulate wealth. That was a pressure many people succumbed to, buying anything they could get their hands on, while ignoring the need for a rational analysis of whether or not they could really afford it.

Interestingly enough, when we later moved to Little Rock, Arkansas, the difference between the costs of renting and buying was proportionately much smaller. In Arkansas, the cost of renting our dream home was roughly $2,000 per month, whereas the cost of ownership was only $2,450 per month. Based on those numbers, it should only take me 7 to 10 years to come out ahead by owning a home.

In the Know

In deciding what makes the best financial sense for you (as opposed to what is more of a preference and convenience), I'd strongly recommend that you play around with any of the numerous rent vs. buy calculators you can find online. These will help you to perform a similar calculation and determine whether or not you're truly missing the boat by not owning. Be sure to use a calculator that includes estimates for the annual increases to rent and the effects of tax deductions on the costs of ownership. To get you started, check out the real estate calculators at Yahoo! Real Estate (realestate.yahoo.com), as well as others listed in Appendix B.

Who's Making the Money?

While first-time home buyers may feel completely blindsided with all the hidden fees and charges in the home buying (or sales) process, experienced owners don't fare much better.

Since most people only own three to five homes during their lifetime, it's easy to forget how many people line up to take a whack at your pocketbook. The whole process is not unlike the piñata you see at children's birthday parties. There's you, trying to hold on to as much of your hard-earned money as you can. And then there's a line of professionals, waiting for their chance to knock what treasures they can out of you.

In protecting yourself, it's of the utmost importance that you understand how everyone from your real estate agent to the notary public makes his or her money. Only then can you avoid unnecessary fees while simultaneously negotiating those that you can't do without. Here's an overview of who everyone is and how they're going to try and make a living at your expense:

- ◆ **Real estate agent.** At the core of most people's home purchase or sales experience is the real estate agent and the broker they work for. These professionals, when at the top of their game, can easily pay for themselves in helping you to get the price you were looking for and navigate the ensuing field of paperwork. But then again, for providing a service that can cost as much as 5 to 6 percent of your home's value, they darn well better. Unfortunately, many of these professionals still operate in their own best interest instead of their clients'. I'll talk more in depth about the pitfalls of agents and their fees later in this chapter.

> **Your Bottom Line**
>
> When the smoke clears, it is typical for a seller to pay 4 to 6 percent in commission, and a buyer to pay 2 to 4 percent of a home's value in closing costs. If you're provided with estimates over this amount, don't be afraid to get a second opinion from a competing professional.

- ◆ **Lenders and mortgage brokers.** While I'll talk more about lenders and mortgage brokers in the next chapter, it's important to realize that as much money may disappear from your pocket thanks to lenders and mortgage brokers than any other financial professionals you'll encounter during your life. In fact, a mortgage broker may cost you 1 to 2 percent of your loan's value up front, on top of the hundreds of thousands of dollars in interest you'll pay to your lender over the life of your loan.

- ◆ **Escrow and title services.** The professionals who help ensure the "safety" of your home-buying experience are some of the most valuable professionals you'll encounter—a fact not lost on them.

The fees charged by your escrow and title company are some of the heftiest fees in your closing costs, easily tacking on 1 to 2 percent of your home's value. Thankfully, they are also some of the easiest to shop around and negotiate due to their relatively low overhead.

◆ **Third-party providers.** If you've ever bought or sold a home, you've discovered that there are all kinds of other mandatory and optional expenses along the way. Whether it is termite or home inspections, home warranties, or notary public services, these fees can quickly add up to a few thousand dollars. Potentially making matters worse is the fact that most of the providers of these services are in some type of relationship with your real estate agent or your lender.

◆ **The government.** Uncle Sam, as well as your state and local governments, love to get their hands on transactional money, and home sales are no exception. And while you won't be paying sales tax on the purchase or sale of your home, don't think for a second that they won't use it as an opportunity to collect income taxes on certain profits or reassess (code for "raise") your property tax basis.

Getting Hosed on Housing

As I've previously mentioned, when I was first in the financial industry, I worked as a stockbroker on a commission-only basis. It left me with a deep respect for people who make a living without a safety net, as well as a deep disgust for the conflicts of interest that many professionals fail to navigate ethically.

Real estate professionals, just as much or more than investment advisors, have to walk a fine line between serving their clients and serving themselves. This is especially true when your month-to-month survival may depend on a single sale. It doesn't mean they can't do it; it just means that a lot don't. While I can promise you that there are honest real estate agents out there (my daughter married one), I can also promise you you'll never find one without knowing some of the major tricks to watch out for.

Now's the Best Time to Buy (or Sell) …

If there's one stereotype about many real estate agents that never seems to disappoint, it's that they think "now" is always a great time. It doesn't matter what you're doing, be it buying, selling, or leasing. It doesn't matter if the real estate market is skyrocketing or getting clobbered. In fact, it wouldn't even matter if Earth was about to crash into the Sun—the bottom line is that they always think now is a great time to do whatever you're considering doing. In fairness, they're not lying, they're just omitting a key piece of information. The reality is, now is always a great time for someone living solely on commission.

It's a rare occasion when I meet a real estate agent who will give me an honest assessment of a lousy market, instructing me to wait 6 to 12 months before making a purchase or selling my home. That's because in doing so, they're shooting themselves in the foot financially. Not only are they losing the immediate ability to make a living off of you, but they're also risking the possibility that you'll decide against buying or selling altogether. It's too bad though; when I find those rare men or women who give me their honest opinion, free from all the real estate market hype, they're the people who get every single referral I come across.

In the Know

One of the best sources for broad real estate statistics is the website for the National Association of Realtors. The free research section of their website provides very useful data that helps you gauge where home prices are versus historical trends. Visit www.realtor.org/research for more info.

When it comes to discerning the right time to buy or sell, the rule of thumb I'd suggest you use would be to measure how close to the asking prices homes are selling for. If they're selling for 95 percent or more of their asking prices, it's a great time to be a seller. If they're selling at 90 percent or less, it's a great time to be a buyer and a time where only motivated sellers will probably want to put homes on the market. Anywhere in between is probably a fairly valued market and both parties are getting a fair shake.

Under or Overbidding the Comps

There's no worse situation for a buyer or seller than an agent who needs a deal and needs it quick. Agents in these situations have a much higher likelihood of offering an opinion that gets them paid, even if it's at your expense. One way they often do this is by under or overbidding the *comps*.

The comps are the sales of comparable properties within a few months prior to when you're looking to buy or sell a home, and are used to help both buyers and sellers shape their pricing. For example, if another three-bedroom, two-bath home very similar to yours sold for $300,000 just a week earlier, that'd be a good place to start your pricing when you go to sell. Likewise, if the home you're considering buying is being priced at $120 per square foot but all similar homes have sold for $105 per square foot, you know the seller's price may be a tad high.

def•i•ni•tion

Comps, also known as comparable sales or as a competitive market analysis (CMA), are a look at what other similar homes in the area have sold for in the most recent 3, 6, or 12 months. Since every home is slightly different, comps are often quoted in a standardized price-per-square-foot format.

In an effort to expedite a quick purchase or sale, some agents have been known to quote just the comps that would lead to a faster sale, even though it may cost them a little bit of commission over the long haul. For example, if they show a seller who's listing with them only the lowest comps they can find, chances are the home will list for less and result in a quicker sale. Likewise, if they only show a buyer the higher-priced comps, it may make a potential home look like a good deal, avoiding prolonged negotiations or even a soured deal.

To avoid this situation, be sure to ask your agent for the actual list of all comparable sales for the prior six months, even if they think they're irrelevant to your transaction. This will help you determine if your agent is omitting information that could be useful to you. If nothing is missing and the comps seem fair, it serves as another sign that you've potentially found a trustworthy agent.

Also, while they won't give you as exact a comp as a Realtor who truly knows your area, websites like Zillow.com and RealEstateABC.com can give you a reasonably accurate picture of what different homes are valued at in a given neighborhood.

Avoiding For Sale by Owner (FSBO) Properties

Aside from the fact that most agents I've run across won't advocate selling your home yourself, many agents won't waste time showing you for sale by owner (FSBO) homes either when you're a buyer. That's too bad, since many owners who go the FSBO route do so because they've put a lot of time and effort into their home and think it's very special. They want to ensure that they get as much out of it as they put into it, and paying an agent to list it can cut pretty deep.

Since many FSBO homes don't have a listing agent and many of the owners are not real estate mavens, they haven't figured out how to work with an agent representing a buyer. They're not sure if they want to pay a commission to the buyer's agent, much less the standard 3 percent. They don't speak the language, know how to handle the paperwork, etc. In short, they can be an underpaid nightmare for many agents representing buyers.

The solution for some agents, of course, is to just avoid showing these homes. Not because they're not exactly what the buyer is looking for (they often are), but because it can be much harder to make a living as an agent with FSBO homes mixed in with agent-listed properties. To avoid this, you need to ask your agent on the front end whether or not they'll be showing you FSBO homes and how they'll get compensated if the seller refuses to pay a commission. It's not uncommon for an agent to have a contingency fee of a few thousand dollars which is paid to them by the buyer of a FSBO if the seller refuses to pay a commission.

In the Know

Feel like you've got a lot to learn about real estate? Considering that the typical American may buy or sell a few million dollars of real estate over the course of their life, boning up on the process can pay huge dividends. Many local community colleges offer standardized real estate courses (the same ones future agents take) for less than $100.

The Referral Circle

One of the things they teach you in Real Estate Agent 101 is to never stop networking. You're always handing out cards, not just to potential customers, but to people who could send you potential customers. In fact, the dream of most real estate agents is to be in a "referral circle" with a mortgage broker, a home inspector, an insurance agent, a stockbroker, and a CPA, among others. The real estate agent sends all their clients to each person for their respective needs, and the others in the circle send all their clients to the agent for their real estate needs.

It's not a bad idea on the surface, until you stop and wonder whether or not they're really referring you to the most capable person they know. Perhaps the best mortgage broker they know refuses to play the game and won't send any referrals their way, but the guy they know who just got his mortgage broker's license is more than happy to swap business. It's a "you scratch my back and I'll scratch yours" kind of arrangement, with no one too concerned about whether or not you're getting *your* back scratched. To avoid this, high financial IQ individuals always ask for multiple recommendations, as well as do their homework on the referrals they receive.

Representing Both Sides

One of the most basic and honored principles of agency relationships of any kind is that the agent is working for the exclusive benefit of the party they represent. If a buyer or seller enlists the help of a professional agent, they should reasonably expect that agent to do everything legally within their power to ensure they get the best deal, regardless of what is best for the other party.

Thus, a major conflict arises when a real estate agent attempts to represent both the buyer and the seller in the same transaction. In essence, by best representing one party, they by definition have to neglect the interests of the other party. Because of this, many states do not allow or frown on dual-agency relationships. Yet a noticeable number of agents and brokers continue to enter into these relationships, often lured by the promise of receiving both sides of the commission.

In reality, dual-agency relationships are sometimes unavoidable or preferable due to the nature or timing of a transaction. However, high financial IQ individuals know that they need to pay extra close attention to the details of these deals and take all advice with a grain of salt.

Watch Your Back

Most agents talk a good game and are quick to make promises about their ability to help you find or sell a home. To find out if they can really live up to their promises, ask them for a rundown of the homes they've helped to buy or sell in the last 12 months. This will give you a much clearer picture of whether or not they're making a mountain out of a molehill.

The Fine Print

When most people think of real estate fine print, it's of the multi-hour ordeal of signing paperwork to complete their purchase. And while there are plenty of pieces of noteworthy fine print within this paperwork, some of the most frustrating for consumers is found elsewhere.

Failure to watch out for fine print throughout the entire sales process, not just during closing, can lead to thousands of dollars in unexpected losses. If information on these different types of fine print is not readily offered to you, do not hesitate to ask.

Taxes

Most residential real estate transactions are primarily lifestyle choices. In other words, people buy or sell a home because they want things like more space, a smaller backyard, or to be closer to a certain part of town.

Since most transactions are based on their preferences and needs, buyers and sellers don't often consider the tax consequences until late in the process. When they do, they often base their decisions off the advice of a real estate agent who has no real experience as a tax professional. This can lead to pricey mistakes that end up costing people far more or saving them far less than they ever imagined.

I cannot begin to tell you the number of real estate agents I've run into over the years who incorrectly describe to their clients how the mortgage deduction works or what it is worth. Likewise, I consistently hear misinformation about how and when capital gains taxes are calculated when someone sells their residence.

Here's some of the IRS's fine print that is most often omitted or incorrectly explained:

- **The mortgage interest deduction.** A common error made by real estate agents (and lending professionals) has to do with the value of the mortgage interest deduction. Quite often, you'll hear real estate agents estimate the monthly dollar value of this deduction by simply multiplying the interest portion of a buyer's monthly payment by their income tax bracket. Of course, this fails to take into account that most people who do not yet own a home are currently taking the standard deduction, which already saves them a substantially similar amount of money. If they were to receive the mortgage interest deduction, which would likely replace the standard deduction, many people would only save a small amount more than what they currently do without a mortgage.

- **Capital gains tax.** Under the current law, you can protect up to $250,000 per owner from capital gains tax on your primary residence. However, as many agents don't realize, there are a plethora of rules that apply to this calculation that may decrease the protected amount or eliminate it altogether. You should be sure to check out the most current version of IRS Publication 523 for the rules regarding taxation of home sales.

- **Home buyer tax credits.** In the last few years, a number of tax credits have been introduced by Congress in an effort to make home buying more affordable and to stimulate the real estate market. Naturally, some overzealous agents are quick to throw around these credits as if they are something every person can qualify for, with many home buyers realizing far too late that they do not. Likewise, many agents fail to mention that these credits come with substantial recapture provisions that require the taxpayer to pay them back if they sell their home too soon.

◆ **Short sales and loan forgiveness.** While real estate agents aren't typically the ones encouraging distressed home owners to pursue *short sale* strategies, this piece of tax fine print still begs mentioning in this section. In some cases, loan amounts forgiven or erased due to a short sale may result in a substantial amount of phantom income on the taxpayer's return. For example, a short sale that results in $100,000 in loan forgiveness could easily result in $25,000 or more in taxes due to Uncle Sam by the seller. Home owners considering a short sale should consult a CPA and IRS Publication 4681.

def•i•ni•tion

A **short sale** is when a home owner who is experiencing financial trouble gets permission from their bank to sell their home for less than what is owed on their mortgage. Both the home owner and the bank often find this arrangement beneficial since it avoids the more costly foreclosure process.

In addition to IRS fine print that can save you some money, many states offer a homestead exemption or credit for primary residences, to help keep property taxes from increasing too quickly or above a certain amount. While a homestead exemption can save a significant amount, many states do not automatically grant it, requiring taxpayers to file a one-time or annual form.

Lost Deposits

One of the most heartbreaking scenes encountered time and again throughout the last economic crisis was the loss of deposits put down to enter into a purchase contract for a home. In the typical scenario, buyers found the home of their dreams, agreed on a price with the seller, and entered into a purchase contract to buy the property. In the process, they put down a deposit to "hold" the property, ranging anywhere from a few hundred to tens of thousands of dollars. Sadly, because of the growing credit crisis, they soon discovered they were unable to get the financing they had counted on, and in turn forfeited their deposit.

While you might be tempted to believe this is an isolated occurrence, it's happening frequently enough all across America, especially with some of the larger homebuilders who are trying to protect their bottom lines. While the word "illegal" might come to mind, the agreement to the nonrefundability of the deposit was right there in the fine print. To protect yourself, be sure to negotiate as small of a deposit as possible and attempt to include a contingency that allows you to get your deposit back if you cannot secure financing at or below a certain interest rate.

Broken Listings

A risk similar to the loss of a deposit for a potential buyer is the risk of a "forced" commission for a seller. Many agents' listing agreements include what is known as a safety or protection clause, which allows them to still charge their commission if you no longer wish to use them as your agent but sell your home within a certain amount of time.

On the surface, this seems like a fair protection for a real estate agent. It protects them from finding a buyer for your property only to have you and the buyer decide to negotiate the contract without the agent's help, in turn avoiding the need to pay a commission. Unfortunately, aggressive protection clauses can severely limit a seller's ability to ditch a lousy agent for a better one, or even opting to sell it themselves to another party months down the road. To protect yourself, I'd strongly suggest that you refuse to work with agents who require you to sign ironclad listings that don't allow you to leave them or require that you pay them a commission on a for sale by owner unless they directly introduced you to the potential buyer.

Charging for In-House Services

Real estate agents and brokers are up there on my detestability scale when it comes to charging you for the things they would need to do anyway if they hoped to ever get paid. Over the years I've seen or heard of everything from the semijustifiable (notary charges) to the downright absurd (mileage charged by the agent for driving clients around). Regardless of the source or justification of these fees, the effects are the same: hundreds, if not thousands, of dollars out of your pocket.

Why do they charge you for these things, many of which cost them little or nothing? Simply because they can, and because most people are too exhausted to argue over these amounts when they're so close to the finish line. That's why, if you hope to avoid these charges, you need to discuss them up front. When an agent is still trying to land your listing, especially if they know you're considering other agents, they're a lot more likely to waive or absorb these fees out of a future paycheck that they hope to get. Once you're already in a contract with them, they see these fees as something very different. They see them as costs that now reduce their inevitable paycheck.

In the Know

More home owners are opting to sell their home themselves and circumvent real estate agents altogether, saving tens of thousands of dollars in commissions in the process. Making it easier than ever are full-service websites like FSBO.com, ForSaleByOwner.com, and Owners. com, which assist with the sales paperwork as well as the listing itself.

Saving on Real Estate Commissions

For those who have never worked in and around residential real estate, you may have no idea what a cutthroat field it can be. While the most established agents can easily earn six figures, the industry as a whole suffers an incredibly high turnover rate. In fact, most new agents quit after struggling to break $25,000 per year in income. Even many middle-tier agents are only a few slow months away from looking for a new career. All this is in the favor of buyers and sellers who are willing to shop around for the best deal, pitting hungry Realtors against one another.

The classic real estate commission is 6 percent of a home's value, which is paid out of the seller's proceeds and split by the buyer's and seller's agents. However, this has become (and will remain) more and more negotiable, thanks to the Internet, increased competition from discount agencies, and a sustained period of slower sales. In fact, the only people who are paying the full 6 percent are people who don't bother to push for a discount.

The easiest way to get a discount is simply to send out a couple dozen e-mails to local agents informing them that you are shopping for an agent who will work for a certain percentage. If you're in no rush to sell your home, consider naming a commission in the range of 4 to 4½ percent. If you need to sell in a rush, or feel like you're going to need a substantial amount of handholding, you should name a price closer to 4½ to 5 percent.

Remember, every .5 percent you get your commission reduced will save you $500 per $100,000 in sales price. So a $350,000 home that sells with a 4 percent commission instead of 6 percent saves the owner $7,000!

Other Tips for Boosting the Bottom Line

Negotiating with your agent isn't the only way to swing yourself a better deal when you buy or sell your home. By planning ahead and showing a little chutzpah, you can easily save a few thousand dollars on either side of the transaction.

For buyers:

- **Ask the seller to pay closing costs.** Especially if you're considering paying at or near the asking price, you should consider asking the seller to pick up the closing costs. It is often easier to negotiate these up-front fees, which can easily run $5,000 to $10,000, as opposed to getting the seller to lower their price by the same amount.

- **Use a flat-fee notary.** The fees to get your signature notarized can easily run into the hundreds of dollars for a home purchase. With a few phone calls, though, you can usually find a notary who will do all the notary work needed for your transaction for a set fee as low as $100.

- **Ask for a repair allowance.** Many times, after a home inspection, the seller is presented with a list of items that need repairs. If the items are nonessential or aesthetic details, consider asking the seller to just credit you the estimated cost of these repairs at closing. Then you can either pocket that money or do the repairs yourself, if they truly matter to you.

For sellers:

- **Spend on the little things.** A fresh coat of paint, a carpet cleaning, and some seasonal color in the garden can strengthen your selling price just as much as more major improvements.

- **Avoid remodeling to sell.** While remodeling may seem to add a lot of zing to your home, it's arguable whether or not you'll recoup the value of major upgrades when you sell. This is especially true when you subtract the incremental commission, the potential for cost overruns, and the effects of a weak real estate market.

- **Consider home staging.** Home staging is one of the newest trends in real estate sales. Home stagers, which can charge anywhere from $250 to $5,000 or more, help to make your home look as presentable as possible, often bringing in their own furniture. While the cost may seem a bit extreme, home staging can easily add 2 to 5 percent to a home's sale price.

Another wrinkle that can be exploited to either party's advantage is the temporary renting back of a home to the seller. This can occur when the seller or the buyer needs anywhere from a few extra days to a couple of months to complete their transition. For buyers, they'll want to set this fee as high as possible, while the sellers will want to push for it to be as cheap as possible, or even free if just for a few days.

The Least You Need to Know

- Do your homework so you won't give in to unfounded pressure to buy or sell simply because "now is the best time."

- Make sure that you understand all the aspects of an agent's contract before you commit to their services.

- Don't take an agent's word for the tax consequences of a transaction; be sure to consult IRS publications and check with your tax professional.

- Keep an eye out for how agents might be serving their own needs above yours, such as dual-agency situations and referral relationships with certain vendors.

- Negotiate the best commissions by contacting multiple agents and being up front about the commission you're willing to pay.

Chapter 9

Mortgages

In This Chapter

- ◆ Mortgage meltdown 101
- ◆ Getting milked by mortgage professionals
- ◆ Fees you can (and can't) negotiate
- ◆ The refinancing trap
- ◆ Perspectives on paying points

When most Americans think about home affordability, they think solely in terms of the purchase price and the size of their monthly mortgage payment. But then what else could there be, besides occasional maintenance expenses and some property taxes? Take, for example, a mid-size home bought for $200,000 (after a small down payment) using a 30-year fixed mortgage at 6 percent. The monthly payment is only $1,199.10, which may seem like a relative steal compared to housing costs in many parts of the country. But that's where most people stop crunching the numbers and make a decision. If they were to drag out the calculator and do some simple math, they might think twice about owning that home (after they recover from the initial heart attack).

If they were to perform just the easy computation of multiplying their monthly payment ($1,199.10) by the number of months they're going to make it (360), they'd realize that that mortgage is actually going to cost them $431,676 out of pocket! That's right, their $200,000 home will cost them more than twice what they thought they were paying.

How is that possible? Where does all that money go?

It goes to the mortgage lenders, and the people who help them market their loans. That's right, the people who loan you the money on your home will actually make more profit than the people who built it. If that doesn't cause you to take pause for a moment, then I'm not sure what will.

Of course, as an owner, you're at least ensuring that a portion of the money you spend each month remains part of your net worth—something that doesn't happen when you're a renter. And naturally, most of us would not be able to buy homes if it were not for banks and other lenders being willing to loan us the money. But the fact that a home buyer often pays 100 percent of the home's purchase price in interest is something that high financial IQ borrowers are keenly aware of. They know that this represents huge potential profits for everyone from the lender to the loan officer or mortgage broker, and this in turn can lead to business practices that don't put the consumer first. Further, high financial IQ individuals know that anything they can do to lower their costs may save them tens of thousands of dollars that can be diverted toward other financial goals.

What Caused the Mortgage Meltdown?

Just after the turn of the twenty-first century, the North American economy began experiencing a financial meltdown unparalleled since the Great Depression of the 1920s and 1930s. At the heart of this meltdown was one of the most overinflated housing markets (if not the most overinflated) ever. And at the heart of that overinflated housing market was one of the "easiest" mortgage environments ever. Anyone, almost regardless of their credit history and income levels, could borrow hundreds of thousands of dollars to purchase a home. Making matters worse, they could do it using fancy products that arguably weren't even fully understood by the companies and people offering them.

Before we begin looking at how some in the mortgage industry seek to take advantage of you, it's important to realize that the mortgage meltdown was as much the fault of consumers as it was big corporations, unscrupulous mortgage professionals, or *subprime lending.* Failing to realize the consumer's role in the crisis can lead to your own private mortgage meltdown, even amidst an otherwise stable economy.

def•i•ni•tion

> **Subprime lending** refers to loans made to borrowers with below-average credit who consequently pay higher rates and fees for their loans. Subprime mortgages serve an important role in the lending markets for some borrowers, but were clearly overused in the last housing boom.

In the end, most people who lost their homes simply reaped what they had sown. If that was you, don't feel too bad, since you weren't the only one. If it wasn't you, it doesn't necessarily mean you were extraordinarily smart so much as you were lucky, so don't get too cocky. In either case, examining the key decisions troubled home owners made will help you to avoid them in the future.

Using the Lowest Rates

It's a fairly simple relationship—lower interest rates mean lower payments. And being that we as humans like to avoid pain, many people automatically chose the lowest interest rates available without even looking at the type of loan it came with. Of course, the loans with the lowest rates and payments (at least at the start) are usually adjustable rate mortgages. But when these rates began to ratchet up, as they will inevitably do at some point over a 30-year mortgage, many home owners found themselves barely hanging on. If they had taken the slightly higher interest rate on a 30-year fixed mortgage, most of them would still be in their homes without foreclosures, late payments, and other black marks on their records.

Buying Too Much Home

Sadly, many people did not simply use the lower interest rates of adjustable rate mortgages to ensure a lower mortgage payment. Rather, they used it to buy a larger home, for the maximum monthly payment their budget could bear. It didn't matter that a home was larger than someone needed or had amenities they'd never use, those were all things they didn't have to worry about thanks to low rates. Naturally, when rates started climbing and home sales got sluggish, these people with the loans on the largest of homes got hurt the most. The moral of the story is to avoid buying more home than you need, just because you can.

In the Know

When it comes to "too much home," there are a couple of good financial rules of thumb to keep in mind. Most importantly, you should try and keep your housing costs under 50 percent of your household's total income. Second, your total fixed expenses, including your mortgage, should be less than 65 percent of your household's total income.

Not Expecting a Downturn

As the housing market crashed, high financial IQ consumers groaned what was perhaps the largest collective "we told you so" in the history of mankind. They watched in horror as most home owners built a financial house of cards, expecting the wind to never blow. They borrowed the maximum available, under the assumption that both their home prices and wages would continue to go up, while rates would continue to go down. Like an elephant perched on a three-legged stool, instability in any one of those areas would likely cause the whole thing to come crashing down. Ironically, all three legs seemed to give way at the same time. Most home buyers who survived were the ones not counting on a financial utopia for their mortgages to stay out of trouble. The smart (or lucky) ones had bought a home they could afford even on a reduced income, they locked in their rates, and were comfortable staying in those homes for the long run should the need present itself.

Drawing Out Their Equity

Like the foolhardy pilot who was so sure that his plane would never crash that he used his parachute for a tablecloth, many home owners tapped the equity in their homes for foolish and temporary things. When the real estate market came crashing down, their depleted equity left them owing dramatically more than their homes were worth. In turn, this kept them from being able to sell a home that they could no longer afford the payments on, forcing many into foreclosure. The high financial IQ borrower knows that their home equity not only represents an investment that can be used in the future, but also a parachute and a safety net in the present, should home prices come crashing down.

In the Know

Despite what many people think, not all mortgage interest is deductible, especially when it comes to home-equity lines of credit. If the loan is not used to buy or improve a home, the home-equity interest is deductible only on the first $100,000 borrowed, and is further limited if the combined value of the line of credit and their primary loan exceed the total value of the home. See IRS Publication 936 for more details.

How the Mortgage Industry Gets You

The business model in the mortgage industry is torn between two realities—they need your money today, but they can earn much more on whatever you finance over 30 years. In other words, you paying up-front fees keeps the lights on, but increasing your loan balance makes them rich.

With this in mind, borrowers typically encounter a mix of up-front fees and attempts to push up both the borrowed amount and the rate at which it's borrowed. To protect yourself, you've got to be aggressive at negotiating on both fronts, as well as knowing the tricks and traps that can leave you paying more than you originally signed on for.

Playing the Shell Game with Rates

The most classic trick of course, is the "bait and switch," where consumers are shown one rate and then get stuck with another. Usually this happens under the guise of a certain rate no longer being available or the property, borrower, or loan type not qualifying for that rate. Worst of all, as some borrowers have recently found out, the rate adjustment rules on their adjustable rate mortgage were tweaked at closing, leaving them far more vulnerable than they had bargained for.

There are a couple of ways to handle discovering a bait and switch on your promised rate or terms. Most simply, you should point out the change and demand it revert to the discussed terms, not taking no for an answer. If your mortgage professional shows any signs of dragging their feet, you shouldn't hesitate to immediately contact another mortgage professional for a counteroffer, letting your original mortgage professional know you're doing so.

Origination Fees and Commissions

The vast majority of mortgages issued every year involve face-to-face interaction with some kind of lending professional. In many cases, this is an employee of the bank or lending institution where a consumer does their normal banking. Other times, it is a broker who works independently and has relationships with multiple lending institutions. Either way, these individuals usually receive all their compensation in the form of *origination fees* or commissions on the front end of a mortgage transaction, based on the amount of money loaned, the rate it is loaned at, and the length of the loan.

def•i•ni•tion

> **Origination fees** refer to a fee paid by the lender to an employee or outside mortgage professional for starting or "originating" the loan process between a borrower and that lender. Origination fees may be as small as .25 percent for a lender's own employees, and can exceed 1½ to 2 percent for independent mortgage professionals who partner with the lender.

All that means that these professionals have a vested interest in you borrowing as much as you can, for as long as you can, at as high of a rate as you can bear. Now as always, some professionals successfully navigate this fine line between their payday and your white picket fence. But others are constantly in a mode of sizing you up and offering (or pushing) as much lending product as they can.

Typically, a loan officer or mortgage broker earns a base amount somewhere between .25 percent to 2 percent, which is actually referred to as "points" instead of "percent." In other words, a half-point origination fee is equal to one-half of one percent (.5 percent) of the loan amount.

As a rule of thumb, a loan with a one point (1 percent) origination fee is fairly priced, but has some room to be negotiated. Anything above 1 percent should be shopped around since this amount, even though initially paid by the lender, ultimately ends up raising the cost of your loan over time.

But the mortgage origination fee or commission is not the only place that the mortgage broker or lending officer may try to take advantage of you. Most lenders allow brokers and lending officers to try and lock you into a rate above the going market rate, keeping or splitting the difference in revenue. This difference between rates, known as the yield spread premium, increases their profits by 2 percent of the loan amount for every .5 percent they raise your rate. So a mortgage broker that gets you to pay 6 percent instead of the going rate of 5½ percent will earn $5,000 more for every $250,000 in mortgage balance.

Cutting down both the origination fee (or commission) and the yield spread premium is as easy as walking the *good faith estimate* (GFE) you receive from your lender across the street to another lender (or five). Once they know they are all competing for your business, they'll begin undercutting each other. Don't be afraid to keep circulating the other brokers' and banks' revised good faith estimates since you'll never see most of these folks again, but you'll have to look your mortgage payment face-to-face every month for the next 30 years!

def•i•ni•tion

The **good faith estimate (GFE)** is a form provided by a potential lender to a borrower within three days of completing an application. This allows the borrower to get a full picture of all the estimated costs before committing to the loan, and thus should be reviewed carefully and compared to other offers.

Loan Fees

Just like the actual process of purchasing a home, mortgages come with a stack of fees that are often kept under wraps until right before you close on your mortgage. Since most people are at the end of their sanity at this point, they usually just swallow the fees, especially if they're being "financed," meaning they'll be spread out over the life of their loan.

Not surprisingly, many of these fees simply represent additional profit for the mortgage broker, lending officer, and the institutions they represent. Getting some of these fees reduced is not overly complex, since there is no real cost underlying them. In other words, many lending professionals would rather reduce these sources of pure profit than lose you altogether.

Fees you should try to negotiate:

◆ **Administrative fee.** Many brokers add on an administrative fee that may range from $500 to $1,000. While the term "administrative fee" sounds official, it's generally code for "extra profit." Often, this fee goes straight into the pocket of the person who's also receiving the commission or origination fee on the mortgage. When shopping for a competing bid, make sure to mention your displeasure about this fee so that other mortgage professionals begin whittling away at it as well as your rate.

◆ **Application fees.** As hard as it is to believe, many mortgage professionals charge an application fee on top of their administrative fee. High financial IQ individuals view either fee by itself as a stretch, and view the presence of both as preposterous. Especially if you have solid credit, meaning that your loan application will likely get approved, you should tell your broker that you're bothered by this fee and will be shopping elsewhere unless he'd like to rethink it before you make your final decision.

◆ **Credit check fees.** While many smaller mortgage brokers and hometown banks may legitimately have to pay $10 to $20 for a credit report, most large lenders receive these at a greatly discounted rate. While it's not worth finding a completely new lender over a $20 fee, you should not be shy about asking them to absorb that fee.

◆ **Wiring fees.** Sending money from one institution to another usually costs something on the sender's end, but not on the receiver's end. If your lender is charging you money to receive a wire, it's a bogus fee and should be challenged.

Fees that you generally can't negotiate:

◆ **Third-party fees.** Generally, the fees for services charged by outside vendors such as title insurance, appraisal fees, escrow, and county transfer fees, are going to be hard to negotiate. In fact, your mortgage broker or bank probably has nothing to do with the fees set by the third parties who perform these services. Your best bet to getting a discount on these services is to call a couple of each type of provider to see if they're willing to compete for your business.

Regular Refinancing

Just like some stockbrokers churn their clients' accounts for profits and some insurance agents incessantly replace policies for a new commission, some mortgage professionals push their clients to refinance every time rates drop even slightly. Worst of all, the most unscrupulous (or clueless) mortgage professionals really position themselves as doing you a favor every three to five years by recommending this.

Of course, if you are constantly refinancing a mortgage that has less than 30 years left back into a new 30-year mortgage, *you'll never pay off your loan!* The only thing you'll do is pay an ever-bigger mountain of interest to your lender, who then pays an additional commission to your mortgage professional.

Once you begin doing the math, you see how absurd continuous refinancing can be. Imagine having a $200,000 loan at 6½ percent for 30 years, with a monthly payment of $1,264.14. After five years of making payments, the loan balance will have dropped to $187,222. If the home owner continues to pay on that loan from that point on, the remaining payments of the 25 years will amount to $379,242.

If the $187,222 remaining balance is refinanced at 6 percent, it would result in a new payment of just $1,122.49, roughly $140 less per month. On the surface, that sounds like a great deal, until you do the simple math of multiplying that monthly payment by the new 30-year mortgage term. Only then do you realize that this refinancing, which is seemingly saving you money each month, will cost you $404,096. That's $24,854 more than if you left your mortgage alone, because your mortgage professional did the favor of helping you refinance!

So when it comes to refinancing a mortgage, there are a couple of rules you should try to live by:

1. **Three-year cost recovery.** I generally recommend that anyone refinancing a mortgage should be able to recover their up-front costs within three years through their lower monthly payments. For example, if it costs you $2,500 out of pocket to refinance, you should save at least that much over the first two to three years.

2. **Continue with original amount.** The real financial geniuses use refinancing to lower their interest rate, but not their payment. In other words, whatever new payment they're given by their lender, they continue to pay their original monthly payment. This ensures that their mortgage will get paid off in less than 30 years, while actually costing them less than before.

3. **Don't take money out.** "Cash out" refinances are one of some mortgage professionals' favorite tricks to make an extra $500 to $1,000. By getting you to take out $50,000 to $100,000 for home repairs, a dream vacation, or paying off other debt, they generate a higher commission for themselves due to the higher balance.

Watch Your Back

In an effort to increase their profits through increasing the size of mortgages, many lending professionals pushed negative amortization mortgages (NegAms) on their clients during the last housing boom. These mortgages, which promised greater flexibility by allowing home owners to pay less than they actually owed, led to ballooning loan balances that eventually strangled many home owners' finances.

Mortgage Fine Print to Watch For

Many people, when they're trying to protect themselves during the home buying process, will spend hours going through the sales contract with a fine-tooth comb, negotiating away a few hundred dollars in fees if they're lucky. Then ironically, they spend almost no time comparatively going through their mortgage agreement, where surprise changes in terms can cost them tens of thousands.

Luckily, the Real Estate Settlement Protection Act (RESPA) and other government regulations require lenders to provide some of the clearest disclosures of any financial industry, including:

◆ **The good faith estimate (GFE).** As mentioned earlier, the good faith estimate is an itemized list of all the estimated costs associated with your loan that must be provided within three days of applying.

◆ **The Truth in Lending (TIL) statement.** This form must also be provided by your lender within three days of applying for a loan. It clearly outlines the annual percentage rate (APR) of the loan, which may vary from the rate you were quoted; the monthly payments; and the total of all your payments after the loan is paid in full.

◆ **HUD-1 statement.** The HUD-1 statement must be provided to a borrower no less than 24 hours prior to closing on their loan. It includes itemized details of all the final (not estimated) settlement costs associated with the loan. This HUD-1 statement should be compared to your original good faith estimate (GFE) to see if anything has changed.

It's important to ask your lender about potential prepayment and early payoff penalties, which are often buried in your mortgage's fine print. These penalties occur when a borrower pays off their mortgage too quickly through additional principal payments, a sale, or refinancing, and can add thousands of dollars of costs to your new loan.

Saving Big on Your Mortgage

While nitpicking the up-front cost of your mortgage should be a given, the best way to save big money is by simply locking in as low of a fixed rate as possible. In fact, for every .25 percent your initial rate drops on a 30-year fixed mortgage, you save $41.76 per month, or $15,033.60 over the life of your loan.

In a similar fashion, reducing the size of your loan upon which that rate is calculated can have a profound effect. Simply making one extra mortgage payment per year or putting $10,000 toward your balance early on can shave five to seven years off your mortgage. While people with high financial IQs know that paying off a house won't likely outperform the stock and bond markets over time, they do realize that speeding up the payoff process is a great way to diversify their net worth and lower their long-term income needs.

Should You Pay the Points?

Most mortgage professionals will show a borrower multiple interest rates on the same loan, that vary solely based on whether or not the borrower pays additional "points." These optional points, equal to 1 percent (or portion thereof) of the loan value, are equivalent to pre-paying a portion of your interest to the bank in return for lowering your annual interest rate.

In the Know

As with many other personal finance computations, numerous websites provide free calculators that help you to determine if paying points makes sense. Check out www.bankrate.com and www.lendingtree.com for easy-to-use versions.

Assuming they have cash to pay down the loan, many people feel conflicted about paying the points. They know intuitively that a lower rate by itself is a good thing, but wrestle with whether or not they're saving more than they're paying.

In short, if you don't think you can invest your money elsewhere and significantly outearn your base mortgage rate (with zero points), you'll likely come out ahead by paying the points. If you do think you can outperform the rate by a significant margin (at least 1 to 2 percent), then you may want to invest the money elsewhere besides your mortgage.

Another important consideration with points is to make sure you've considered how long you'll be in that loan versus how much you expect to save. Since each point paid on a $250,000 mortgage will cost $2,500 (plus some additional fees) and save approximately $2,000 per year in the earliest years of the mortgage, you should plan on owning that home and not refinancing for at least two years for the out-of-pocket costs to make sense.

The Bimonthly Payment Option

One mortgage cost-reduction technique that has proven itself time and time again is the biweekly mortgage payment strategy. When successfully used, this program can help a home owner pay off a 30-year mortgage in 20 to 25 years, saving $100,000 or more in interest in the process. While the strategy may sound complex, it's based on a simple principle: the more money you pump into your loan early on, the smaller the balance that your interest is calculated on over time.

To enact this strategy, all you need to do is pay one half of your mortgage payment every two weeks. If that doesn't seem anything different than what you're already doing, it's because you're assuming that there are only four weeks in a month. In reality there are an average of 4.3 weeks in each month. So since there are 52 weeks in a year, making a payment every two weeks would equal 26 half payments per year. And, since 26 half payments actually equals 13 full payments, this strategy forces you to make one extra mortgage payment per year. While that may not seem like a lot, it makes a huge mathematical difference.

Be forewarned—there are services and even software programs that promise to help you do this. While they might add a layer of convenience, they can often cost you $1,000 or more over the life of your loan. In reality, all you need to do is set up an automatic transfer from your bank account and adjust your other household spending around that regular withdrawal. Be sure to inform your lender that you wish for any additional funds received to be applied toward your loan's principal, since some banks don't do this automatically.

Wholesale Lending

In the late 1980s, you could find insane deals on designer clothes and goods at outlet stores. I can recall visiting a Ralph Lauren Polo shop and spending $500 on clothes that would have cost me $2,500 elsewhere. But by the mid-1990s, after people began flocking to outlets, the manufacturers themselves slowly began raising prices and putting their newest merchandise in these shops. Before long, much of what you found at the outlet stores wasn't any cheaper than what you'd find at your local mall. The term "outlet" ceased to represent a good deal and simply became a marketing gimmick to make people think they were getting a good deal.

The same has become true of wholesale lending. A few decades ago, there were a small band of lenders and mortgage brokers who made a decent living by offering mortgages directly to the public, without fancy retail branches. This allowed them, when necessary, to undercut many of their full-service competitors. They worked on slim profit margins and high volume, but they truly provided many borrowers with deals they could not find elsewhere.

But in the waning days of the housing boom, as every slight interest rate drop equated to a bigger home, more and more borrowers began to seek out these lenders. So of course, everyone started claiming that they offered wholesale lending or were wholesale brokers to grab some of this market, even though few offered the good deals that were previously obtainable.

That doesn't mean you can't save money now by using a wholesale lender. The problem, of course, is finding someone who is truly a wholesale lender. If you end up using someone who only claims to offer these services, but gives you the same rate they did before they called themselves "wholesale," you won't truly be saving anything.

The best bet for getting a deal through a real wholesale lender is to first get a couple of rate quotes from your local brick-and-mortar bank and a few standard mortgage brokers. Then contact a few real estate agents (or ask the one you're working with) specifically for a few referrals to mortgage professionals who *only* work on a wholesale basis. When you contact these individuals, you can then compare their quoted rates and settlement fees with what you received from the other professionals to see if they're truly "wholesale."

Loan Modifications

At the time of this writing, loan modifications are still in their infancy. These agreements, which essentially change the terms of your loan without actually issuing a new loan, are being used to keep home owners from losing their homes to unaffordable payments. In part, these programs are backed by new government legislation and funding that makes loan modification attractive for both the borrower and the lender.

 Watch Your Back _____

Your lender has an obligation to ensure that the terms and mechanics of your loan are clear enough to understand. If you're suffering because they failed to do this, you should not rule out legal action. A growing number of home owners and former home owners are beginning to recover significant damages from some of the largest lenders, due to the lack of professionalism, honesty, and client care on the part of their representatives.

Unfortunately for many borrowers, lenders are not (and will likely never be) forced to participate in these programs. To do so seems to run against the grain of capitalism and a truly free market economy. Even companies that currently offer these programs will likely discontinue them as soon as their companies' bottom lines and housing prices stabilize. In short, getting your mortgage lender to restructure your loan is a great strategy (be sure to read the fine print, as always) while the opportunity lasts, but shouldn't be counted on as a fallback strategy that will always be there.

The Least You Need to Know

◆ Even safe mortgages can yield disastrous consequences if you buy too much home, don't lock in your rate, or don't leave room in your budget for a lousy economy.

◆ Since even slight differences in rates can cost you tens of thousands of dollars, you should make at least two to three lenders compete for your business.

◆ The mortgage administrative fee and yield spread premium represent additional profit for your mortgage professional and should be actively challenged.

◆ Regular refinancing will likely cost you hundreds of thousands of dollars unless you continue to pay down your mortgage using your original monthly payment amount.

◆ If you plan on being in your home at least a couple of years and don't think you can significantly outearn your mortgage rate, you should consider paying up-front mortgage points.

Chapter 10

Living with Your Landlord

In This Chapter

- The right time to rent
- Games landlords play
- Defining the fine print
- Getting the best rental rates

In Chapter 8, I talked about the financial myth of home ownership. This was the idea that, for many people in certain high-priced parts of the country, it may make very little sense to try jumping through the hoops required to own a home. For these people, it may make far more sense to rent the roof over their head instead of buying it for twice the monthly cost. In fairness though, there's one major variable I left out that potential renters need to evaluate—the joy of having a landlord.

Since my wife and I were in college, we've probably had a dozen landlords between us, who have ranged from downright wonderful to completely nightmarish. Some proved to be, over time, exactly the same person they were the day we signed the lease. They stuck to their word on rent increases, didn't try to nickel and dime us, and gave us every cent of our security deposit back. Others essentially tore up the lease agreement, held our security deposits hostage, and stuck us with every kind of expense they could dream up.

Whether you're renting out of necessity or out of choice, it's important to realize that the landlord you meet when you're considering renting their property often undergoes a major personality shift once you're their tenant. Consumers with high financial IQs know what to watch out for on the front end, and how to take a stand once they're a tenant, and how to ensure their deposit doesn't take up permanent residence with their landlord.

The Best Time to Rent

Like all financial transactions, there are great times to be a renter and lousy times to be a renter. Knowing the difference is the bedrock of all your other financial conversations with your landlord. When the market favors renters, you'll want to push for better rates, lower deposits, and less expenses passed on to you. When the market begins to favor landlords, you can pretty much expect your landlord to become more aggressive in their financial dealings with you.

In the Know

Interested in some real-time statistics about rent levels in your part of the country? Check out RentSlicer.com, which allows you to search for recent rental amounts based on criteria such as zip code, number of bedrooms, and type of property.

Despite what most people think, the strength of the overall economy has relatively little to do with rent prices and landlord practices. Rather, the strength of the residential real estate market, and in particular the ability of renters to become owners, has the most profound effect on the costs of renting.

Of course, you can have strong housing markets in flat economies, and flat housing markets in strong economies. You can also find certain geographical areas that are booming residentially while the broad housing market is suffering, and vice versa. Knowing where you stand in your tenant/landlord relationship is about knowing what the local and overall housing market looks like:

♦ When it is easy for renters to become owners, because mortgage rates and/or home prices are low, landlords in general will have a tougher time attracting and retaining tenants. Because finding and keeping tenants ultimately means months of a house or apartment sitting empty with no one paying rent, landlords will keep their terms (and their ongoing demands) friendly, because they don't want to have to find new tenants.

♦ When the housing market becomes overpriced, preventing potential home owners (younger adults, current renters, and geographic transplants) from buying homes, there is an increased demand for rentals. This allows landlords to have their pick of potential renters while simultaneously demanding higher rent and less favorable terms.

♦ Housing markets that are subject to special circumstances, such as a seasonal influx of people, loss or creation of jobs, or an extreme over- or underabundance of rentals, may allow landlords to keep costs unreasonably high, or force them to be artificially low.

In the end, high financial IQ individuals keep their eyes on the horizon, knowing what could affect the financial outcome of their rental relationship. If a market is currently favoring landlords, they're going to work extra hard to watch their backs, protect their deposits, and get rental rate agreements set in stone. If the market favors tenants, they're going to press hard for discounts and lax terms.

How Landlords Get You

I would hesitate to call these tricks of the trade, because most landlords I've met view themselves as well within their rights to operate in a fashion that protects their huge investment in the real estate you're renting. They (and I think they might be correct) feel that they should manage their properties in a way that protects their assets and compensates them fairly for your use of their property.

The problem, of course, is that some landlords almost become adversarial with their tenants once they move in, adopting a little bit of an "all's fair in love and war" attitude. It essentially becomes your wallet against theirs. Since it's hard to predict in advance what kind of personality your landlord is hiding beneath that smiling exterior, you need to be on guard for a number of red flags.

Small, Regular Rent Increases

When I was first married, our apartment complex raised our rent every six months when we renewed our lease. In the letter explaining the increase, they'd always cite increased costs, nationwide increases in rent, etc. For the first couple of increases, I didn't question it too much. That was, until I met someone who had just moved into the building and was being charged the same amount for rent that I was originally charged over a year earlier. When I confronted our property manager about why the higher costs we were paying had not also been passed on to our new neighbors, I was told that someone would get back to me. Of course, no one ever did.

In the Know

For a full rundown of tenants' rights by state, visit the website for the Department of Housing and Urban Development at www. hud.gov/renting.

Many landlords will increase your rent every chance they get (usually when you sign a new lease, every 6 to 12 months), though they may only bump it enough to make you roll your eyes. While the amount may seem more annoying than anything else, keep in mind that two or three smaller increases in rent over a few years can quickly add up to hundreds of dollars more per month. To protect yourself from landlords who slowly hike your rent, knowing that $25 or $50 a month more isn't worth packing up your life and starting over elsewhere, you should consider doing the following:

◆ **Sign at least a 12-month lease.** Month-to-month and six-month lease agreements give landlords more opportunities to increase your rent. By signing a 12-month lease, they'll only be able to force the discussion once per year. Even better, if you know you're going to stay put for a longer period of time, consider asking for a discount for an 18- to 24-month lease. Many landlords will jump at the chance to lock in such a long-term revenue stream.

- **Prenegotiate the increase.** By getting your landlord to commit in advance to a set amount that your rent will be increased by (especially if you need to use a month-to-month lease for any reason), you'll avoid nasty surprises. Many landlords are happy to do this since it makes their future revenue more predictable and saves them the pain of bringing it up later. Shoot for 2 to 3 percent annually, which is a ballpark estimate of the historical rate of inflation in the United States over the last century.

- **Contact them early.** Again, landlords often raise rent, and raise it by a larger amount, because they think they can get away with it. Since many landlords love to pop the increase on you last minute ("your rent will be going up next month"), you can use the fear of a vacant house or apartment to keep the increases in check. Call them 2 to 3 months before your lease ends and ask them if they plan on raising the rent, because you want to have enough time to consider your options. Chances are they'll either take some of the bite out of the increase or skip it altogether out of fear that they'll have to replace you.

> **In the Know**
>
> Your landlord isn't the only one who can check references. Before you sign a lease, especially for a higher-priced property or a longer-term lease, consider asking your potential landlord for permission to contact one or more former tenants about their experiences.

Keeping Security Deposits

There are few tenant experiences as maddening as taking excellent care of someone's property, only to have your former landlord nitpick your security deposit down to just a few hundred bucks. Yet it happens all too often, leaving most tenants feeling frustrated and helpless, seemingly with no other option than just accepting it and moving on with their life. In reality, there are plenty of landlords who are counting your security deposit as income the moment you hand it to them. And the longer you stay in the house or apartment, the easier time they're going to have justifying their right to keep it.

One very questionable practice that always seems to sneak up on tenants is the landlord practice of using security deposits to pay for routine maintenance and wear and tear—things that should come out of their pocket. It's not uncommon to hear of landlords keeping tenants' security deposits to replace carpet that was already 10 years old and out of style when the tenant originally moved in. Or landlords subtracting money to replace furnaces, garbage disposals, or front doors, claiming that the tenant's use is what brought on their demise.

> **Your Bottom Line**
>
> As a rule of thumb, losing 5 to 10 percent of your security deposit for every year you're in a property should be considered reasonable if your landlord has done a good job of maintaining the property.

Of course, many landlords don't send you the itemized list (if they do at all) until weeks or even months after you've moved out and moved on. They know this makes it highly unlikely that you're going to go back and try and contest their decisions. To ensure that you get as much of your security deposit back as you truly deserve, be sure to do the following:

- **Do an initial walk-through.** Whenever you rent a new place, you should be sure to walk through the property with both the landlord and a camera. If things are already damaged, carpets already stained, etc., take pictures for later comparison. This will ensure that the landlord both acknowledges previous damage and you document it to help remind them, should they conveniently forget.

- **Get specifics in writing.** Chances are, if you ask a landlord before you sign the lease whether or not they're going to charge you for normal wear and tear, they'll say no. At this point, they are still trying to get you into the property and will be more flexible and apt to make favorable promises. Be sure to get this in writing, especially with regards to appliances, carpet, paint, etc.

- **Get a receipt.** Especially on longer-term leases, it's not uncommon for tenants to forget how much of the cash they paid up front was the first month's rent, last month's rent, and security deposit. By getting a receipt for your deposit, you'll help your landlord avoid the temptation of pulling a sleight of hand with your money.

◆ **Demand a final walk-through.** While it may feel a lot more convenient to just move out and let the landlord send you a check, you'll likely end up getting much less back. By walking through with your landlord, you'll be sure that every expense is both legitimate and attributable to your time there.

◆ **Threaten legal action.** If your landlord has taken more than their fair share of your deposit, don't hesitate to threaten legal action in small claims court, especially if the security deposit terms were clearly spelled out in your lease agreement and you have pictures from the initial walk-through. Landlords tend to settle discrepancies of a few hundred dollars very quickly if it's going to help them avoid a day of sitting around the county courthouse.

Using Credit Checks to Gouge You

Credit checks are a normal part of the rental process, with many prospective tenants even being required to pay the fees to run the report. However, it is not unheard of for landlords to use subsequent credit checks, after you've already become a tenant, as a justification to increase your rent. In doing this, they also know that they're putting you between a rock and a hard place, since your change in credit status may prevent you from even finding another place.

While it is not illegal for landlords to continue to check your credit (if you've given them expressed written permission—usually in your rental application), there are very specific rules in place to protect tenants from landlords who use your credit report as a basis for changing your rent or denying your rental application.

 Watch Your Back

It is illegal for anyone, including your landlord, to check your credit without your express permission. If you discover an unauthorized inquiry, you should contact the party immediately and insist they have it removed, since unauthorized inquiries can lower your overall credit score.

Under the Fair Credit Report Act (FCRA), when a landlord denies your application or raises your rent based on your credit report, they are required to provide you with a "notice of adverse action." This notice, which can be delivered verbally or in writing, explains the reason for their decision and gives you an opportunity to view the information they retrieved. By requesting an explanation of their decision, as well as the information to review, you can ensure that your landlord's decision is legitimate and not simply a tactic to bilk you out of a little more money each month.

The Fine Print

One of the greatest temptations with the rental agreement fine print is thinking that things that are clearly outlined in there won't apply to you. Of course you don't plan on trashing the place, breaking your lease after only a few months, or paying your rent late—so why should you worry about negotiating those terms before you sign the agreement?

Yet, it's this fine print, laid out in very clear terms in the comparatively simple lease agreement, that often comes back to haunt the financial situation and reputations of renters. Before you sign a lease, make sure you clarify with your future landlord how these pieces of fine print may apply and how any unusual situations or exceptions might be handled.

Some landlords may prefer to go paperless and avoid a formal lease agreement. While it might feel like avoiding the fine print altogether could actually protect you, think again. A properly structured lease agreement can protect you from surprise rent increases, lost security deposits, and other shady tactics. Consider doing an online search for sample lease templates for your state and encouraging your landlord that signing protects him as well.

Fees for Late Rent

Many people sign their lease agreements without ever stopping to consider what the fine print says about rent due dates and penalties for late payment. This often trips up tenants who get paid on the last day of the month or odd days like the 7th and 22nd of every month. These tenants, who generally make enough money to pay their rent in full, find themselves continually paying substantial late fees that they initially overlooked, all due to the timing of their paychecks.

With many landlords charging $25 to $50 for late payments, even a couple of late payments a year can waste significant amounts of money. By checking the lease agreement for both the rent payment dates and late fees, you can make arrangements with your landlord ahead of time to account for irregularities in your paycheck cycle.

Breaking Your Lease

The ultimate goal of a landlord is simple and straightforward—find someone to occupy his or her rental. So if you break a lease unexpectedly, your landlord is going to be none too pleased that you've stood between her and her number one goal. By breaking your lease, you're disrupting their cash flow and forcing them to find new tenants on short notice. Thus, it's understandable that breaking your lease will likely result in an upset landlord and some lost money on your end.

But life is life. Sometimes people have to break leases, and no landlord should be in that business without expecting it to happen (perhaps for legitimate reasons) every now and then. Unfortunately, some landlords use it as an opportunity to take their tenants to the cleaners. Before you ever commit to more than a month-to-month rental agreement, you need to understand what it could cost you to get out early.

In the Know

Just as violating provisions of your lease can give your landlord the right to evict you, your landlord's violations, especially in the areas of privacy and maintenance, can allow you to exit your lease without consequences. Be sure to check the tenancy laws in your state before making a decision.

Most typical rental agreements (and state laws) allow the landlord to collect rent from you until they can find another tenant, which can easily take two to three months from when you give your initial notice. Some rental agreements, however, include even more restrictive language, incorporating both forfeiture of deposits as well as additional financial penalties.

If you do find yourself in a situation of needing to break your lease, review your lease agreement for the right to sublet the property to someone else. Finding a replacement tenant, whether they pay you or pay directly to the landlord, can greatly smooth over this process and save you a good deal of money.

Prohibited Activities

Would you believe that there are some landlords out there who secretly *hope* that their tenants will break the rules? It's true! It's not that these landlords enjoy kicking out tenants, but rather that tenants who don't live up to rules give up many of their rights. This means that if and when a landlord decides they need to raise the rent, break their end of the lease, or keep more of the security deposit than is otherwise explainable, they can blame it on you. They can claim that their actions are simply a necessary response to you failing to uphold your end of the bargain.

That's why it's crucial to pay very close attention to the prohibited activities in rental agreements, especially things with vague definitions like "no parties" or "no excessive noise." It is not unheard of for a landlord to conveniently use the birthday party you threw for your spouse or the noise your children make when they play in the backyard as a justification for certain actions.

Here are some commonly prohibited activities that you should define and clarify with your landlord in advance to stay out of trouble:

- No pets (does this include fish?)
- Excessive noise (how does your landlord measure this?)
- No parties (how many people constitutes a party?)
- No smoking (does this include outside the home?)
- No unapproved tenants (can you have overnight guests?)
- No renovations (can you use nails to hang pictures?)

Saving Money as a Tenant

Many renters view themselves as helpless victims of both the rental markets and deadbeat landlords. But those with high financial IQs are well aware of the fact that there is much they can do to lower their out-of-pocket rental costs:

- **Be the "right" tenant.** Few things can help you as much as standing out from the other potential tenants your landlord interviews. Dressing professionally, having references ready, and emphasizing your desire for a mellow renting experience will usually move you to the top of a landlord's list of potentials.

- **Be up front about your budget.** I've known a number of landlords over the years who have lowered their rent to help entice their preferred tenants, but it has always been in response to those people communicating their concern that the rent was just a tad out of their range.

- **Rent out of season.** The best time to shop for a lease is when no one else is. Landlords get desperate like everyone else, and are often more apt to commit to lower rent or a lower up-front deposit when they're having trouble filling a vacancy. For many areas, winter and the holidays are the best time to shop for a new living situation, while summer is the worst.

- **Pay multiple months.** If you're sitting on a pile of cash, consider negotiating the prepayment of your rent at a discount. If you can arrange a percentage discount that is greater than what you could earn on the money in the bank, you've made a great move. It's not unheard of for tenants to get 10 percent off their rent by prepaying cash-strapped landlords two to three months in advance.

- **Deduct repairs from your rent.** While this one is bound to get your landlord's blood boiling, most states allow their tenants to pay for necessary repairs out of pocket and then deduct it from the rent that is due. For this to avoid getting you evicted, you need to ensure that you gave reasonable notice and time to your landlord to repair a problem before you take action.

The Least You Need to Know

◆ Smart renters know when the market favors them, and when their landlord is prone to tighten the financial screws.

◆ Minimize regular rent increases and lost deposits by proactively discussing the terms of your lease with your landlord.

◆ Be sure to perform a walk-through with the landlord when you begin and end your lease.

◆ Ask for documentation when a landlord claims your credit is the source of changing rental terms.

◆ Be sure to define and avoid prohibited activities so that your landlord can't later use them against you.

Part 4

Life's Big Expenses

The road to financial freedom has more than its share of pot-holes. If you don't know how to steer clear of them, you can easily spend a decade trying to pull your "financial car" out of the proverbial ditch. In this part, we'll look at some of the most common black holes that suck money away from your financial dreams—health-care costs, automobile purchases, college expenses, and life insurance. You'll learn how professionals and institutions work to grab your hard-earned money, the fine print that leaves so many frustrated, and ways you can cut your costs and redirect money back to your long-term goals.

Chapter 11

Health Care

In This Chapter

- ◆ The sickening costs of health care
- ◆ How insurance companies avoid paying your claims
- ◆ Life changes that change your coverage
- ◆ Saving without sacrificing

Have you ever watched a little kid build a tower out of blocks? They diligently work to stack one block on top of another, slowly working toward the sky. Of course, since they're stacking the blocks directly on top of each other, without building a base of any kind, the tower becomes increasingly wobbly as it grows. When there's just a few blocks stacked up, you can jump up and down right next to it and it won't budge. But by the time it's a few feet high, just looking at it wrong will cause the whole thing to come crashing to the ground.

This is not unlike the state of health care for many Americans, who can get away with a lot medically in their early adult years, but become more and more financially vulnerable to a major health event as the years pile on. In fact, spend a day hanging out in the back of a bankruptcy court and you'll begin to see that unplanned and unprotected medical costs are one of the leading causes of financial ruin for many people.

The High Cost of Staying Healthy

Most westerners are no doubt thankful for the quality of health care that can be obtained, often in the same day as it's needed. But until they lose their health insurance, most people don't have any clue how pricey that privilege is. Consider what some fairly common procedures can cost (including of related costs):

Cost of Common Procedures/Treatment at U.S. Hospitals

Tonsillectomy	$2,500–$5,000
Pregnancy (regular)	$3,000–$7,000
Pregnancy (cesarean section)	$5,000–$20,000
Hysterectomy	$7,500–$12,500
Pneumonia	$7,000–$15,000
Heart attack	$15,000–$45,000
Heart bypass	$100,000–$250,000
Cancer	$250,000–$1,000,000

Of course, it's not just big-ticket procedures or treatments like these that are ruining the finances of otherwise successful Americans. Uninsured preventative and prescription costs can easily add thousands of dollars per year, per family member, to a household's medical costs. That's enough to leave many families with no ability to save, much less avoid racking up a mountain of debt that they'll never recover from. When it comes to protecting themselves from a major wallet-ectomy, high financial IQ individuals know that their number one enemy is ignorance of how the system works.

Protecting Yourself from a Sick System

Make no mistake about it, the health-care system in America is sick. This system is comprised of an "axis of expensive" that consists of corporate hospitals, health insurance providers, and pharmaceutical companies. Between the three, which all operate with the intent of maximizing their profits, it's no mystery why costs have gotten so out of control.

Watch Your Back

One classic health insurance rip-off is "dreaded disease" policies, which may be sold by themselves or as riders on existing policies. These policies promise, for a relatively small premium, to cover all the additional costs of certain traumatic illness. Unfortunately, these policies rarely pay off as promised, usually due to company instability or unreasonable rules and requirements.

Because most health-care providers operate on a for-profit basis, they find themselves dealing with a major conflict of interest just like all the other financial professionals I've discussed so far. Specifically, they find themselves caught in a tug-of-war between what is best for their patients and what is best for their shareholders, with the costs of services being the rope in between. As financial pressure increases on medical providers, whether it is the individual doctor with a mortgage and kids in college, or a hospital system's board answering to displeased shareholders, the party that will inevitably suffer the most is the patient.

Confusing Co-Pays, Coinsurance, and Limits

Many consumers, especially younger adults who've never experienced a high-cost medical event, have a false sense of confidence about what their health insurance covers. Since they've only had a few minor procedures and maybe a prescription here and there, they have no idea that even good insurance coverage can leave you with substantial bills.

I'm continually surprised at how many otherwise financially savvy individuals cannot tell me of the basic differences between a co-pay, deductibles, coinsurance, and annual out-of-pocket limits. Since these costs can still equal thousands of dollars for an insured individual, ignorance of health insurance mechanics often leaves individuals owing thousands to a hospital or their credit card companies. Here's how it works.

◆ **Co-pay.** These fees, which are usually a benign amount ranging from $25 to $50 per visit, lure many consumers into believing that any visit to a medical provider will only cost a small amount. More than a few new parents have been shocked when the bill for their child's birth finally comes and is thousands of dollars, instead of the $50 co-pay they're used to.

◆ **Deductible.** Often confused with the co-pay, the annual deductible is an amount that must be paid out of pocket by the insured person before the insurance company begins kicking in any money. Many consumers are surprised to learn that they may still have to pay a co-pay even once their deductible has been met.

◆ **Provider-specific co-pays.** Many plans will have higher co-pays or limits on the number of visits allowed for certain kinds of providers such as chiropractors or mental health professionals. Sadly, since many consumers initially visit these types of professionals a large amount in a short period of time, they do not realize until later that these services may be covered at a much lower rate, if at all.

◆ **Coinsurance.** If there is one health insurance concept that leads to more tears, it's *coinsurance*. In fact, most people never fully understand this concept until it ends up costing them an arm and a leg. Coinsurance, also known as the "corridor payment," requires the patient to absorb a certain percentage of the costs of major medical procedures, above their deductible and below their maximum. For example, a policy may require a patient to absorb 20 percent of the costs of major medical procedures on all expenses above their $1,000 deductible and below their $10,000 annual out-of-pocket maximum, or an additional $1,900.

def•i•ni•tion

Coinsurance refers to the portion of health-care costs that you and your insurance company share on a percentage basis. Coinsurance usually kicks in after you've met your deductible and before you reach your out-of-pocket limit for the year.

◆ **Annual out-of-pocket limits.** The best health insurance plans will have out-of-pocket limits on annual medical costs. In other words, in a worst-case scenario, you can expect that your annual costs (not counting your premiums) will not exceed a certain amount.

- **Lifetime maximum.** Most plans come with some type of lifetime maximum on what can be paid out, usually ranging from one to five million dollars. While this is usually something that cannot be avoided, many consumers make the mistake of choosing a plan with much lower limits in an effort to cut out a little cost. However, considering that some fairly common major medical procedures can cost hundreds of thousands of dollars, this is usually a poor idea.

Reasonable Premiums—Until You Get Sick

One of the things that can make health insurance feel like a scam at times is the fact that insurance companies are happy to sell it to you when you don't need it, and are even quicker to get rid of you when you do. Over the last decade there have been a number of landmark lawsuits that have brought much-needed attention to how health insurance companies abandon their sick clients.

One practice in particular, known as rescission, involves insurance companies going back and reviewing the policies of high-cost patients to find errors, and then raising the premium or even canceling the policy due to inadequate disclosure on the application. Of course, if you fail to tell your insurance company that you've had previous heart attacks, they have every right to refuse to pay on later heart attacks. But insurance companies have been known to cancel policies of sick clients over minor discrepancies in weight or the omission of unrelated and minor medical conditions that a client had legitimately forgotten about.

To protect yourself from both raised premiums and canceled policies, you should be sure to do the following:

- **Be thorough.** When you apply for new health insurance, it's crucial that you get every piece of medical information that you can recall on these forms. Be sure to include every prescription medication you've taken, every diagnosis, and every procedure, no matter how routine. Failure to do this gives your insurer a foothold to later rescind your policy or raise your premiums.

- **Do your homework.** Picking a health insurance provider with a good reputation for service and reliability shouldn't come down to luck. To minimize your chances of choosing a health insurance company that will abandon you when you need them the most, be sure to review third-party consumer ratings available at websites like www.jdpower.com/insurance and reportcard.ncqa.org.

♦ **Check for legal troubles.** Each state has an insurance commissioner who regulates and oversees insurance procedures, which can usually be accessed by visiting your state government's official website (www.ca.gov, www.ny.gov, etc.). These offices often track consumer complaints and can help you discern whether or not your canceled policy or increased premium is legal.

> **Your Bottom Line**
>
> Self-employed individuals who pay their own health insurance premiums are allowed to deduct this on their tax return in a more beneficial manner than other health costs. These premiums are deducted on an "above-the-line" basis, which means that they may be deducted even if your other health-care costs are too small to be deducted.

♦ **Don't let your coverage lapse.** Especially if you are experiencing a major medical event, accidental lapses in coverage can literally cost you hundreds of thousands of dollars. If you fail to pay your premium (something that can easily occur for a single person who becomes seriously ill), it can result in the irrevocable cancellation of coverage. While you might be able to purchase new coverage, the premiums will now take into account the condition you're experiencing.

Billing You Before Your Insurance

One of the most despicable practices employed by some doctors is billing patients for the full amount of their care even before they've billed insurance. Since the amount on this initial bill may be significantly greater than what they pay after insurance kicks in, many consumers often end up overpaying their medical bills with money that was needed to meet other very necessary expenses.

Theoretically, this overpayment will be refunded later by either the medical provider or the insurance company. But it is not uncommon for this money to just disappear into the abyss of the medical billing process, or even worse, into the pocket of shady providers. To protect themselves against this evaporation of money, smart consumers communicate directly with their insurance company when a bill is received that has not had insurance applied to it.

Pre-Existing Conditions

One of the most common backdoors that insurance companies use to escape payment is the pre-existing conditions clause, which usually doesn't get much attention from the person selling you the policy. The rationale behind this clause is for insurance companies to adequately protect themselves against "adverse selection," when sick people run out and buy insurance only when they need it. In general, pre-existing conditions are not covered for the first 6 to 12 months of a new policy.

Sadly, many consumers do not realize until a few months into their policy that certain conditions will be deemed pre-existing by their insurance companies. This leaves them shelling out a monthly premium for something that is not currently and may never be covered by the policy they've purchased. To protect themselves from this, high financial IQ individuals explicitly ask about a policy's pre-existing conditions policy and are sure to disclose any conditions that they think they may need coverage for.

In the Know

The Health Insurance Portability and Accountability Act, also known as HIPAA, created strict guidelines about how and when pre-existing conditions could be excluded from an employer-sponsored health plan. This means that consumers who are denied individual coverage based on a pre-existing condition may still have a good chance of getting it through their employer.

Preauthorization and Denied Claims

One of the favorite techniques employed by insurance companies to avoid their duty to pay your claims is the requirement to get certain procedures preauthorized. Under this process, a consumer submits a request to their insurance company to pay for a future procedure. The insurance company performs a review of the reasons for the procedure, the selection of providers, and the potential for other forms of treatment, and either approves or denies the request. And while there is some logic behind this, similar to that of pre-existing conditions, insurance companies have found it to be a handy loophole for making consumers shoulder the entire cost.

Unfortunately, many consumers don't realize until it's too late that minor procedures their doctor might recommend may need preapproval. And while you can hope that your doctor makes it clear which of his or her recommendations require this approval, it doesn't always happen that way.

I experienced this a few years ago when a dermatologist recommended that I have a few moles removed so I wouldn't nick them every time I shaved. Only later did I find out that my insurance considered this a procedure needing preapproval, that my claim was subsequently denied as elective, and that it was going to cost me hundreds of dollars out of pocket. I would have never guessed since my doctor seemed to be recommending it. Thus, a best practice is to always request preauthorization for any procedure other than routine exams and life-saving procedures.

Watch Your Back

Under the government's expanding regulation of employer-sponsored health plans, the Newborns' and Mothers' Act was signed into law in 1996. This law requires (without preauthorization) that mothers and newborns be allowed to stay in the hospital for a minimum of 48 hours after birth (96 hours for a cesarean section).

Discount Cards

Discount cards are a health insurance product that consistently costs more than it delivers. With these cards, which are often deceptively marketed as insurance policies, the consumer supposedly receives a substantial discount at local hospitals and doctors. Of course, when participants go to pay their bills, the hospital informs them that they do not participate in that company's program and are under no obligation to honor the discount.

Nasty Surprises with Your Policy

Some of the nastiest surprises with health insurance aren't the tricks companies pull to get out of paying for care. In fact, many consumers expect and fear these insurance fights and are proactive in trying to make sure all their ducks are in a row. Rather, it's the fine print about how their policy deals with major life-stage transitions that leaves many people's jaws on the floor. By looking down the road and anticipating these situations, high financial IQ individuals don't get caught being financially unprepared and personally unprotected.

The Killer Cost of COBRA

For those unfamiliar with it, the Consolidated Omnibus Budget Reconciliation Act (better known as COBRA) is one of the most important employee protections enacted in the last few decades. It essentially allows employees who have been terminated from or quit their full-time employment to continue their group coverage at no more than 102 percent of the cost. The problem that most people don't realize until after they've lost or quit their job is that the cost of COBRA includes both what they paid *and what their employer paid*. For many consumers, this can easily double the out-of-pocket expense required to maintain their health coverage.

In addition to coming to terms with the price of COBRA coverage, there are a number of key rules that consumers must pay attention to in order to protect themselves:

- **Eligible employers.** Some employees may not be eligible for COBRA coverage, depending on the size of their employer and certain other factors. Generally, the health plans of businesses with fewer than the equivalent of 20 full-time employees do not offer federal COBRA coverage.

- **Discontinued plans and bankrupt employers.** COBRA coverage is only available if an employee's former company stays in business and continues to offer a health plan. If there is no health plan, then the COBRA benefit ceases to be available.

◆ **Election periods.** COBRA coverage must generally be elected within 60 days of the loss of employment.

◆ **Coverage periods.** Under most circumstances, an employee may receive COBRA benefits for a maximum of 18 months, though this is extended to 36 months in certain instances. It is important for consumers relying on COBRA to make other health insurance arrangements well in advance of the end of their COBRA coverage.

Long-Term Care and Disability

Those with a high financial IQ have looked at the fine print of their health coverage and know exactly where they stand when it comes to long-term care and disability-related medical expenses. As many people discover all too late, most health-care policies do not include coverage for long-term nursing or disability care. Addressing these gaps in coverage is critical considering that roughly 40 percent of Americans will experience a disability during their lifetime, and 60 percent of Americans will require skilled nursing care in their senior years.

Often, these provisions can be added as riders to existing plans for a lower cost than purchasing them as individual policies. Even then, it is crucial to examine the coverage closely, especially in regards to what type of event triggers this extended coverage. Further, due to the relatively high cost of long-term care and disability policies or riders, consumers should check to see what coverage is provided for them by their employer, their state, and under Social Security and Medicare.

When many people realize that their policies don't protect them against disability or long-term care costs, they begin shopping for separate policies that do. Sadly, this money is often wasted since many long-term care and disability policies are extremely expensive, while providing minimal benefits with a laundry list of exclusions and rules. If you are considering one of these policies, be sure to get an opinion from someone besides the person selling you the policy.

College Kids and Coverage

While college students may still seem like children to their parents, many insurance companies view them as adults needing separate health insurance coverage. This can come as a huge shock to parents who haven't done their homework and get a surprise emergency room bill.

That's not to say that insurance companies are looking to stick it to the parents of college students. In fact, financial hiccups in this area are usually because parents and students didn't follow the steps required to receive the coverage that is offered by their carrier. Most plans actually cover children through the college years (up until a certain age), as long as certain criteria are met.

In the Know

Additional provisions have been added to the COBRA and ERISA acts (ERISA is an act similar to COBRA that protects employee benefits) over the years that protect the health coverage of dependent college students who become ill and must withdraw from full-time school, spouses and children affected by a divorce, and adopted children with pre-existing conditions.

Here are some important questions to ask regarding continuation of coverage for your college-age child:

◆ **Student status.** Are part-time students covered, as well as students who decide to take time off from school for any reason?

◆ **Age limit.** How old may a student be and still receive coverage?

◆ **Marital status.** What happens if your child gets married partway through college? Are they still eligible for coverage?

◆ **Network coverage.** If your child is going to college away from home, and especially if you use an HMO (which may provide very limited coverage outside your hometown), are approved and participating doctors available in their area? If not, you may want to consider switching to a PPO plan, which offers much greater geographical and provider flexibility.

◆ **Student coverage.** Does your child's school offer group health insurance coverage to students at a low cost? Be sure to look into this, even if your student still qualifies under your plan, since the savings may be significant.

Ways to Save

Even for those who are lucky enough to never experience any major medical crises in their lives, most people still spend more on health care than they need to. Through a careful combination of planning, creativity, and self-care, you can easily save from a few hundred to a few thousand dollars per year.

Go Group, Save Big

One of the best ways to save money on health insurance, especially for those with less-than-perfect medical histories, is by participating in a group health insurance plan. These plans, most often used by businesses, are usually regulated by state law and are required to accept all participants at the same rate, regardless of pre-existing conditions.

While most consumers who are offered these plans through their employer participate, many small business owners and self-employed individuals overlook these plans as a way to significantly decrease their health-care costs. For example, a business owner with a medical condition that makes him virtually uninsurable as an individual may be able to set up a small business plan covering him and his few full-time employees. In fact, some states require insurance companies to provide price-controlled insurance to small businesses with as little as one or two full-time employees.

Use an FSA

Flexible spending accounts (FSAs), which are offered by many larger employers and can be set up very easily for smaller employers, allow employees to set aside money on a pretax basis for medical expenses. This is similar to how money you put into a 401(k) account comes out of your paycheck before the IRS gets its hands on it, allowing you to invest more of your overall income. Except, with an FSA, the money is not meant for retirement, but for medical expenses you'll incur during each calendar year.

The funds set aside in these accounts is then accessed as needed by the employee by either using a special debit card, or by submitting their medical receipts to the plan's administrator, who then issues a reimbursement check. Either way, the amount spent completely avoids having federal or state income taxation removed.

Flexible spending accounts can result in substantial savings, especially over the traditional tax method of deducting your expenses on your return, since medical expenses are only deductible to the extent they exceed $7\frac{1}{2}$ percent of your adjusted gross income. For example, if you earn $30,000 per year, you would only be able to deduct any expenses above $2,250 ($30,000 × $7\frac{1}{2}$ percent). So if you spent $2,500 on medical costs, only $250 would be deductible. However, by channeling that money through an FSA plan, the entire $2,500 is removed from the W-2, in turn lowering your taxable income by that entire amount.

There's only one significant drawback to these plans. Whatever has been deducted from your account that is unused at the end of a calendar year is permanently forfeited. So it's recommended that consumers guess low on what amounts they commit to their FSA, including only those things they are sure will occur (prescriptions, regular check-ups, a birth, etc.).

Use an HSA

While a health savings account (HSA) might sound like the same thing as an FSA, they function very differently. Like the FSA, an HSA allows a taxpayer (including the self-employed) to set aside money into a special account to be used for medical expenses. Also like an FSA, this amount reduces a taxpayer's income in the eyes of the IRS by whatever amount is contributed. Unlike an FSA, however, money that goes unused in an HSA is allowed to grow until retirement and withdrawn for general living expenses.

In order to set up an HSA, a taxpayer also needs to participate in what is known as a high-deductible health plan. These plans offer significantly lower monthly premiums than standard plans, but this is because the consumer is committed to paying 100 percent of the first few thousand dollars in medical expenses out of their HSA balance. For taxpayers who are in generally good health and do not expect a large amount of medical expenses, the use of an HSA can potentially put tens of thousands, if not hundreds of thousands of dollars, back in their pockets.

In the Know

For more information on the rules and requirements of FSAs and HSAs, check out IRS Publication 969.

Miscellaneous Ways to Save

Over my years of managing my own family's health needs and working with hundreds of financial-planning clients doing the same, I've pretty much seen or tried every cost-cutting trick out there. Aside from the ones I've already mentioned, here are a few others that seem to consistently work:

- **Opt out of unneeded coverage.** Upon closer examination, many people discover that they're paying for coverage that they don't foresee needing, especially for things like maternity, prescriptions, chiropractic, or mental health. Getting rid of unneeded maternity coverage can easily save $100 to $200 per month alone.

- **Raise your deductible.** If hospital visits are a rare occurrence in your household, consider raising your deductible amount by $500 to $1,000. Since most plans allow you to visit the doctor for a small co-pay, even if your deductible has not been met, you may be paying for a lower limit that you will never use.

- **Switch to an HMO.** Since many health insurance companies offer both an HMO and a PPO option, the same doctors that you trust are offered under both plans. If you're using a PPO and your current physicians are often offered in the HMO as well, you can save a significant amount by switching plans.

- **Look into state plans.** A number of states offer state-subsidized insurance for higher-risk individuals who cannot get insurance elsewhere. While these plans are not the cheapest available, they are still far less expensive than having an uninsured major medical event.

◆ **Ask for generic medications.** After checking with your doctor (some have a medical reason for prescribing name brands), ask your pharmacist to use generic medications to fill your prescription. While the savings may be small if you have insurance ($10 to $50 per prescription), it can save you hundreds if you're not insured.

◆ **Ask for prescription samples.** Did you know many doctors have cabinets full of the medications they prescribe? Thanks to pharmaceutical company reps that are trying to win your doctor's business, a polite request may get you a bag full of brand-name samples.

◆ **Invest in preventative care.** Do you want to know the number one tip for lowering heart bypass costs? Easy—avoid needing one! By investing in proper preventative care as you go, as well as getting regular medical screenings, you greatly increase your chances of avoiding costly and life-threatening problems. Best of all, many insurers will pay for 100 percent of preventative screenings since it saves them money down the road—the only thing the screenings end up costing you is a little bit of your time.

The Least You Need to Know

◆ To ensure that you get what you bargain for, learn how the different co-pay, deductible, coinsurance, and out-of-pocket limits in your plan work.

◆ Do everything you can to ensure that your pre-existing conditions are covered and your treatments meet preauthorization requirements.

◆ Anticipate potential life changes (college, unemployment, long-term care) and research how your coverage and costs may change.

◆ Use FSAs or HSAs to lower your after-tax costs of health care.

◆ Consider raising your deductible and switching to an HMO plan to lower your monthly costs.

Chapter

The Car Dealer

In This Chapter

- ◆ Disarming car salespeople
- ◆ Tricks of the auto trade
- ◆ Avoiding fine print traps
- ◆ Getting the best deals

One of the darkest chapters of my working life, one that is usually left off of my resumé, came during my college years. I was desperate for money and willing to do just about anything. I'm not sure I can ever live down the shame.

What was this dark profession I turned to during my most desperate hours? No, it didn't involve a bowtie and Speedo … I was a used car salesman. Oh, the humanity!

Actually, it was one of the most educational jobs in my life. I learned a ton about sales, ethics, and cars. I worked with people I admired and people I despised. And, perhaps most importantly, I learned things that have saved me more money than I ever made in my few years of offering test drives. Hopefully, through you reading this chapter, I'll be able to pass on this car buying IQ to you.

The Big Leagues of Bamboozlement

There are few things as dreaded for most people as stepping onto a car lot. Within seconds a salesperson is hovering over you, beginning to pepper you with questions. It can be so bad that you almost can't hear yourself think. In fact, attempting to do the thinking for the customer is at the heart of an effective salesperson's routine. Before long, you find yourself sitting at a desk with a pen in your hand, not quite sure how you got there.

But it doesn't have to be that way. Avoiding a salesperson's tractor beam is as easy as understanding the three main stages in the auto sales process: getting you on the lot, getting you to take a test drive, and getting you to sit down. By understanding these, you take the power out of the salespeople's hands, turning them into sad creatures, fearful of losing their precious sale.

Getting You on the Lot

For all the ease of the Internet and the growth of online auto sales, the vast majority of transactions still only occur after you step foot on the lot. That's because most people have enough common sense to not spend tens of thousands of dollars on a vehicle without seeing it, test driving it, and going over the terms in person. That means that job number one for car dealerships is still attracting you to their lot. That's the whole goal of their advertising, including some of the most deceptive techniques of any consumer product.

The most famous of these is the loss leader technique, which fills every Sunday's auto section. Under this technique, a dealer will advertise a make and model of a car at a ridiculously good price. But as high financial IQ people know, there's a major piece of fine print tucked into that ad. Somewhere, usually near the bottom of the page, is an asterisk that notifies you that there is "only one vehicle available at this price," or something even more appalling, such as that price only being available to previous customers, first-time car buyers, etc.

In reality, all the similar makes and models on the lot are priced substantially higher. But since you've now stepped onto the lot, the chances of you buying a car, regardless of the price, increase substantially.

Between you showing up with the intent of buying something, and most salespeople's skills at roping you in, there's a good chance you'll be going home in a new car.

Aside from reading the fine print, one of the easiest ways to avoid finding yourself ensnared is to call or e-mail a dealer midweek (since these ads usually run on the weekends), and ask for a price list of the type of cars you're interested in. That way, when the ad comes out, you can get a feel for how deep of a discount their advertised loss leader is going for. This will also help you determine if a trip to the lot is worth your time if the loss leader is sold before you get there.

Getting You to Test Drive

The chances of you buying a car go up even further once you get behind the wheel, something that salespeople are happy to exploit. Additionally, a test drive usually requires you to share your personal information, including address and phone number—info that will later be used to market to you.

By refusing a test drive when it's first offered, the salesperson will usually give you some space to breathe, especially if there are other people on the lot. In fact, consider refusing to even give the car a test drive until after you hear a price that you can live with. This helps you to avoid falling in love with a car, something that is easily exploited to wring the most amount of money possible out of you.

Getting You to Sit Down

The cardinal sin of car sales is letting someone walk off the lot. Few things earn the disdain of a sales manager as a salesperson's inability to get you to "sit." That's because, once you sit, the probability of you buying a car (assuming you can get financed) jumps to nearly 100 percent. Very few people have the strength to walk away once the salesperson starts throwing monthly payments at them.

As a rule of thumb, I don't think you should ever buy a car on the same day you visit the lot, unless you just can't live without a certain car. By learning to walk off the lot (even if you walk back on later), you take control of the negotiation process before it even starts. Because you haven't yet sat down, the dealer is more prone to offer you the terms you want to avoid losing the sale altogether.

I recommend getting the salesperson's number and either calling it a day or going and grabbing some lunch. After a few hours (or days) pass, call the salesperson and tell him you're interested in the car, but just not at that price. Tell him what you're willing to pay for the car and tell him to call you back if he thinks he can swing you a deal. Be sure to act indifferent (even if you aren't) and refuse to make another trip down to the lot until he gets back to you with a different price. I can guarantee you'll get a response within a day, if not within just a few hours.

> **Watch Your Back**
>
> Whatever you do, don't give a dealer a deposit to hold a car. Aside from horror stories of dealers keeping the money or charging a restocking fee, it's a way for the dealer to ensure you'll come back before you can go anywhere else.

How Dealerships Stick It to You

Aside from the song and dance they go through just to get you onto the lot and sitting at a desk, there are a number of things dealers do to boost their profits throughout the process. Many of these additional costs can be minimized or completely avoided, but it takes a heads-up approach, some homework, and making decisions in advance about some of the things you'll be offered.

Sticker Price Tricks

The window sticker is generally the starting point for all pricing discussions. Understanding what a dealer chooses to include (or leave out) is crucial in keeping your "out-the-door" price as low as possible.

There are two numbers at the center of most car purchase negotiations: the dealer's invoice price and the manufacturer's suggested retail price (also known as the MSRP or sticker price). But in addition to these, there are all kinds of other fees and costs tacked on that are open to negotiation. Those with a high auto IQ focus on starting their negotiations from the invoice price (instead of the MSRP) and on getting some of the line item fees waived.

In the Know

Most car window stickers now include EPA mileage estimates and annual estimated gas costs, something many consumers are interested in when gas prices spike. Unfortunately, these numbers are often unrealistic, failing to reflect how most people drive. To be on the safe side, consider shaving 10 percent off the miles per gallon estimate, and adding 10 percent to the annual fuel cost.

While we'll focus more on negotiating with the invoice price instead of the MSRP later in the chapter, let's take a look at other things included or left out on the window sticker that can be used to jack up your final price. Again, you should inform the salesperson before you ever sit down that you're concerned about these fees and that they may keep you from buying the car.

- **Document fees.** I've always been amazed that dealers have the audacity to charge you for less than a dollar's worth of forms and the 15 minutes it takes to print them out. While some dealers may or may not drop this fee, you should avoid dealers who charge more than $50 to $100.

- **Delivery fees.** While this fee, also known as the destination charge, is often required by manufacturers, many dealers raise it to pad their pockets. The best way to avoid getting ripped off is to call other dealers in your area and ask what their delivery fee is. If yours is out of line, don't be afraid to quote the dealer what you've heard the competition charges.

- **Prep fee.** Yet another fee that the dealer charges you simply to increase their profits is the prep fee. This includes the cost of keeping the car looking pretty and maintained while it sits on the lot. Again, by researching competitors' fees in advance, you'll have more leverage to threaten the loss of the sale if they don't negotiate.

The Add-Ons

When I was working in car sales during college, salespeople were judged (and paid) as much on what after-market products they could

sell as anything else. That's probably why I wasn't the best salesman—
because I didn't believe that rust proofing was a huge need in Southern
California!

Most of these add-on products represent 50 to 90 percent profit for the
dealers and big commissions for the salesperson. So you shouldn't be
surprised when they get pitched to you. In fact, since you have already
essentially committed to buying the car, you can expect the gloves to
come off. You'll be browbeaten, scared, and guilted into buying them.
You'll be told how they'll prolong the life of your car, lower your insurance rates, and keep you safer. And in most cases, it's a load of hogwash.

Watch Your Back

Did you know that many auto lots' service departments make as
much or more than their sales departments? It's true, especially in
economies where car sales grind to a halt. With that in mind, consider
shopping around and getting a second opinion and an outside price
quote on any major maintenance recommended by your dealer.

Here's the breakdown of what you're likely to get pitched to you, and a
few thoughts on making the right decision:

- **Paint and fabric protection.** There may be no greater rip-off
  than the magical sealant the dealer is happy to apply to your car
  for $200 to $300. In most instances, these services do nothing to
  tangibly protect your car that you couldn't do with some Scotch
  Guard and a regular waxing. This is especially true since most
  people only keep their cars five to seven years—long before rust
  would set in or fabric deteriorates. Just say no to any type of paint
  and fabric protection.

- **Radio and entertainment systems.** If your car needs a little
  more bass than the factory provides, or the idea of your kids
  watching DVDs quietly in the back sounds like heaven, you'll
  want to shop around before you pay your dealer to install these
  items. Typically, the markup is greater and the quality lower than
  if you have these installed by a company that specializes in auto
  electronics.

- **Anti-theft devices.** Especially if you own a car that has ranked in the top 10 stolen cars in any year, you can expect to get pitched on some kind of anti-theft device. These devices range from vehicle location beacons to alarms to kill switches. While these items by themselves may be worth buying, you need to do some homework before saying yes. Most importantly, to counter the salesperson's claim that it will pay for itself by lowering your auto insurance, you need to actually call your insurance company and find out. Further, you should research other people who sell after-market products to see if you can find a better deal.

- **Insurance policies.** In addition to trying to pitch you regular auto insurance, more and more dealers are offering *gap insurance* and credit life insurance. Both of these can usually be purchased cheaper elsewhere, if they are needed at all. Check with your lender to see if either of these are required or recommended, as well as your current insurance company to see what options they provide.

def•i•ni•tion

> **Gap insurance** is a special type of policy that is meant to protect you in the event your car is totaled and your insurance payout is less than what you owe the bank. If you put down a sizable down payment, this type of policy would probably be a waste of money.

- **Extended warranties.** Extended warranties can be a financial lifesaver or a complete waste of money, depending on the cost and terms. Many dealers mislead buyers to believe that these products extend warranties by five or six years, when in fact they only extend them *to* five or six years. In other words, customers pay $1,000 to $2,000 for a warranty that only protects them a couple years longer than their factory warranty. As a rule of thumb, a warranty shouldn't cost more than $200 to $300 per year it adds to your existing coverage.

Financing Tricks

A huge, hidden source of revenue for dealerships is financing (providing loans). It's not uncommon for a dealer to make as much or more off of your loan as they do on the sale of the car itself. And while buyers often secure great rates through their dealer, there are plenty of consumers who also get ripped off through a number of common tricks.

All of these tricks, just like with the credit cards in Chapter 3, revolve around bumping up your interest rate. And while you don't need to worry about your rates jumping to 20 to 30 percent, even a jump of a couple percentage points can cost you big money. For example, if they can find a reason to raise your rate on a $20,000 five-year loan from 6 percent to 8 percent, that increases their profits on the loan by over $1,000!

Here are some of the top tricks dealers use to change your rate without losing your business:

◆ **On approved credit.** We've all seen those commercials offering new car financing for no or ridiculously low interest rates. Of course, those commercials contain fine print, like many of life's other great deals. Those rates are O.A.C., or on approved credit. This means those rates are reserved for people with nearly perfect credit and higher levels of income. For the other 90 percent of America, they're happy to finance you at 7 to 10 percent. To ensure you don't fall into this trap, consider getting approved for an auto loan by your bank prior to visiting the dealership, and letting the dealer compete with that rate.

◆ **Stretching payment periods.** One of the most alarming trends in auto financing is the increase of six-, seven-, and even eight-year loans. These longer financing periods are simply marketing gimmicks that help dealers sell cars at more profitable interest rates. By stretching the payments out over long periods, the payments themselves become smaller, even though the interest rate is going up. Again, walk into the dealer armed with outside financing and make them compete for a good rate on either a four- or five-year loan.

In the Know

Auto refinancing, which was virtually unheard of a decade ago, has grown immensely in popularity and availability. If you are in a long-term car loan at an unfavorable rate, check with your bank or credit union about the possibility of refinancing.

◆ **Couldn't get your rate.** Unscrupulous dealers and finance departments have been known to call you days, or even weeks, after your deal is done to inform you that they couldn't get your loan approved. They go on to tell you that they've done you the favor of getting you approved at a slightly higher rate and they'll just change your paperwork without you even needing to come down. Of course, you've been driving the car and have grown attached to it, so what are you going to do? You take the car back, that's what you do. March into the dealership, demand to talk to the manager, and promise to notify everyone in town of their lousy business practices if the mess isn't cleared up immediately.

Your Trade-In

You might have heard the saying, "One man's trash is another man's treasure." Never has this been so true as when it comes to your trade-in. Dealers know that most people buying a new car are ready to wash their hands of their old ride, and thus lowball their trade-in offers accordingly. In reality, dealers know that they can often get 5 to 10 times what they offer you by placing your car back out on their lot or even selling it south of the border.

When it came to our family's last three auto purchases, a dealer offered me less than $500 each time for our less-than-beautiful trade-ins. In all three cases, I was able to sell them for between $2,000 to $3,000 to private parties within a week of placing an ad in my local paper, which went a lot farther toward lowering my new loan than what the dealer was offering me.

 Watch Your Back

> If you're going to sell your car to an unknown private party, be sure to ask for cash or a certified money order. More and more scam artists have been buying used cars with phony checks and riding off into the sunset with people's cars. Don't forget to have the buyer sign a "Release of Liability" form, which can be found at any DMV and on most state's DMV websites.

The Fine Print

If any one industry has contributed to fine print having a lousy reputation, it's probably auto sales. Whether it is rules restricting your rights to return a lemon or buried wording that leaves your lease costing a lot more than promised, the auto sales industry is all about protecting their right to profit off of you.

In general, like many other industries' fine print, there is not much you can do besides study that 10-point font in the hopes of navigating the fine line between your rights and your responsibilities. People with a high financial IQ make sure they know the rules, know how to play by them, and avoid dealerships that tilt them too far in their favor.

Lemon Laws

In the last few decades, most states have passed lemon laws that help to protect consumers from buying a car that turns out to be a piece of junk. Under these laws, if you are forced to make a certain number of repairs within a certain period of time, you are entitled to receive your money back. Unfortunately, a number of the states' laws require you to use an attorney to pursue damages.

In regard to fine print, educated consumers do the homework on their state's lemon laws and make sure they are not signing any paperwork that could negate some or all of the coverage. Further, they make sure that the car they're buying is actually covered under that state's laws, since many slightly used cars, which a salesperson won't hesitate to call "new," don't fall under these laws.

To research your state's laws, visit the website for your Consumer Affairs Department or state attorney general. A handy list of links, including an easy-to-read summary of each state's laws, can also be found at www.carlemon.com.

Warranty Conditions

Dealers love to wave warranties in car buyers' faces. It helps them to feel like nothing can go wrong with the huge investment they're about to make. Unfortunately for many consumers, most warranties have numerous exclusions and rules that can leave a consumer exposed to major costs soon after they buy the car.

Never take a salesperson's word for the warranty on the car you're buying. If it is a new car, ask to see the full warranty paperwork. If it is a used car, ask the dealer to provide paperwork documenting the remaining coverage period in terms of both miles and the actual termination date. Keep the following points in mind:

♦ **Deductibles.** It's not uncommon for a warranty to contain a deductible on certain services, especially if it is a nonfactory warranty. While some of these warranties are a very reasonable $25 or $50 per service, some can be as high as $250 or $500.

♦ **Wear-and-tear parts.** You need to read this portion of your warranty the most carefully since I've seen numerous salespeople claim that wear-and-tear parts like brakes were covered under the warranty. When pushed to clarify, they would say that they actually meant that the brake system is covered, not the brakes themselves. Yeah, right.

♦ **Bumper to bumper vs. powertrain.** Again, you'll hear salespeople casually throw around warranty lengths in an intentionally unclear manner. They'll claim (to people who don't know any better) that a car has a five-year warranty against any problems, when in fact the warranty they're speaking of is a *powertrain warranty* that primarily covers the engine. Other things like power windows and electrical systems are only covered under the bumper-to-bumper portion of the warranty, which is typically much shorter.

> **def•i•ni•tion**
>
> A **powertrain warranty** typically covers the engine itself, some parts of the transmission, and occasionally the drivetrain and the axle. Most of a car's other systems, those that it could drive without, are not covered.

♦ **Transferability.** It's not unheard of for some warranties, especially extended warranties, to only cover the original owner. If the car is resold or even given away, the warranty coverage may not extend to the new owner. Other times, it can be extended to the new owner, but requires a transfer fee to be paid or the company to be notified within a short window of time.

◆ **Scheduled maintenance and accessories.** Some warranties become void if you cannot prove that you (or the former owner) performed the regularly scheduled maintenance on the vehicle. Additionally, if any after-market accessories are added, such as bigger tires, it can void the warranty.

Leasing Options

When you do the math, there are few car financing options worse than a lease. That's because a lease is nothing more than a rental car that requires a substantial down payment, and has the potential for heavy penalties when you're done. Though they look cheap on the commercials, you've got to study the fine print to guard against three major costs:

◆ **Early termination fees.** In today's flailing economy, many consumers are coming to discover that you can't just turn your leased car in whenever you like. In fact, the fine print often requires a consumer to pay both the remainder of all payments and an early termination fee that ranges between $250 to $1,000.

◆ **Mileage fees.** Most leases only permit you to drive a certain number of miles per year (usually 12,000) without paying an additional mileage fee. With fees ranging from 10 to 25¢ per additional mile, it's not uncommon to hear of people being hit with $5,000 or more in mileage fees at the end of a lease. If you find yourself in this situation, you should investigate how much it would cost to just buy the car outright, since you're already going to spend a substantial sum.

◆ **Money due at signing.** While it's not really a piece of fine print that comes back to haunt people, since it actually hits you on the front end, it's still worth mentioning. Leases that otherwise look like a bargain become a lot more expensive when you do the math on that "money due at signing" fine print you see in the lease commercials. Paying $2,500 up front as part of your lease agreement is the equivalent of adding $104 to your monthly lease amount. Ouch!

If you find yourself in a lease that's not working for you, or are just looking for a great deal on a lease, you should look into lease swapping. Under a lease swap arrangement, one or more lease holders switches places with another lease holder, usually for a small fee. Check out websites like www.swapalease.com for more information.

How to Save

Since cars are an essential, expensive, and recurring expense for most of us, it's in your favor to learn the art of getting a deal. By being wise about when you shop, where you shop, and what you buy, you can easily save yourself a few thousand dollars every five to seven years. That's a lot of money you could devote toward other goals.

When it comes to saving big on cars, the name of the game is patience. Dealers make their heftiest profits off the people who can't wait to buy a car. These are the folks who miss opportunities in the natural auto manufacturing and sales cycle to get the best deals.

The Best Times to Shop

While most salespeople would lead you to believe that car prices are the same no matter what time, day, or month you walk onto the lot, they're not. In fact, the sticker price, the dealer's willingness to bargain, and the salesperson's willingness to give up some of their commission, all coincide with the word "end."

Because everybody in the car business is paid to perform, and because older cars need to move to make room for newer cars, anytime you can catch car lots at the "end" of anything, you're bound to come out ahead:

- ◆ **End of the day, week, or month.** At the most basic level, salespeople and their managers are tracked on a daily, weekly, and monthly basis. Most showrooms have a "leader board" in the staff lounge that shows how everyone is performing. Often, the salespeople who have performed well cut out early to enjoy life. That means the people floating around at the end of the day, week, or month are often hungry for a job-saving sale. That makes them an easy target for negotiation.

In the Know

By shopping on the days when the fewest numbers of people visit car lots (Monday through Wednesday), you'll also avoid feeling like someone is about to steal the car you want out from under your nose. Go when the lots are empty, and you'll cease to be your own worst enemy when it comes to making a well-thought-out decision.

◆ **End of the model year.** Next year's models usually begin hitting the lots around the end of summer and the beginning of fall. This means that dealers need to begin moving out the older models to make room for the new. This is a great time to look for deals.

◆ **End of the calendar year.** Actually, just after the end of the calendar year in January is a great time to shop for deals on the previous year's models. The lots officially need to get rid of those cars, because most people are going to be mainly interested in the newer models.

Buy Away from Town

One of the things many high IQ car buyers have noticed over the years is that auto prices are often more expensive in the large cities than they are on the outskirts. If you're willing to drive out into the rural areas, they often get even cheaper. This difference in prices is attributable to both the lower costs of operating a car lot away from large cities, as well as a potentially lower volume of sales, which can force dealers to sell at or below cost to generate some cash flow.

A bonus comes if the sales tax rate changes as you cross over city or county lines. A 1 percent difference in sales tax would save you $200 on a $20,000 car. All other things being equal, that alone may be worth an hour or two drive. Just be sure you don't get too smart and buy a car over state lines without checking the import rules. Many states levy heavy fees on cars brought in from out of state.

Buying Slightly Used

If you haven't read *The Millionaire Next Door* by Thomas Stanley, I'd highly recommend it (see Appendix B for that and other recommendations).

In the book, Stanley looks at the purchasing habits of millionaires and discovers that they're actually more frugal than most people—part of the reason they've become millionaires.

One of the spending items Stanley looks at is the car-buying habits of millionaires. Despite what you'd think, most millionaires don't cruise around town in new BMWs or Mercedes. *Just the opposite.* Most millionaires actually tend to buy reasonably priced cars. What's more, they buy them used!

Considering that most new cars experience a sharp drop in value as soon as you put any real mileage on them, financially savvy people know that buying a used car with 10,000 to 30,000 miles on it may be the best deal going. These cars, many of which are now *certified pre-owned* vehicles, may be anywhere from 10 to 25 percent less than a brand-new car. Yet, they have little or no wear showing and are still under their manufacturer's warranty. Pair them with a good extended warranty, and you've managed to essentially buy a new car at a major discount.

def•i•ni•tion

> **Certified pre-owned** cars are used cars that have been thoroughly inspected according to manufacturer's standards. If manufacturer-mandated repairs are needed, they are made prior to the car being offered to the public for sale.

Negotiating a Price

Most car buyers make the mistake of trying to chip away at a car's MSRP or sticker price. Doing this is like trying to climb a muddy hill with a blindfold on. You have no real idea how low the dealer can go, and may even feel afraid of insulting them or sounding stupid.

By starting your negotiations with the dealer's invoice price, something that can be found for free on websites like Edmunds.com, you'll have a fairly good picture of what the dealer paid for the car. Instead of dickering over how much to lower the sticker price, you can make the dealer a simple offer such as buying the car at or slightly over invoice (i.e., $500 over invoice). Expect your offer to be countered, so be sure to start your bidding below the maximum price you want to pay.

The Least You Need to Know

◆ To get the best deal, keep a salesperson living in fear of a lost sale.

◆ Always walk into the dealer with competitive financing already arranged elsewhere.

◆ You should generally avoid leases, paint and fabric protection, dealer-sold insurance, and leaving a deposit.

◆ For the best deal, always shop at the end of the day, week, month, or year.

◆ Buying a barely used car will save you as much as any negotiation technique.

13

The High Costs of Higher Education

In This Chapter

◆ Nasty college costs surprises

◆ Collegiate fine print

◆ Tax benefits for college costs

◆ College funding tips and tricks

A few years ago, my wife and I were walking around in San Francisco when I saw a missing-dog sign that I'll never forget. To this day, I get a good laugh every time I think of it. It read: "Missing Dog: Blind in right eye, left ear missing, broken tail, three legs, recently been fixed. Answers to the name Lucky."

In my experience, many parents feel like Lucky after putting a kid, or four, through college. While people pat them on the back and congratulate them, they can't help but feel like they've been run over by a financial semi truck. They've tapped every asset they have, stopped saving for retirement and other goals, run up some debts, and have a general feeling of having been very

184 Part 4: Life's Big Expenses

profitable to a nonprofit institution. While their kids graduate with wide-open futures, many parents feel like they've been sent back to square one with just 10 to 20 years left in their working lives.

Those with a high financial IQ know that it doesn't need to be this way. Putting your child through college doesn't need to cost an arm, a leg, and your sanity. They know that even the most esteemed institutions come with fine print and nasty surprises they conveniently leave out when you're touring the campus. In short, they study up on how the finances of college work, so that they can pass the test of paying for it when the time comes.

College—Life's Most Expensive Party

The college experience comes with certain givens—late nights, pizza, road trips, and dirty laundry. More certain than all of these, though, is that the real cost takes most parents' breath away. The problem is not that parents didn't expect college to be a significant expense, but rather that they failed to realize two key facts.

First, the cost of college doesn't just arise from a single source. In fact, the high cost of college is actually the combination of a number of separately priced factors that join forces to steamroll a parent's pocketbook.

Second, college costs are increasing faster than they ever have. Whereas the normal increase in the cost of living (known as inflation) runs about 2 to 3 percent for most of life's expenses, college costs have historically increased at a rate of 5 to 6 percent.

> **Your Bottom Line**
>
> Many parents make the faulty assumption that their child will finish college in four years, just as they did. Unfortunately, even the most focused students are finding it increasingly hard to finish in four years due to an inability to get the classes they need when they need them. Smart parents budget for five years and hope for four.

College costs are comprised of four main components, as well as a few extras that often end up on Mom and Dad's credit card. By understanding each one of these components, parents with a high financial IQ are often able to lower them significantly through creativity and planning:

- **Tuition.** The single largest chunk of your child's college bill will be tuition. This is the cost for the actual "education" portion of their college experience. For full-time college students, there is generally a standard tuition fee, which allows a student to take a certain range of units per semester. Smart parents make sure that students take the maximum number of units allowable under their flat fee, to effectively lower the overall cost per unit of their child's education.

- **Housing.** Also known as the "room" portion of "room and board" costs, housing is the second-largest expense in putting a student through school. It can easily amount to $5,000 to $10,000 per year in many parts of the country. Thankfully, this is one of the places where financially savvy parents know they can lower their costs significantly. Whether it is having their students live at home, securing lower cost off-campus housing (if permitted), or encouraging their student to become campus residential advisors (who get free housing), there are numerous ways to lower this cost.

- **Board.** If freshman year of college is known for one thing, it's probably the weight gain known as the "Freshman 15." College students are like locusts, devouring whatever is put in their path. Out of a fear of their student being malnourished, many parents sign up for the "unlimited" cafeteria plans offered by their school, never realizing that their student would have to eat five or more times a day to justify the high cost of these plans. Educated parents do the per-meal math on their campus meal plans, as well as research off-campus dining opportunities for the best deal.

- **Books.** If there is one cost that leaves parents wondering what exactly they've gotten themselves into, it is books. Many a parent has bemoaned the ill-fated phone call from their student during the first week of school where they learned that textbooks were going to cost $500 every semester. Parents in the know get their student's list of required texts well ahead of time and do everything from scouring eBay to using textbook rental services.

◆ **Technology.** When I went through college, in the early days of computers, a laptop was a luxury reserved for the most well-to-do students. The rest of us had to hoof it to the computer lab to write our papers. Now of course, laptops are a virtual requirement, with many schools burying the cost in your tuition bill. Since many schools use the sale of technology to students as an additional source of revenue, forward-thinking parents lower their tuition or out-of-pocket costs substantially by purchasing the required technology directly from the manufacturer or an electronics mega-store.

More Money, More Tricks

One of the great financial truths is, the more money that's at stake, the more people will work to take it from you. And when it comes to money at stake, there are few opportunities as the large amounts of money parents dish out for college.

This extraordinary opening of parental wallets is like blood in the water for sharks. Just a hint of it can turn companies, professionals, and even the colleges themselves into financial predators. When it comes to making it through college in one piece, much of it depends on you knowing how to defend yourself against a financial feeding frenzy.

Your College's "Dear Parent" Letter

It's truly amazing how many schools completely ignore the topic of annual tuition increases in their promotional materials and conversations with prospective parents. In fact, I'd call it downright unethical that the topic is ignored.

Why such harsh words toward colleges? Because the vast majority of colleges, most of which never mention tuition increases, will increase your tuition every year like clockwork. I like to call it the "Dear Parent" letter. It usually comes somewhere between March and May of each year, when you've already committed your child to another semester of study at their school. The letter, which is worded to garner parental sympathy for the plight of the college, informs you that tuition will be increasing by a certain percentage the following year. Ironically, the schools very rarely include a hard dollar amount, since percentages seem to invoke less sticker shock.

The first year you get this letter, you actually feel half bad for the school and their need to increase costs. The second year, though, you begin to scratch your head and wonder if this is going to become a pattern. Of course, by year four, you realize that this is the song and dance most schools engage in every year! Even if there is not a truly pressing need to raise tuition, schools are going to, just because they can.

In the Know

The annual Dear Parent letter is a great time to ask your school's financial aid department for an increase in aid. Most schools' departments know that Dear Parent letters create a hardship for a percentage of the students and are prepared to offer slight increases in aid to the squeakiest wheels. Act quickly, though, since plenty of other people will be looking for help.

While there's really nothing you can do to argue the tuition increase (and trust me, many a parent has tried), parents with high financial IQs do their homework ahead of time. When their students are still choosing a school, they press their admissions officer for hard facts on the history of tuition increases. In doing so, they can make an educated decision about whether or not they can afford to send their child to that school, and begin preparing accordingly.

To help you gauge a school's tuition increases, consider the following statistics from the College Board for the 2008–09 school year:

- Public four-year college tuition: Increased by 5.9 percent

- Private four-year college tuition: Increased by 6.4 percent

- Public two-year college tuition: Increased by 4.7 percent

- Room and board at all schools: Increased by $395

In-State Tuition Rules

If there's a bait and switch when it comes to college costs, it's with how schools advertise in-state tuition. In case you're unfamiliar with the concept, most public colleges charge students substantially more if they are not considered residents of the college's state. In fact, out-of-state tuition can easily increase the cost of attendance to the level of many private schools.

Over the years, numerous schools have been accused of leading out-of-state parents to believe that their students could easily qualify for in-state tuition after a short period of time, such as 6 or 12 months. However, when the student or their parent later goes to claim this benefit, they find out that the rules were much more strict than the school communicated and their student may in fact never qualify for a tuition discount.

If your student plans on attending a public school in another state, you need to be sure to request a copy of the school's in-state residency requirements at your time of enrollment. Be sure to check the fine print for the following requirements:

♦ **Residence.** If you're talking about earning residency status, then you better know what defines a "residence." Many parents attempt to maintain PO boxes in states in order to qualify for residency, only to find out that this is not accepted.

♦ **Duration.** While the minimum length of residence usually appears straightforward, it often has hidden catches that deny residency for students who live out of state during the summer or over extended holiday breaks.

♦ **Age.** Some programs do not offer residency to students under a certain age, sometimes ranging as high as their early 20s.

♦ **Employment.** Some states only offer residency to students who also hold at least part-time employment in that state, thereby contributing income taxes to the state's budget.

♦ **Financial independence.** A number of states do not consider a student a resident if their financial support originates in another state.

Financial Aid Offices and Preferred Lenders

The financial aid office is an on-campus department that exists to help students figure out how to pay for college. They're the gateway for all types of financial aid, including both federal and school-specific programs. The average financial aid office at a large public university may very well be responsible for helping students to secure hundreds of millions of dollars in loans each year. That represents a huge amount of revenue and profit for banks and lenders, who compete against each other to attract new borrowers.

Not surprisingly, the number of high-profile scandals involving financial aid officers is growing. In fact, a number of these officers have been caught accepting compensation (a nice way of saying bribes) for positioning certain lenders to receive more business. You should be wary of any lender your school recommends over another, since many of the loan programs themselves are standardized. Be sure to do your homework on the loan product and lender, instead of just taking a school employee's word on it.

Private Student Loans—Too Good to Be True

One of the most alarming trends surrounding college educations is the explosion of private lenders. These lenders, for whatever reason, do not participate in government-backed financial aid programs such as the Stafford, Perkins, or PLUS loans. They do, however, participate in an immense amount of advertising that leads many parents and students to believe that they are the most cost-effective and efficient borrowing option available. In fact, one company has recently run a series of ads essentially mocking parents who use government-sponsored financial aid programs made available through their school's financial aid office.

In reality, these lenders almost always charge substantially higher interest rates than are available to parents through the government programs, often exceeding 10 percent annually. Additionally, these loans do not qualify for juicy loan forgiveness programs available in many professional fields, or for the interest deduction available for student loan borrowers.

We Only Sell Some Section 529 Plans

Not surprisingly, one of the key players in helping your child get a college education may be a financial advisor. For many parents, navigating the crowded field of account choices and investment options is something that they'd much prefer to hand off to a pro, even if they manage all their other long-term investments themselves.

One of the most exciting things to happen to college planning in the last decade, and the go-to choice for most financial advisors, is the Section 529 college account. Thanks to generous tax provisions, such as state income tax deductions for contributing and tax-free growth of your investments, these accounts have attracted over $100 billion dollars in just over a decade of existence.

Unfortunately, much of the money directed to these plans has been through commission-based financial advisors. While the idea of commissioned advice is enough to turn off most high financial IQ parents, there's an additional wrinkle that you should be aware of—most financial advisors only get paid to sell certain plans. In other words, if your state offers a great plan but doesn't pay a commission to advisors for selling it, you're not likely to hear about it. Rather, you'll hear about another state's plan, along with a weak argument why its higher expenses are justifiable. Before you decide on a plan, visit a third-party website that ranks Section 529 plans based on their value to you, not to your advisor.

In the Know

Interested in finding out how much financial aid you may qualify for? Visit www.fafsa4caster.com, a website run by the Department of Education.

Visit About.com to read my regular column on "Saving for College." You can also visit collegesavings.about.com to read reviews and rankings of different Section 529 plans.

The Fine Print

Aside from some of the downright dirty-tactics schools, lenders, and advisors use to beef up their bottom line at your expense, there's also a mess of fine print you need to be aware of. While none of these things are designed to directly stick it to you, they do end up coming back to haunt many parents and students who didn't take the time to understand them.

We May Take Back Your Scholarship

According to *The Wall Street Journal*, one of the most well-known and well-managed college endowments, that of Harvard University, dropped 22 percent in the last four months of 2008. That amounts to a loss of roughly $7 to $8 billion dollars of money that help fund scholarships.

What does all that mean? It means that many schools that had been previously generous with scholarships are being forced to tighten their belts. It means that students who do not live up to the terms of their scholarships are promptly having them yanked with the money being used to attract new students. If your student is lucky enough to get a scholarship, you need to double-check the terms of that scholarship, as well as have a backup plan, just in case.

Here's a list of the most commonly violated terms of scholarships that catch families off guard:

- **Grade point average (GPA).** More and more scholarships, not just academic scholarships, are including GPA provisions. If your GPA falls below a certain level, you are either put on probation or may even immediately lose your award. Since grades cannot be turned around overnight, parents need to be actively communicating with their students to make sure they're pulling their weight.

- **Minimum number of units.** It's not uncommon for students to drop a class early in the semester, only to realize that their scholarship required them to take a minimum number of hours to be eligible.

- **Behavior guidelines.** While many parents expect their children to have a few wild college moments, many universities are not so understanding. If your student violates behavior guidelines, most often associated with alcohol and drugs, they can instantly lose the scholarship.

We're a Private School—We Define "Need" Differently

Thanks to the recent economic downturn, more parents than ever have had to rely on financial aid to put their child through college. For many parents, this financial aid is actually a mix of federal financial aid from the Department of Education and private financial aid from their child's college. This leads to yet another piece of fine print that catches many parents unaware.

While the federal aid formula for determining a family's "need" on the FAFSA form is the same from school to school, financial aid that comes from a private school's war chest may be awarded using a completely different formula. In fact, many private schools use a separate form, known as a CSS PROFILE, to determine if you qualify for aid. The application, which is available through www.collegeboard.com, also costs a fee to submit, unlike the Free Application for Federal Student Aid (FAFSA) form.

The reason this fine print ends up leaving parents pulling their hair out occurs when there is either a major change in their financial situation or they enroll an additional child in a different school. In both of these cases, a parent is prone to assume that things will work the same way they did the year before or at the other school. Of course, they come to find out that they work completely different, and the amount of aid they receive may drop substantially. Naturally, if they haven't prepared for this by doing their homework in advance, it creates a major financial hardship.

Transfer Students

One of the best ways to save money on college is to attend a community college or public four-year school for one to two years, and then transfer to a more expensive or exclusive school for the remainder of a degree. In fact, many students graduate high school with this being their exact plan.

Unfortunately, failing to read the fine print of a school's transfer policy is a mistake that has cost countless students substantial time and money. By substantial, I'm talking about adding an extra year to their college career, which can easily cost $5,000 to $10,000 in tuition, room, and board.

Following are some of the main hiccups in the transfer process that you need to be aware of.

◆ **Maximum transferable units.** Many schools put a limit on the number of units you can transfer into their school. In other words, they don't want you getting 90 percent of your degree at Joe Bob's College of Taxidermy and Accounting, and then transferring to Harvard just long enough to get the degree. Be sure to check with your transfer school so you don't waste time taking classes that are over the limit.

◆ **Downgrading your classes.** Many schools that let you transfer your prior work refuse to count it toward core curriculum or major requirements. Instead, they classify the classes as electives, which means you may have to take many of them over at your new school to fulfill degree requirements. As you or your student registers for classes each semester, be sure to call your eventual transfer school to make sure the classes count as you want them to.

◆ **Financial aid.** Many students who transfer after a couple of years at a local, lower-cost school are shocked to find out that some or all of their financial aid doesn't transfer. This is especially true with students who were receiving financial aid from their state government, which often does not transfer to out-of-state schools. Before you commit to a transfer, be sure to check with both your previous and future schools' financial aid offices about how your financial aid may be affected.

Federal Loan Interest Rates

While federal student loans are generally the way to go when it comes to borrowing money for college, there is still some fine print buried in there that can make graduation day a less than joyful event—specifically, the fact that interest is charged and added to many federal student loans while students are still attending college.

This specifically applies to what is referred to as "unsubsidized" Stafford loans and PLUS loans. Under these programs available

In the Know

Through 2012, subsidized Stafford loan rates are scheduled to decrease to an eye-popping 3.4 percent! After 2012, however, they are bumped back up to 6.8 percent. For more info on student loan rates, visit www. salliemae.com.

to students who *do not* demonstrate financial need, interest is charged and begins being added to the total of the loan from the day it is issued, even though repayment may not begin until after graduation. While that may not seem like that big of a deal, for students borrowing $10,000 per year, this can easily add $5,000 to their balance by the time they graduate.

One of the tricks used by students and parents to lessen the sting of this interest calculation is to attempt to pay the interest each month as it is added to the loan, during the college years. While this may cost $50 to $100 per month in beer and pizza money, it gives graduates a huge leg up when they graduate.

Tips for Covering the Costs

The only people who pay full price for college are the ones who haven't taken the time to explore the numerous options out there for creative parents and students. Whether it is financial aid for the upper-middle class, student loan cancellation programs, or tax credits from Uncle Sam, there is plenty you can do to lower your tab by thousands.

Like many techniques used by those with a high financial IQ, these work best if they're not left until the last minute. Making the most of some of these techniques takes planning, decisions about where your child might go to school, and even discussing with them what type of careers might be a wise choice.

Financial Aid for the Rich

Okay, it may be a stretch to call yourself "rich." But it can definitely feel that way when it comes to who most financial aid programs seem to be available to. In fact, most middle and upper-middle class families believe that there's no way a school would consider them for financial aid or that they'd qualify for loans. Luckily, that's just not the reality.

Many schools, especially private schools, offer financial aid to a large portion of their student population. While students with parents making six figures may not get a full ride, a large percentage still receive some type of assistance. But it typically only goes to students who fill out the Free Application for Federal Student Aid form (FAFSA) or the CSS PROFILE. If you don't fill out these forms, you'll never know what you've missed out on, including:

- **Major-specific scholarships.** Many departments within schools offer scholarships to students choosing a specific course of study. Since these are offered to a much smaller population of students, there's a greater possibility your family may qualify.

- **Unsubsidized Stafford loans and PLUS loans.** One of the best-kept secrets in college financing is unsubsidized Stafford loans. These loans, with single-digit interest rates, are available to a much broader base of students than other need-based loan programs.

 Watch Your Back

One of the most common college planning scams is the "scholarship search," where a consultant promises to help you find obscure scholarships that are going unused or that your student would easily qualify for. The reality is, all scholarships are extremely competitive and these services promise something they cannot deliver.

Tax Deductions and Credits

The U.S. government offers a number of major tax deductions and credits that can take a big bite out of your tuition bills. In some cases, these programs can put as much as $2,000 to $3,000 back into parents' pockets. Be sure to talk to your tax advisor to ensure you properly claim these credits:

- **The American Opportunity Tax Credit (AOTC).** Formerly known as the Hope Scholarship, this credit directly lowers the amount of tax you owe (making it better than a deduction that lowers the amount your tax is calculated on). For 2009 and 2010, this credit is equal to 100 percent of the first $2,000 you spend on qualifying college costs, and 25 percent on the next $2,000. That's a combined total of $2,500! As with all the education tax credits, the AOTC is subject to a number of rules and restrictions. Be sure to check out IRS Publication 970 for more details.

- ◆ **The Lifetime Learning Credit.** This credit lowers your tax bill by the equivalent of 20 percent of your college costs for any given year, on the first $10,000 of expenses. Unlike the AOTC, this credit can also be used for graduate school, continuing education, job improvement, etc.

- ◆ **Student loan interest deduction.** This deduction allows the first few thousand dollars in student loan interest paid (not just accrued) to be deducted from your return each year.

- ◆ **Tuition and fees deduction.** While this deduction has been touch and go when it comes to getting canceled, its benefits have been extended through the 2009 tax year. Under this deduction, the first $4,000 in tuition and fees is deductible from the income you show on your tax return.

In the Know

A number of the education tax credits (as well as other noneducation credits) are doubled for residents affected by certain natural disasters. Previous programs have included the Midwestern Disaster Tax Relief and the Heartland Disaster Tax Relief programs. If you live in an area that has been affected by such a disaster, be sure to check with a tax advisor or the IRS for special treatment.

Prepaid Tuition May Be a Great Investment

For parents considering a Section 529 savings plan or Coverdell Education Savings Account (similar to a Roth IRA, but used for college expenses) for their child's college fund, a prepaid tuition plan may be one of the best options available in a turbulent economy.

Since these plans allow you to buy future tuition at today's costs, your effective rate of return is whatever the college increases tuition by between now and when your child enrolls. Since many schools are raising their tuition at a rate of 5 to 7 percent per year, this is an attractive alternative for risk-averse parents or those with only a few years to go.

The only catch is that many prepaid tuition programs require your child to attend either the school whose prepaid tuition plan you used, or a school within your state if you used a statewide plan. But if you can live with that or have a family tradition of attending a school, these plans are a great option.

Student Loan Cancellation Programs

If I could stand on a mountaintop and shout just a few financial planning tips to the world, student loan cancellation programs would be at the top of my list. That's because these programs can literally wipe out tens of thousands of dollars in student loans by a student simply working in the profession they trained for in their studies.

Most commonly encountered in the teaching, medical, and public service professions, these programs are used to help steer qualified graduates toward places where a need for their skills exists. For example, the Teach for Texas program erases the student loan debt of teachers in "shortage" areas—subjects and locations where there are not enough qualified teachers applying.

Of course, you still get paid your normal salary when you participate in these programs. The loan forgiveness is actually a tax-free bonus for filling a need in the workforce for one to five years. Be sure to check out the "Financial Aid" section at collegesavings.about.com for a full list of loan forgiveness programs and resources.

Sources of Free Money

There are a couple other sources of free money out there worth mentioning. I say "free" a bit tongue in cheek, because they all cost you something. But they're great ways for many students and parents to add some more money into the mix:

♦ **UPromise and BabyMint.** These two programs offer parents cash toward college for shopping and dining at thousands of locations across the country. The program is free and doesn't increase the costs of your goods, but is simply a gimmick to get you to shop one place over another. The best thing about these programs is that you can register friends and family to contribute as well. Check them out at www.upromise.com and www.babymint.com.

In the Know

One of the best sources for information on education programs for veterans and service people is www.military.com.

◆ **Military incentives.** While many are already familiar with the Montgomery GI Bill, which pays for college *after* military service, there are an increasing number of programs that will also repay previous student loans for service, often for just enrolling in the reserves.

◆ **Work study.** These programs, which are traditionally offered to students demonstrating financial need, often receive far less applications than other programs. Perhaps that's because you actually have to work for the money. If your student is spending their downtime just hanging around the dorm playing video games, you may want to look into these programs to lower your costs.

◆ **The Peace Corps and AmeriCorps.** Both of these volunteer work study programs offer close to $5,000 for a few years of volunteer service. If your student has an itch to see the world, consider having your child earn money through one of these programs instead of dishing out funds for a school's pricey overseas program. Find out more at www.peacecorps.gov and www.americorps.gov.

The Least You Need to Know

◆ While most parents count on tuition, they often forget about the cost of room, board, books, and technology.

◆ Your child's college *will* raise its tuition while they're there.

◆ Most advisor-sold Section 529 plans cost more and offer less than those bought directly from your state.

◆ Prepaid tuition plans may offer a much more stable return over time than traditional college savings plans.

◆ All parents should apply for financial aid, even if they don't think they'll qualify for any assistance.

Chapter 14

Life Insurance

In This Chapter

- ◆ Life insurance sales tactics
- ◆ The problems with cash value insurance
- ◆ Insurance fine print
- ◆ How to do insurance the right way

For my money, there are few cultural icons that match the grandeur of Ron Popeil. If you know the name, but can't quite place the face, let me help you out. Ron is the inventor and late-night pitchman for classics such as the Flowbee, Ginsu Knives, the Pocket Fisherman, and my favorite, the Chop-O-Matic. Ron made a fortune selling sleep-deprived Americans some of the best (and worst) inventions ever dreamt up. (I'm sorry, Ron, but GLH-9, your spray paint for bald spots, really is one of the worst ideas ever.)

One of the things I loved about Ron's infomercials was his classic lines like, "It slices! It dices!" and "But wait, there's more!" In fact, if you took Ron at his word, any one of his products would solve most of your problems and enable you to throw out half of the tools, appliances, and gadgets you owned. I kind of get that same feeling when I talk to some insurance salespeople about their products.

According to some of these people, the life insurance products they sell are about all you'll need to reach your financial goals. "It protects you! It invests for you! You can borrow against it! Even your kids should have one!" Sadly for many consumers who are sold more insurance than they realistically need, it's not available for three convenient payments of $19.95. Rather, it sucks away thousands of dollars from their net worth and delays the achievement of many of their financial goals.

I do want to preface this section by saying that there are some really great insurance agents out there who know their valuable place in the overall process of helping you reach your financial goals. They don't believe their products are the solution to every (or even most) financial problems, and they strive to make a good living by doing right for their customers. My hope is, after reading this chapter, your financial IQ will enable you to tell these men and women apart from the rest, since there will be times where you'll definitely need their help.

Understanding Insurance Commissions

Here's a quick pop quiz for you. What do you think the average commission rate is for someone who sells cars? How about houses? How about stocks or mutual funds? Well, in most of these cases, the commission they earn is somewhere between 1 to 6 percent.

What about a life insurance agent? Are you sitting down? The typical commission on the sale of a life insurance policy is 80 to 90 percent of the first year's premium! That's right, on an insurance policy that costs $1,000 in the first year, an agent may receive between $800 to $900 as their commission. Not only that, in the years following your initial purchase, agents receive something called renewals, which average between 3 and 10 percent of the ongoing premiums you pay.

When you pick your jaw up off the floor, stop to consider what all that means. First, your agent has a ridiculously huge incentive to make each and every sale happen, as well as continuing to sell you more insurance even if you don't need it. Second, with so much commission built into life insurance, you can deduce that most insurance companies are charging you far more than it actually costs to insure you.

The bottom line is that insurance is the highest commission financial services product someone can sell you. This translates into an industry plagued by questionable sales practices, half-truths, and fear-based selling.

Watch Your Back

Although you should always be appreciative of financial professionals willing to give you a competitive discount, many states actually have rules against insurance agents "rebating" a portion of a client's commission. If an agent tries to seal a deal with you by offering such a discount, check your state laws. If they're in violation, it's a sign that you need to find someone more ethical to work with.

Fear: An Insurance Agent's Best Friend

Every golfer I know has a favorite club. One that just feels like it was built for their hands; a club that literally becomes an extension of themselves when they hold it. If they could, they'd use it for every shot.

For insurance agents looking for that next 90 percent commission, that "club" is fear. Few things allow them to tee you up for a hole in one like a good dose of the what-ifs. If they can get you to buy into the fear that they're shoveling, it's a short leap to get you to sign on the bottom line. In boosting your financial IQ, you'll want to have disarmed the most classic fears ahead of time, so an agent isn't able to get their hooks into you.

The Fear of Your Own Death

One's own death is something that most people avoid thinking about for as long as they can. Perhaps it's just one of those "out of sight, out of mind" things that never crosses their mind until they're ill or someone close to them dies. But that's exactly why some insurance agents love to bring it up!

By focusing on something that is uncomfortable for you to think about, they accomplish two things. First, they generally shorten your consideration process. Since you don't want to think about death at all, you probably don't want to think too much about the insurance you may or may not need to protect your loved ones. It's not uncommon to see people sign on the dotted line just to make the discussion go away.

Second, manipulative agents will use language and assurances that almost create the sense that an insurance policy can actually protect you from death itself! You'll hear them talk a lot about the risk to you of not having insurance, or how exposed you are. Statements like these play off emotions more than reality, considering that if (when) you die, you won't be worrying about a thing anymore!

> ### Your Bottom Line
>
> While no one likes to think about their own mortality, you can breathe a sigh of relief when it comes to your life expectancy. In the twentieth century, the life expectancy of the average American actually doubled! It still continues to grow slightly every year, meaning most people have a long ways to go.

To disarm this fear, you need to begin viewing insurance only in terms of what it can realistically accomplish. While it can't extend your life or make every policyholder a millionaire, it can protect your loved ones against being up a creek without a paddle in the event of an untimely death.

Something I repeat ad nauseam is, the only thing insurance is meant to do is cover a financial loss created because you die—if your loved ones are no worse off financially when you die, there is no need for insurance. Thus, the insurance you buy should only cover you for when there is a true exposure, and only be enough to cover that exposure.

The Fear of Your Loved One's Deaths

One of the biggest insurance sales sins, in my opinion, is the sale of life insurance on a nonworking spouse or children. Insurance agents who market these policies are counting on your ignorance and fear, since these policies generally make no financial sense.

Just like the fear of our own death, insurance agents are quick to word the "protection" their coverage provides as something that seems to have the power to stave off death itself. People with a spouse or young children are especially susceptible to this fear, since the thought of their loved one dying is terrifying. Of course, this fear is generally unfounded, since younger adults and children in Western society have one of the lowest death rates on the planet.

Further, going back to our rule of not buying insurance if there is no financial loss created when someone dies, insurance on children and a nonworking spouse just does not make sense. If a child or nonworking spouse dies, it is a huge emotional loss, but not a financial one. If such a person were to die, they would "take" all their monthly expenses (which average $500 to $1,000 per month in America) with them. But since they were not working while alive, there's no simultaneous disappearance of income.

It may sound very callous, but mathematically, it's actually a net positive when you lose someone who is not adding income to a family's bottom line. Even if you had to pay for a childcare provider to take the place of your spouse, the costs are usually offset by the lack of their monthly expenses. Long story short, just say no to insurance on a nonworking spouse or child.

The Fear of Funeral Costs

More than once in my career, I've overheard insurance agents telling people without life insurance, that a good policy will help make sure that they get a proper burial. As if *not* having insurance would result in your kids having to bury you in the backyard next to the hamster that died a few years ago.

For many, illness and death can feel like a very undignified process. Yet, in my entire career, I've never seen someone have an undignified memorial service simply because they didn't have enough insurance. Most people have enough assets to cover the cost of a proper memorial service, and most funeral homes offer payment plans that allow heirs time to liquidate a deceased person's assets to cover the costs. Further, it does not take long for the annual cost of insurance to add up to more than a funeral service will eventually cost anyway.

Your Bottom Line
According to the National Association of Funeral Directors, the average funeral service cost approximately $10,000 in 2007. The cost of cremation is nearly a third of that figure.

The Fear of Becoming Uninsurable

Another classic trick used by insurance agents, especially with younger adults, is telling them that they risk becoming uninsurable should they get sick later. In other words, buy the insurance now, even though you don't need it, and you'll be sure you can get it later.

What these agents fail to tell you is that this virtually never happens. It is extremely rare statistically for younger adults to be diagnosed with a disease or condition that would keep them from qualifying for life insurance later, if and when they need it.

Insurance Is Not a Good Investment

One of the biggest ways agents dupe people into buying both the wrong kind of insurance, and too much of it, is by convincing them that it's a good investment. This occurs with a type of insurance policy called *cash value* insurance, which in addition to providing coverage if you die, contains a built-in savings mechanism. These policies work by charging you more than your actual insurance costs, and depositing the excess into some type of savings vehicle made available through the insurance company.

def•i•ni•tion

Cash value insurance, also known as whole life or permanent insurance, contains a savings feature in addition to providing an eventual death benefit. While these and even more complex versions such as universal life and variable life insurance seem to offer a handy mix of insurance and investing, they're still viewed as substandard by financial planners.

Insurance agents will tell you time and time again that this type of insurance helps cash-strapped consumers kill two birds with one stone. One easy monthly premium takes care of both their life insurance needs and also helps them save for the future. They'll also tout the "loan provisions" of these plans, which lets you borrow money against them similar to your employer's 401(k) plan. What they almost always fail to tell you is that these policies are one of the most inefficient investments ever created. The investment options offered through these plans are lackluster and high cost compared to what you can purchase elsewhere and are riddled with rules and exceptions that make them just not worth it.

Illustrations: Don't Get Sucked In

One of the cornerstones of cash value insurance sales is a fancy look-ing printout called an illustration. This document is generated by the insurance agent to show how your policy might function over the coming years. Typically, an illustration shows a few different things, a couple of which are used to pull the wool over your eyes:

♦ **Premium.** This is the amount you pay for your policy each month. In most cases, with cash value insurance, you're entitled to pay the same premium every year for the rest of your life, as long as the policy remains active. It's important to take note of this amount, because it is going to be the primary thing you evaluate in choosing this kind of insurance over what is known as term insurance, something I'll cover at the end of this chapter.

♦ **Cash value.** This is the amount that the insurance company expects for you to have accumulated in the savings component as each year passes. It's important to note that your future cash value is calculated using hypothetical rates of return, something an insurance company may not be able to deliver on over time.

♦ **Surrender value.** Often times, cash value life insurance policies will hit you with a substantial surrender charge if you cancel your policy and take out the cash value in the first 5 to 10 years. So this amount is essentially the cash value minus the surrender charge.

♦ **Death benefit.** This is the amount your heirs would receive in any given year if you were to die.

Cash Value or Death Benefit—You Only Get One

One of the most misleading things about most cash value policies is how the cash value and the death benefit are represented side-by-side on an illustration, as well as by shady agents.

To look at a cash value life insurance policy that has been in place for 20 to 30 years, you'd think the policyholder has struck it rich. They might be showing a death benefit of $1,000,000 plus a cash value of $200,000 to $300,000. That'd be a whole lot of money!

Watch Your Back

Since insurance professionals are licensed by each state individually, a consumer wishing to check the complaint history and licensing information of an agent should visit the website for that state's insurance commissioner. Most states offer either an interactive search or a number to call for more information on agents and their companies.

It turns out that one of the most odious pieces of insurance fine print is that your heirs only get the greater of these two amounts, not both. In other words, that whole song and dance about your insurance being a great savings vehicle ceases to apply if you die before you withdraw the money.

For those of you thinking you'd be smart enough to just withdraw your cash value while you're still in good health, the fine print gets you there, too. If you withdraw your cash value, you lose your death benefit!

We Charge More Than We Pay

Here's one of those critical thinking moments for you as you build your financial IQ. If an insurance company is reasonably sure that they'll have to pay out on your life insurance, what are the chances that they'll charge you less than you're going to cost them?

The answer is zero. Insurance companies would not stay in business if they consistently paid out more than they collected from their customers. Yet, cash value insurance, which is also known as whole life insurance, promises to cover you for your *whole life* as long as you continue to pay the premiums.

If they're covering you for your whole life, there is a 100 percent probability they're going to eventually pay the face value to your heirs. With that in mind, is it that far-fetched to imagine they're going to charge you more than you're going to get? Purchasing whole life insurance is statistically a bad deal for you, and a great deal for insurance companies. That's why they have such big buildings and can pay their agents 90 percent commissions!

The IRS and Your Cash Value

While life insurance proceeds paid to your heirs are generally income-tax-free, the accumulated cash value in a whole life insurance policy may not be if you withdraw it. In fact, if you've managed to accumulate more than you've paid in on the policy, the excess is going to be taxed at ordinary income tax rates, just like your paycheck.

Watch Your Back

A major tax drawback to the use of insurance policies as savings vehicles is the lack of a tax deduction for contributions that normally come with 401(k)s and employer-sponsored plans. This could cost the average consumer anywhere from $150 to $250 per $1,000 contributed to a cash value policy instead of a deductible retirement plan.

When compared to the tax treatment of things like your company retirement plan, a Roth IRA, or even plain old mutual funds held in a taxable account, this pokes yet another hole in the argument that cash value insurance is a great investment.

More Fine Print

The cash value portion of life insurance isn't the only place consumers are getting ripped off and experiencing nasty surprises. Many insurance policies (including term policies) have complex rules about the type of deaths they cover, cancellation of coverage, incomplete facts on your application, etc. Here are some of the main wrinkles you need to watch out for:

- ◆ **Exclusion periods.** Most life insurance policies don't cover people who die within the first 6 to 12 months of purchasing a policy. If this happens, the company typically refunds your premiums paid and sends you on your way.

- ◆ **Risky behavior.** Also known as the Darwin Clause, many policies state that they will not pay benefits on a death resulting from behavior that is deemed highly risky. While you might be tempted to breeze through this section when reviewing your policy, don't. Risky behaviors that have resulted in nonpayment of a death benefit have been known to include scuba diving, snowmobiling, and learning to fly a private plane.

◆ **Murder or suicide.** While we've all seen the murder mystery shows where the wife ended up bumping off her husband for the insurance money, insurance companies are not usually this dumb. Most policies carry provisions that eliminate benefits if the insured person is taken out by one of the beneficiaries or commits suicide.

◆ **Incomplete application.** The premium you pay is based on the level of risk the insurance company believes you are exposed to. If you fail to include something that is considered a risk factor on your insurance application, an insurance company can and will wiggle out of paying. For example, if you claim you don't smoke, but the insurance company uncovers the picture of you smoking a cigar at a poker game, your heirs may be out of luck.

There's one additional piece of fine print worth mentioning, but it's one that can help you rather than hurt you. Let's say that times get tight and you miss a payment on your insurance. Don't panic; all is not lost. Even if you find out you've come down with some tragic tropical disease, and missed a payment or two, there's probably hope. Go back to your insurance policy and look to see if you have reinstatement privileges, something required by most states. This fine print allows you to catch up on your unpaid premiums and reinstate coverage as if nothing ever happened.

Insurance the Right Way

You might think, based on what I've discussed so far in this chapter, that you should run for the hills whenever the topic of life insurance is brought up. That's not the case. You should only run for the hills when someone tries to convince you to do insurance the wrong way. When insurance is done the right way, like those with a high financial IQ do it, it's an indispensable part of protecting your progress toward your financial goals.

As I've mentioned, you should only buy insurance that covers your loved ones for a financial loss that is created because of a death. If there is no *financial* loss, there is no need for insurance. If there was a potential financial loss, but it went away (because your children grew up, you retired, etc.), then it's likely that you no longer need life insurance.

In the Know

If you purchase an insurance policy only to change your mind or discover some unreasonable fine print, you may be able to demand your money back. Most states require insurance companies to provide a free-look period during which a consumer can cancel a newly issued insurance contract for a full refund. Since these periods can range from a few days to a month, you should be sure to check your state's rules.

If there is a potential financial loss, however, the size of that financial loss will help you gauge exactly how much insurance you need. My rule of thumb is that you need 20 times the annual loss created because of a death. In other words, if someone's death represents a $25,000 annual net loss (their annual income minus their annual living expenses), then they should have roughly $500,000 in insurance coverage.

The reason for this rule of thumb is that it provides a family with a large enough pool of money that the interest earned would sufficiently cover the financial shortfall created. Historically, relatively safe investments like government bonds have paid in the ballpark of 5 percent, which means a $500,000 portfolio would pay $25,000 per year, indefinitely.

Becoming Self-Insured

The goal of the financially intelligent is to eventually become self-insured when it comes to their life insurance needs. This in fact is not a separate goal from saving for your future, but a by-product of doing it well.

If you do a diligent job of saving for life's big goals and managing the money (or your advisors) wisely, you at some point will cease to need life insurance on yourself. This occurs because your assets become more than sufficient for your heirs to live off of for the rest of their lives, even if your income disappears.

For most people, this doesn't occur until at least their late 40s or early 50s. But it generally occurs for most people by the time they fully retire in their mid-60s. With the exception of someone whose pension will disappear if they die, there is no reason to continue to spend hundreds or thousands of dollars every year on life insurance coverage. Chances are that this money would be better spent elsewhere, even if just on increasing the quality and longevity of life itself.

Buy Term and Invest the Rest

Between the combination of most people only needing life insurance for a specific window of time (raising children, growing their net worth to a sustainable level, etc.) and the fact that cash value insurance is a generally poor investment, term life insurance is the best solution for most people. As the name implies, term insurance covers you for a specific window of time, such as 10, 20, or 30 years, after which you are no longer covered.

However, since the likelihood of you dying during that window is much lower than the 100 percent likelihood of you dying while you own whole life insurance, your costs will be dramatically lower. In fact, it's not uncommon to see a term life insurance policy cost one tenth of what a cash value policy costs.

Now some of you may rightly point out that a term policy doesn't have a cash value savings component. But this is where I'd like to introduce you to one of the favorite sayings of the financially astute—*buy term and invest the rest*. Under this theory, a consumer fares better much longer over time by purchasing lower-cost term insurance, and investing the savings elsewhere besides in their insurance policy.

Let's look at an example of how the numbers might pencil out. At the time of this writing, I requested a quote for $1 million in whole life insurance on a healthy 35-year-old nonsmoking male, as well as a 20-year term policy for the same amount. The term policy came back with a quote of $490 annually from an A-rated insurance company, and $10,460 annually for a whole life policy. That's a difference of almost $10,000 per year!

If that difference between the cost of the term policy and the whole life policy, $9,970 per year, were invested earning an average of 8 percent per year over the next 20 years, you'd accumulate $492,747. By comparison, the cash value life insurance policy will only have accumulated $225,192 over the same time frame—not even half as much. Furthermore, if you died during that 20 years, a term policy would pay you the full $1 million, in addition to the money you managed to accumulate in a separate account. However, the whole life policy would only pay you the $1 million, with the cash value reverting to the insurance company.

Insurance Company Ratings

Unlike banks, credit unions, and even brokerage houses, there's no agency or organization that backs insurance companies. In other words, if an insurance company goes belly up, your policy (including cash value) can disappear overnight. That's why, if and when you need insurance, it's crucial to choose an insurance company whose financial history and future both look rock solid.

Thankfully, there are companies that provide third-party ratings that take the guesswork out of selecting an insurer. I'd strongly recommend that you consult these before you make a decision to purchase insurance. Further, I'd suggest that you don't settle for a lower rating just to save some money. If you're going to spend the money on insurance, it better darn well be there when you need it.

In the Know

It only takes a few seconds to look up your life insurance company's ratings at www.fitchratings.com or www.ambest.com. Both websites also offer an e-lert feature that will inform you when an insurance company's ratings change.

While there are a significant number of organizations that rate life insurance companies, there are three in particular that have industry wide respect—Moody's, A.M. Best, and Fitch's. If a company has a good rating from another group, but not one of these three, you should skip them. As far as the ratings themselves, their scales vary slightly, but anything with an A or above is generally considered high quality.

Section 1035 Exchanges

One of the great insurance tricks the financially savvy keep in their back pocket is the Section 1035 exchange. This little-known IRS rule allows owners of a whole life insurance policy to move their cash value to a better life insurance policy without incurring any income tax on the transaction.

While many who have been sold an unsuitable or costly whole life policy may have no interest in simply replacing a bad policy with another similar policy, the Section 1035 exchange rule also allows a policy owner to move the money to a variable annuity. As mentioned in Chapter 6, variable annuities are not an ideal long-term investment, but they're likely to perform much better than your average cash value life insurance policy.

Just be sure to purchase your replacement insurance policy before you perform the Section 1035 exchange, just in case you cannot qualify for a new life insurance policy. Also, when selecting a variable annuity, consider a lower-load option available through one of the no-load mutual fund families. Although there will still be some cost attached to these annuities, it'll be substantially less than one bought through a full-service financial professional.

The Least You Need to Know

♦ Don't let an agent use fear to bully you into buying a policy or increasing your amount of coverage.

♦ Be sure to read the fine print to understand exactly what your policy does and does not cover.

♦ If you do a good job planning and saving for life's big goals, you won't need life insurance after a certain point.

♦ For most people, buying term and investing the rest is the best insurance choice.

♦ If you're stuck in a bad cash value life insurance policy, consider performing a 1035 exchange *after* purchasing better term insurance.

Part

5

Dealing with Your Uncle Sam

Individuals with a high financial IQ don't leave anything to chance when it comes to the government and their personal finances. They know how to take advantage of key programs when they need them, and how to stay off the radar when it comes to the IRS. In this final part, we'll look at everything you need to know, from how to avoid IRS audits to how to make the most out of programs like Social Security and Medicare. You'll also get an overview of some of the financial safety nets the government offers.

THIS IS THE THIRD YEAR IN A ROW THAT STANLEY'S BEEN AUDITED!

BARR

Chapter  15

Your Taxes

In This Chapter

- ◆ IRS audit selection process
- ◆ Red flags on your return
- ◆ Taxes you never knew you owed
- ◆ Resolving IRS conflicts

Throughout much of this book, I've talked about financial IQ as if it was something you couldn't have too much of. In most cases, that's true. But when it comes to the IRS, there's such a thing as just the right amount of financial IQ. Too little, and you'll find yourself getting stuck in tax traps and not knowing how to deal with the IRS if an audit comes your way. Too much financial IQ, trying to be too smart and play the system too much, and an audit is probably inevitable.

What most people don't understand—and something that you're about to—is that the smartest people play the tax system as straight as possible. They take every legal deduction they can while avoiding questionable strategies that grab the IRS's attention. They also take a regular look down the road to make sure they minimize the chances that they'll fall into one of the supplementary tax systems that exist.

How You Help Them Get You

Do understand this about the IRS—they are people just like you and me. In fact, they're some of the most overworked government employees in all of the United States. They're not sitting there trying to dream up ways to persecute innocent taxpayers, nor do they make it their goal to wring every penny out of every American. In fact, they don't even make the rules, Congress does. They simply attempt to enforce the ever-expanding 9,000 pages and one million words of tax code.

The reality is, if you leave the IRS alone and play within the rules, they're likely to leave you and your money alone as well. Most people who end up in trouble with the IRS, especially the ones who end up in the deepest trouble, are people who carelessly disregard the rules or downright break the law.

How Audits Get Selected

Despite what many people think, most IRS audits are not the result of random selection. The IRS does not sit around and draw Social Security numbers out of a hat or throw darts at a list of names. Rather, the vast majority of audits selected fall into one of two categories.

The first category is what is known as targeted industries, in which the IRS performs audits primarily on small business owners and self-employed individuals in industries that are prone to tax abuses. Typically these are industries that rely heavily on cash transactions that would be easy to hide from taxation. If you work in one of these industries, you better run a tight ship. If you don't, you've got one less thing to worry about.

The second category is audits selected by one of the more advanced computer programs ever designed. Known as the DIF system, which stands for Discriminant Function, this program sorts through all filed returns measuring different elements against a pool of closely guarded statistics. Based on the presence of different factors on a return, such as a certain deduction being above a certain percentage of income, a return's DIF score increases. Once a DIF score crosses a certain threshold, it gets flagged for review.

The vast majority of returns that get audited are selected using the DIF system. Because this system measures numerous aspects of returns using a statistical analysis, there is no one way to protect your return from getting selected, besides being extremely honest. In reality, the DIF system is designed to catch tax cheats, and it is very effective at doing so.

The Biggest IRS Red Flags

While the IRS system for selecting audits in any given year is kept relatively secret, there are some things that are historically known to be red flags. Most importantly, the failure of the income numbers reported on your return to match to the numbers submitted to the IRS by your employers on your Forms W-2 and 1099 is one of the surest audit triggers out there.

Aside from that, there are certain types of deductions and income sources that are considered audit triggers. The presence of any one of these won't necessarily cause an audit, but as the number and magnitude of these red flags increases, so does your chances that the DIF system will take a liking to you.

Watch Your Back

Just because you have a professional tax preparer doesn't mean she'll be there if you get audited. While some tax preparers promise to represent any of their clients should an audit arise, many charge an hourly fee for this service. Be sure to check with your preparer to find out what services she provides if the IRS comes calling.

While you shouldn't avoid any of the following (unless you have something to hide), you should be aware that these can definitely increase the scrutiny of your entire return:

- ◆ **Excessive charitable contributions.** While the IRS is more than happy to help you help your favorite charity through charitable write-offs, people donating an excessively large amount of their income, as well as those donating cash or appreciated property, are also subject to increased scrutiny.

- **Excessive entertainment expenses.** If you entertain a lot for business and intend to write off these expenses, you need to be sure to keep accurate records and receipts, just in case.

- **Home office deduction.** Since the IRS requires home office space to be used exclusively for business purposes, as well as meeting other strict criteria, they recognize that many people taking this deduction are doing so incorrectly or illegally.

- **The hobby loss rule.** Many people attempt to convert their hobbies into a side business, which the tax code encourages by allowing small business owners to deduct their losses in the early years against their other income. But if your business continually loses money, the IRS becomes leery of your deductions related to it and may drag out the microscope and start dissecting your return.

In the Know

When it comes to getting your taxes done, not all tax preparers are created equal. In fact, the only people tested and licensed directly by the IRS to prepare income tax returns are enrolled agents. Visit the National Association of Enrolled Agents at www.naea.org to find one in your area.

- **Excessive business mileage.** At over 50¢ per mile, the IRS knows it is tempting to beat down your taxable income by being a little too generous in estimating your work-related mileage. If you're a road warrior when it comes to your job, be sure to keep a detailed log of the purpose and distance of each road trip.

- **Round numbers.** Since most people when they make up a number usually choose round numbers ($500, $1,000, etc.), the IRS is quick to look at returns that contain an excessive amount of milestone numbers.

- **The earned income credit.** The EIC, which is an extra refund meant to assist lower-income taxpayers, has historically been subject to a higher amount of abuse. If you're claiming the EIC and also sizeable deductions, there's a good chance you'll get up close and personal with the IRS's finest.

- **Using a "watched" preparer.** The IRS maintains a list of tax preparers that are known or believed to file questionable returns on behalf of their clients. If your preparer gives indications that they don't mind pushing the limits of the law, you may want to think about finding someone else to avoid getting lumped in with those kinds of questionable practices.

- **Participating in abusive tax shelters.** The IRS has greatly increased its scrutiny of questionable tax shelters and strategies in recent years. If you participate in something designed to shelter income or provide excessive write-offs, you may be drawing unwanted attention.

The Fine Print of the IRS

While the tax code may seem like one giant mess of fine print, it's not intended to be. Nothing in it is meant to ensnare or take advantage of innocent taxpayers. But because of its overwhelming nature, many people don't realize that some of the most painful fine print are rules that apply alternative or supplementary taxes just when you think you don't owe anything else.

In the Know

If your tax return simply consists of a few W-2s, Form 1098s, and Form 1099s, there's a good chance you can prepare it yourself and save a few hundred dollars. Computer programs like TurboTax and TaxCut are easy and intuitive for most people to use and can even help you file your return electronically for free.

While you can't always avoid the alternative minimum tax, estate and gift taxes, and self-employment taxes, you can recognize in advance how these systems work and when they'll apply to you. In turn, you can seek out expert help before it's needed, and in turn minimize your surprise tax bills.

The Alternative Minimum Tax

Can you believe, that if you do a good enough job of legally lowering the amount of taxes you owe, that there's an alternative tax system that may require you to pay higher taxes anyway? It's true, and it's called the *alternative minimum tax (AMT)*.

def•i•ni•tion

The **alternative minimum tax (AMT)** is a tax system designed specifically to tax high-income taxpayers who have otherwise legally avoided taxation. Unlike the traditional tax system, it only has two tax rates, 26 percent and 28 percent.

The AMT, which was originally put in place in 1970 to help tax a few hundred households that had escaped taxation, now penalizes three to four million households per year. That means if you haven't been hit with the AMT, but make at least $75,000 to $100,000 per year as a household, your time may be coming. And, with a minimum rate of 26 percent, that's a lot of money that can disappear from your wallet.

The problem with the AMT is that according to the IRS rules, it is your responsibility to calculate your taxes under both the AMT system as well as the traditional system, and pay the greater of the two. But since most taxpayers have never heard of the AMT, most don't do the double calculation. This of course leads to thousands of people each year who get a nasty letter from the IRS saying that they owe thousands, even tens of thousands of dollars more (plus interest), for a previous year's return that was subject to the AMT.

Ironically, many people who find themselves in an AMT situation could have avoided it by timing certain types of income, avoiding certain investments, and choosing certain types of deductions over others. Here's a list of the top differences between the AMT system and the traditional tax calculation, which could result in you having to pay the alternative minimum tax:

- ◆ **Incentive stock options (ISOs).** One of the most common AMT tax triggers is the exercise of incentive stock options. These are options given to employees that contain special tax deferral and capital gains benefits not found in the more common nonqualified stock options. But exercise too many in one year, and the IRS declares that you've avoided too much income and will slap you with the AMT to recoup some of it.

◆ **Home mortgage and equity interest deduction.** The interest you pay on a home mortgage or home-equity line of credit (borrowing against your house) ceases to be deductible under the alternative minimum tax if not used to buy or improve your main or second home. The loss of this often-substantial deduction presents a nasty surprise for taxpayers who find themselves suddenly qualifying for the AMT.

◆ **Capital gains.** If you have made profits on the sale of your investments (capital gains), it will still be taxed at the lower, more preferable capital gains tax rates even if you qualify for the AMT. But this income does count toward the total amount of income the IRS allows to be protected from the AMT. That means that if you have a large amount of capital gains in a given year, you raise the risk that the rest of your ordinary (wage) income will be taxed at AMT rates.

◆ **Private municipal bonds.** Normally, the income earned from municipal bonds (issued by a state, county, city, etc.) pay interest that is federally and state income tax-free to the holder. But certain types of municipal bonds, known as private activity bonds, generate income that may be subject to the AMT even if they avoid traditional income taxes. Be sure to check with your broker and mutual fund companies to determine your exposure to private activity bonds.

In the Know

If you've grown sick of the complex U.S. tax system, you're not the only one. In recent years, a number of alternative tax systems have been proposed, including the increasingly popular FairTax championed by Georgia Congressman John Linder. For an easy-to-read explanation of the FairTax, check out my book *The Pocket Idiot's Guide to the FairTax* (see Appendix B) and www.fairtax.org.

Gift and Estate Taxes

As hard as it is to believe, you can actually be taxed in the United States for being too generous during your lifetime or dying with too much money. You've got to love the American tax system!

While you might be tempted to brush off this section because you don't plan on dying with millions, or giving away millions, don't. Currently, dying with roughly $1 to $4 million dollars in total net worth (including your home's value) can subject you to the estate tax. Equally as surprising, something as simple as adding someone to the title of a house or to a bank account could trigger eventual gift taxes.

While these are very complex matters, there's some basic fine print you need to know to stay out of trouble. Most importantly, the gift and estate taxes are actually the same tax, calculated on the combined total of all money transferred before and after you die, minus a few exceptions. While the calculation is beyond the scope of this book, the overall methodology is fairly easy to understand.

The IRS provides a limit on the amount of wealth that can be transferred at your death to a nonspouse (you can transfer unlimited amounts, in life and death, to your spouse). If you exceed this limit, which changes depending on the year you die, you can owe up to 55 percent in estate taxes on the excess amount.

To keep people from giving away their net worth on their deathbeds and thereby escaping the estate tax, the IRS has also put a limit on the amount that can be transferred in any one year to any one person. If amounts over this annual exclusion limit are gifted to any one party, you have to file a gift tax return. While you will not be required to pay the taxes now, the excess amount gifted over your annual exclusion reduces the future amount that can be transferred at death.

Due to the ever-changing rules and limits associated with estate and gift taxes, high financial IQ individuals know that they need legal and tax professionals to help them navigate this maze. The good news, though, is that these professionals have developed a number of legal strategies that can help you shelter far more than the standard limits from eventual taxation. Be sure to check out IRS Publication 950, *An Introduction to Gift and Estate Taxes*, for more information.

Self-Employment Taxes

If there was a collective groan heard at tax time during the last economic downturn, it was from people who were self-employed for the first time in their careers. Chances are that you, or someone you know, were among the resourceful people who sold their unique skills after hours and on weekends to help make ends meet. Most of these people however, didn't realize that the joys of self-employment came with an unavoidable pain—self-employment taxes.

Normally, employees working for someone else (W-2 employees) are used to seeing some money go out each paycheck for FICA or OASDI. This 7.65 percent is what each employee contributes to the Social Security and Medicare system, on top of the normal income taxes they pay. But what they fail to realize until they're their own boss, is that their employer is required to match that 7.65 percent, for a grand total of 15.3 percent of your income.

 In the Know

If you've got self-employment income, you need to start thinking about taxes before April 15th. Most self-employed individuals need to file quarterly estimated tax returns that include a prepayment of income and self-employment taxes due. Failure to file these quarterly returns can result in a penalty just like failing to file your annual return. For more information on filing quarterly estimates, review IRS Publication 505.

Of course that means, when you're working for yourself, you're on the hook for the full 15.3 percent! Even worse, this amount cannot be reduced by your other normal deductions, since it is not technically part of your income tax. In other words, even if you can reduce your taxable income to zero through legal deductions, you still have to pay self-employment tax.

The one silver lining, if you can call it that, is that you get to reduce the amount the 15.3 percent is calculated on by all the expenses you paid operating your side business. This includes things like depreciation on equipment, home office deductions, and even possibly medical insurance premiums. Take a look at IRS Publication 334, the *Tax Guide for Small Businesses*, for more information.

Pain in the IRS

It's said that the famed Royal Canadian Mounted Police, or Mounties, always get their man. While many a proud Canadian will tell you that it's true, any American who's owed Uncle Sam money knows that the Mounties can't hold a candle to the IRS. In fact, the IRS arguably has one of the most unparalleled abilities to enforce legal judgments of any organization on the face of the planet. They'll tap into your paychecks, siphoning off money without you being able to stop them. They can and will find your assets, seize them, and sell them. They're relentless.

That doesn't mean that the ultimate of financial arm-twisters doesn't have a few soft spots. Play your cards right, cooperate to make their job easier, and you might just get off the hook for a little less dough.

Getting Your Auditor to Go Easy

If you do find yourself sitting across from an IRS agent, it's important to remember that your attitude can affect the intensity and outcome of the process. While the IRS would officially tell you that all audits are conducted in the same manner for all taxpayers, common sense and anecdotal evidence would tell you that auditors have good days and bad days, like anyone else. If you help them to have a good day (without breaking any bribery laws), then there is a good chance they'll take your word for certain things, let tiny discrepancies slide, and treat you with respect. Be a jerk and your audit will feel like a cross between high school detention and an airport strip search.

Following are some tips on how to make life easier for your auditor, and thus yourself.

◆ **Don't blame them.** It wasn't the cop's fault that you were doing 60 in a 40 mph zone, and it isn't the auditor's fault that you've been deducting something incorrectly for the last decade. Show that you understand that they're just doing their job and you're likely to receive some understanding in return.

◆ **Get organized.** Nothing peeves auditors like someone who comes in with two years of receipts stuffed in your pockets (except maybe someone who doesn't have any documentation whatsoever). Get organized in advance, separating the information they've requested by years and category. Be sure to invest in a few staples and paper clips, and stick a descriptive Post-It note on the front of each bundle of paper to speed things up.

◆ **Be on time.** While we may think the world could do with fewer auditors, the reality is there are not enough of them to meet the IRS's goals. That means that most auditors you meet have packed schedules and don't like to be kept waiting. Show up late for your audit appointment and you're sure to start with a strike against you.

◆ **Keep your mouth shut.** There's an old World War II saying that "loose lips sink ships." It turns out that they can sink audits just as well. Your agent is coming in with an agenda; let him stick to it without distracting him with your excuses. Besides that, rambling on and on may help him uncover other issues he'd like to investigate.

In the Know

While it might seem like the IRS is only out to get you, they have a whole division of employees whose job is to help taxpayers make sense of their IRS situation, even acting as advocates on their behalf. For more information on the IRS Taxpayer Advocate program, visit www. irs.gov/advocate.

Offers in Compromise

One of the most classic techniques to reduce your IRS woes is what is known as an Offer in Compromise. Under this program, a taxpayer essentially offers the IRS immediate payment of a lesser amount to

settle an outstanding balance due. If the IRS deems the offer accept-
able, the taxpayer pays the bill and moves on with their life.

Watch Your Back

In recent years, the
number of tax profes-
sionals taking to the airwaves
promising to help you settle
your IRS debts for pennies on
the dollar has skyrocketed.
Unfortunately for most consumers, these professionals charge
a substantial fee for filling out
forms that taxpayers can very
easily do themselves.

Unfortunately, Offers in Compromise have been so overused in the
past decade that the IRS has begun
turning more and more of them
down. Only the most extreme cases
that have gone uncollected for a
number of years are usually accepted.
It doesn't mean that you shouldn't
try, but it's important to realize that
your chances of getting approved
for a few-thousand-dollar settlement
that is just a couple years old is
pretty low and may not be worth the
application fee.

Installment Agreements

Due to the increasing number of abuses of the Offer in Compromise
program, especially by a small group of tax professionals, the IRS has
increasingly pushed taxpayers toward installment agreements. Under
these plans, the taxpayer and the IRS agree to a repayment schedule
that usually involves monthly payments instead of actually dismissing
part of the balance.

While that may not sound like a lot of help, it does one key thing—get
the IRS off your back. Once you've made the installment agreement,
and for as long as you continue to pay on time, the IRS will not enforce
any additional collections actions against you for that balance. To pursue an installment agreement, you need to fill out an Online Payment
Agreement for balances less than $25,000, and a Collection Information
Statement for balances over $25,000.

Blame It on Your Spouse

It's not uncommon for one person in a marriage to handle the finances,
with the other person being fairly in the dark about a variety of money
issues, including tax filings. Because of this, the IRS offers some relief

for a spouse who had nothing to do with a couple's tax preparation process, but has gotten stuck with a tax bill nonetheless.

There are three exceptions that may apply, each with different rules about who can claim them and what type of relief is provided. While an overview is provided here, it's highly advisable to seek out a tax professional if you need to use one of these remedies:

- **The Innocent Spouse Rule.** Under the Innocent Spouse Rule, you may be exempted from paying some or all of the taxes and penalties arising from your spouse making mistakes on the tax return. In order to qualify for this, you have to have had no knowledge of the error and have to apply within two years of the start of the IRS collections process.

- **Separate Liability Election.** This election essentially allows the IRS to assign the income tax due to the parties who actually earned it, with some additional calculations for any benefit you received from what the other earned. To use this election, you must be widowed, divorced, or separated (at least 12 months).

- **Equitable Relief.** This relatively new provision allows the IRS to absolve you from unpaid taxes, even if you technically owe them, if relief is not provided under the other two rules. Whereas the other two rules are fairly systematic in their definitions of who qualifies and what relief is provided, this provision allows the IRS to provide relief in unique situations.

The Least You Need to Know

- The best way to avoid an IRS audit is to be honest and accurate in the filing of your return.

- Since the IRS matches your tax return against documents filed by your employers and banks, a difference between what is reported and what you put on your return will almost surely guarantee IRS contact.

- Taxpayers need to plan ahead to make sure they're not caught off guard by the AMT and other tax programs.

- Use an Offer in Compromise or installment agreement to get the IRS off your back for unpaid balances.

Chapter 16

Social Security and Medicare

In This Chapter

- ◆ Social Security 101
- ◆ Tips and traps for retirees
- ◆ Benefits for survivors and the disabled
- ◆ Looking ahead to Medicare

There are probably more 30- to 40-year-olds in America who still believe in Santa Claus than there are who believe Social Security will be around when they retire. The fact that the Social Security Administration has estimated it will not be able to pay full benefits after 2042 isn't helping many people's confidence in the program.

Unfortunately, that leads many younger people to ignore the value of knowledge about the Social Security program and its mechanics. In fact, most midcareer professionals couldn't begin to tell you when benefits become available, how they're affected by continued employment and taxes, or what happens when a Social Security recipient dies.

People with a high financial IQ, however, realize that even though they personally may not have to deal with these things for decades, there is a good chance that they will be thrust into an advisory role for their own parents in the coming years. They know that a working knowledge of Social Security will help them to help their parents make the right choices, which in turn lessens the strain and pressure on them as adult children.

The Basics of Social Security

To understand the opportunities and pitfalls associated with Social Security, you've got to understand the basics. Most importantly, Social Security by design was never meant to replace 100 percent of a retiree's income. It was only meant to be a supplement to other programs such as company pensions (which have all but disappeared) and personal savings. That means that if you or your parents are counting on Social Security to cover a good portion of your expenses, you're going to be let down unless you have a very low cost of living.

To not get caught off guard, it's crucial now to begin looking at your (or your parents') Social Security estimates when they're mailed out each year. If you haven't seen one of these recently or would like a fresh estimate, you can order a traditional paper copy or get an instant estimate online at www.ssa.gov/estimator.

 Watch Your Back

> The number of identity theft cases involving Social Security fraud has skyrocketed in the last few years. In extreme cases, thieves steal people's annual benefits statements, change the address, and then report the person as dead in an attempt to claim survivorship benefits. If you can't remember the last time you received your annual benefits estimate, you may want to give the Social Security Administration a call. Get contact information at www.ssa.gov.

To receive retirement benefits under the Social Security program, you generally have to earn 40 "quarters" of credit. In its most basic definition, workers would receive one-quarter credit for each calendar year quarter that they earn above a certain amount ($1,090 for 2009).

Workers who earn more than the minimum in one quarter may receive credit for additional quarters, up to the entire year's amount. So someone earning $5,000 in the first few months of the year would be credited with four quarters credit (their entire year's worth) toward the 40 required to qualify for Social Security.

The monthly benefit amount eventually received in retirement is based on your highest 35 years of earnings, indexed for inflation. This amount may be increased or decreased initially based on what age you choose to start drawing Social Security, as well as increased as you age for inflation.

Social Security Tips and Traps

Few, if any, government programs give as much control to the recipient as Social Security. Under the program, recipients can control the timing of their benefits, which in turn controls the dollar amount they receive. But deciding when to take your benefits isn't as simple as holding out for the most money or taking it immediately if you're living on a shoestring. The choice of when to take it also comes with certain pieces of fine print that recipients need to add to their IQ.

Retirement Age and Benefit Amount

The amount of Social Security benefits received is directly affected by how old you are when you begin receiving benefits, in comparison to the "normal retirement age," used by the Social Security Administration. Depending on when you were born, your normal retirement age changes, with younger adults having progressively later benchmarks. Visit www.ssa.gov to see a comprehensive list of normal retirement ages.

Perhaps the easiest way to look at it is that at your normal retirement age, you get 100 percent of your expected benefits. If you begin drawing Social Security prior to that point, you will get a percentage below 100 percent, and if you begin drawing after, you will receive an amount above 100 percent.

For individuals born after 1940, each month of delaying Social Security increases your benefit amount by .66 percent, or 8 percent per year, with no additional increases past age 70.

Each month you take it early, less than 36 months total, your benefit amount decreases by .55 percent or roughly 6.66 percent per year. For each additional month past 36 months, the decrease slows to .416 percent per month, or roughly 5 percent per year.

When it comes to deciding whether to take the money early or to wait, many people base the decision solely on whether or not they need the money. For some people, getting some money, as soon as possible, seems to be a necessity. The fact that taking Social Security early will reduce their overall benefits by nearly 25 to 30 percent is not as pressing as paying their bills. For others, they feel like they might as well wait, so that the amount is as high as possible.

> **Your Bottom Line**
>
> The Social Security Administration has put together a number of handy calculators that can calculate various facets of your estimated retirement benefit. To give them a try, go to www.ssa.gov and click "Estimate Your Retirement Benefits."

Before you decide, you need to weigh a couple of advantages and drawbacks:

- **Waiting equals an 8 percent rate of return.** For people wrestling with whether to tap their nest egg or start drawing Social Security, it's important to remember that delaying Social Security is equal to an 8 percent return on your money. If you reasonably expect your investments to grow at 8 percent or less, it may be more favorable to delay the start of Social Security and use up a larger amount of your retirement assets first.

- **Taking it early and investing.** Since taking it early results in a 5 to 6.66 percent reduction in benefits, savvy investors who do not need the money may still come out ahead by taking the smaller amount a few years earlier, adding the amounts received to their nest egg, and growing it at a rate greater than the percentage decrease they incurred.

- **Remembering that life is short.** While a lot more people are living until their 70s and 80s, you still need to ask yourself if it is worth your (or your parents) putting off enjoying their sunset years for a little extra cash. If they die earlier than they expect and they didn't draw their Social Security, they may be giving up an opportunity to enjoy life to a greater degree.

♦ **Drawing early benefits while working.** It's not uncommon for people to begin drawing early Social Security while still working. Many don't realize, however, that prior to your normal retirement age, working may reduce the benefits you can receive by $1 for every $2 to $3 you earn above certain threshold amounts (benefit reductions start as low as $14,160 in wages). Once you reach full retirement age (if you reach full retirement age), you will recoup earlier lost benefits, as well as be able to earn unlimited amounts without a reduction. Benefits are not reduced at any point for non-work income such as interest, dividends, and investment profits.

Your Bottom Line

Are you interested in knowing how long the government thinks you'll live? Currently, the IRS expects 30-year-olds to live to be 84.2 years old, 40-year-olds to live to be 83.6 years, and 50-year-olds to live to 83.3 years old. For a breakdown of every age, see Appendix C in IRS Publication 590.

Social Security Taxation

Many people are surprised (and slightly disgusted) to learn that their Social Security benefits are taxable. For people who had their retirement cash flows planned down to the penny, finding out that 50 to 85 percent of their benefits may be subject to income tax can put a major crimp in their lifestyle. That's the difference between the chrome-plated shuffle-board stick and the plain old plastic one.

Determining whether or not someone will be taxed on Social Security is based on how their combined income between different sources compares to one of two thresholds set by the IRS. Currently, single taxpayers with combined income between $25,000 and $34,000 will pay tax on up to 50 percent of their income, and up to 85 percent if their combined income exceeds $34,000. This range is adjusted to $32,000 to $44,000 for married couples filing joint tax returns.

While the actual calculation of how much is taxable is beyond the scope of this book, the calculation of combined income which would indicate some type of taxability is not. Combined income, in the eyes of the

IRS, is simply the combination of your adjusted gross income, tax-free interest (usually earned on municipal bonds), and one half of your Social Security benefits.

So for example, a single woman receiving $15,000 in wages, $5,000 in dividends, $5,000 in tax-free interest, and $15,000 in Social Security would have a combined income of $32,500 ($15,000 + $5,000 + $5,000 + half of $15,000). In this instance, up to 50 percent of her Social Security benefits would be taxable, since her combined income falls between $25,000 and $34,000.

Other Social Security Wrinkles

Just when it seems like you've got Social Security figured out, another wrinkle comes along that throws off your calculations. As always, individuals with high financial IQs are looking down the road to see if any of these wrinkles apply to themselves or their loved ones:

- ◆ **The payback provision.** One of the most interesting wrinkles in the Social Security rules is one that allows people who had previously opted to take Social Security before their normal retirement age to go back and now apply for the larger amount. It's not without fine print, though—you have to repay every cent you've received up until that point. This may be beneficial for some people who have come into a windfall and could choose to either invest that money in a private investment or "invest" it in their Social Security and receive a substantial bump in the monthly benefits. This election can be made on the Social Security Administration's Form 521, but you should definitely consult a financial professional prior to deciding.

- ◆ **The windfall elimination provision.** Especially if you are nearing the end of your working career, there's a chance that you've worked for an employer who paid into a pension program for you instead of Social Security on your behalf. In some cases, for workers who had significant careers at other companies that did pay into Social Security, this creates a "windfall" where you receive a monthly benefit that is viewed as duplicative. Thus, for certain older employees, the benefit amount is recalculated to coordinate these two separate benefits, often resulting in a lower overall monthly amount. If your employment history contains such a scenario, the Social Security estimates you receive may give you a false sense of financial security. Be sure to contact the Social Security Administration if you believe this may apply to you.

♦ **Supplemental SSI.** Certain low-income taxpayers (approximately $1,400 to $2,000 per month in income) aged 65 and older, as well as the blind and the disabled, may qualify for an additional Social Security benefit amount each month. Receiving these benefits is not automatic, however, and must be applied for. Further, these benefits can be reduced by things such as the proceeds from reverse mortgages, and need to be monitored carefully to ensure that taxpayers continue to receive their benefits. Contact your local Social Security Administration office for more details.

Tapping Social Security for Emergencies

When you've been helping people with their personal finances as long as I have, you hear your fair share of truly heartbreaking stories. And for most people, there are few things as overwhelming as a loved one's death, compounded by the fact that they were a contributing or primary breadwinner. The fear of not being able to make ends meet, of having to uproot your children, and of having to find additional work, leaves some widows and widowers feeling paralyzed.

That's why it seems like a miracle when people discover that a loved one's Social Security benefits may kick in decades earlier than normal retirement in the event of a death or disability. This piece of financial IQ can literally translate into thousands of dollars in income each month, enough to help a family in crisis maintain the status quo.

Survivorship Benefits

If a taxpayer has paid in their required 40 quarters to Social Security, then both their spouse and dependents are eligible to receive what is known as survivorship benefits. Eligible recipients may even include a surviving former spouse from a divorce or the deceased's parents if they were financially dependent on that person.

For example, if a 35-year-old woman dies, leaving a surviving 35-year-old husband and three small children, they're likely eligible to begin receiving $1,000 to $2,000 per month until the children are grown, assuming she had earned her 40 quarters.

The amount of survivorship benefits varies depending on who receives them, as shown in the following table.

Survivorship Percentages by Recipient

Survivor	Benefit Amounts
Surviving spouse under 60 with children under 18	75 percent of earned amount
Surviving spouse over 60 with no children	71–99 percent of earned amount
Surviving spouse over normal retirement age	100 percent of earned amount
Children under 18	75 percent of earned amount

Source: www.ssa.gov.

Since both a deceased person's children and the spouse can simultaneously receive benefits, the Social Security Administration limits the total amount a family can receive at 150 to 180 percent of the deceased's earned benefit amount. Spousal benefits (not the children's) are also decreased based on the spouse's earnings, and eliminated completely if they remarry before age 60.

In the Know

While it may not seem like a whole lot of money compared to the cost of a burial, Social Security does provide a $255 death benefit for workers who have earned their 40 quarters.

Since these benefits are not automatic and are usually not paid until they are applied for, knowing whether you qualify and applying as soon as possible can mean thousands of dollars more in benefits. An estimate of the survivorship benefits your family would receive is included in the amounts listed on your annual Social Security benefits estimate.

Disability Benefits

In a similar fashion to the survivorship benefits, the Social Security system provides monthly benefits for both adults who become totally disabled, and possibly for children with disabilities. Again, knowing in advance how these valuable programs work will help you to respond quickly should you or someone you know ever face these situations.

Thankfully, the amount of time required to earn disability coverage is much less than is required to earn survivorship and retirement benefits. In fact, an adult 28 years old or younger may have only had to work 1½ years out of the previous 3 years to qualify. For older workers, they may have only had to work for 5 out of the previous 10 years to qualify.

But as easy as it is to earn coverage, the Social Security Administration's definition of disability is one of the strictest you'll find anywhere. In fact, receiving disability coverage often requires extensive case reviews to determine if your disability is expected to last more than a year (or end in death), if you can work at all at any type of job, and how your disability began.

In addition to providing disability coverage for adults who become disabled, Social Security may provide disability coverage for children who have never worked, as well as adults who have been disabled since childhood. Just as with workers who experience a disability, the rules covering these programs are very strict and subject to multiple reviews. However, the goal of these strict guidelines is to guard against people abusing the system, so parents who feel like their child clearly has a need should not feel discouraged about applying.

In the Know

If you receive both disability payments from Social Security and worker's compensation payments, your Social Security disability benefits are reduced to the extent that the combination of the two does not exceed 80 percent of your average monthly income prior to disability.

Medicare

It's often assumed that Medicare and Social Security are the same program because our paychecks are taxed for both of them at the same time. But when retirement comes, they really operate as separate programs. Whereas Social Security is meant to provide for an income in retirement, Medicare is meant to provide basic health-care coverage.

What comes as a surprise to the financially uninformed is that Medicare is not free. Unlike Social Security, which only costs you during your working years, basic Medicare costs roughly $100 per month during your retirement as well. Not only that, Medicare operates like many other health plans in that there are deductibles, limits, and excluded services. Needless to say, those who lack a working understanding of Medicare and thus count on it too much often have their finances turned upside down when the bills finally come.

While this chapter gives you a basic working knowledge, you should spend some time exploring www.medicare.gov and pick up a copy of Lita Epstein's *The Complete Idiot's Guide to Social Security and Medicare, Second Edition* (see Appendix B) for more information.

Medicare Parts A and B

Standard Medicare is divided into two parts, each covering different types of services. Part A, also known as Hospitalization, primarily covers emergency services and major illnesses. Part A is free for people 65 and older who have paid into the system for at least 40 quarters (similar to Social Security). People who have not acquired the full 40 quarters can still purchase Medicare Part A at a discounted rate, which is typically much cheaper than buying private insurance, especially if there are pre-existing conditions. Enrollment in Part A is automatic if you are receiving Social Security benefits at or before age 65. People delaying Social Security past age 65 have to voluntarily enroll if they want coverage.

Medicare Part B, which requires all participants to pay a monthly premium, covers regular medical visits, preventative care, and ongoing outpatient treatments. Most participants pay just under $100 per month for the Medicare B premiums, but this can increase up to 350 percent for higher income retirees—something that catches many people's budgets by surprise. Additionally, failure to enroll in Part B at age 65 results in a 10 percent premium penalty for each year you delay.

Your Bottom Line
Despite what many people think, Medicare will not cover the majority of costs for long-term care needs arising from diseases such as Alzheimer's. Currently, Part A covers retirees 100 percent for the first 20 days, requires a deductible of roughly $135 for each day up until the hundredth day, and then stops long-term coverage altogether. Retirees should plan carefully to cover these additional costs.

While I'd refer you to *The Complete Idiot's Guide to Social Security and Medicare, Second Edition,* for a more detailed breakdown of what specific services are covered, you should add to your financial IQ the list of some major expenses that are not covered by Part B:

- Dental care
- Eye exams
- Hearing aids
- Most prescriptions
- Many long-term care costs

Medicare Parts C and D

Medicare Part C is an optional insurance program that lets retirees receive their entire medical care through a local insurance provider, with the majority of the premiums paid for through Medicare Part A. Some additional premiums might be required, but the overall cost is usually equivalent to what they were previously paying under Part B.

For many consumers, Medicare Part C provides an increased level of benefits and quality of care because the local insurance company is able to operate more cost efficiently. These savings are then passed on to the retiree, who typically receives extra types of preventative care, eye exams, lower deductibles, etc. While you are not required to trade in your Parts A and B coverage for Part C coverage, many find this to be a wise choice.

In the Know

Though less popular than before the introduction of Medicare Part C, Medigap policies are supplemental policies that are sold to cover some of the holes in the existing Part A and Part B coverage. Retirees in rural areas without access to a major medical network may still want to consider Medigap coverage over Medicare Part C.

Medicare Part D, also known as Prescription Coverage, was signed into law under President George W. Bush and began January 1, 2006. Under this program, Medicare recipients can pay an additional premium and receive prescription drug coverage, a cost that was financially crippling many retirees. Unlike Medicare Part A and Part B, which is standardized by the government, the details of a Part D plan vary from provider to provider.

The Least You Need to Know

- By your early 60s you need to think through whether you'll draw Social Security before or after your normal retirement age.

- Build your budget around the possibilities of your Social Security being taxed, and/or reduced for other income you earn.

- Make sure your spouse and dependents know about their survivorship benefits under Social Security.

- Take a look at what Medicare does and doesn't cover and make sure your current savings reflect your potential needs.

- Avoid the potential 10 percent annual penalty on Medicare Part B enrollment by enrolling immediately when you turn 65, unless you're still covered by another plan.

Chapter 17

Safety Nets for Hard Times

In This Chapter

- ◆ Don't feel guilty about getting help
- ◆ Using your own assets first
- ◆ Meeting the basic needs
- ◆ An overview of bankruptcy

I'm not a huge fan of boxing, but there's one type of highlight reel that always catches my attention. It's that rare occurrence where a boxer throws a punch, misses the other boxer, and smacks the referee square in the face. Of course, the referee, not expecting to take one of these monstrous blows, drops like a sack of potatoes.

That's not unlike our personal finances at times. You may do everything by the book, saving diligently, investing intelligently, and spending cautiously. But out of nowhere, life throws you a sucker punch and you find yourself face down on the financial mat. Maybe your company got bought out, you get sued, or the worst economy in a century comes knocking at your door.

If and when these times come, even people with the highest of financial IQs often don't know what to do next. It's like they've been dropped in the middle of some foreign country without a map, a dictionary, or a clue how to find their way home. Thankfully, though, there's an "embassy" on the corner that we can duck into to get help and find our way home.

Don't Let Pride Get in the Way

The lousy economy of the last half decade has tested many people's deeply held beliefs about things like bankruptcy, welfare, and government assistance. When everything was going swimmingly, many people thought these programs and laws unfairly helped people who weren't willing to help themselves. Now they find themselves trying to decide if they're going to give in and utilize these programs.

While there's no doubt that these systems are flawed and abused from time to time, many are now coming to see what they truly are meant to be—safety nets that keep hardworking Americans afloat while they figure out what to do next. As such, I always tell people that if you have no intention of abusing these programs, then you shouldn't feel bad about using them when you truly do need them. Remember, when times were good, it was your tax dollars that you paid into the system to support these programs. You should view it simply as reaping some benefit for the investments you've made out of your paycheck.

> **Your Bottom Line**
>
> With the Federal Unemployment Tax (FUTA) running at 6.2 percent on the first $7,000 in wages, the average American worker is paying at least $400 per year into the unemployment system. With that in mind, you should not feel bad about taking it when you truly need it!

Tapping Your Own Assets

Most people, before they rely on outside assistance, will naturally want to tap their own resources, whether it's their 401(k), insurance policies, or other investments. Of course, there's a right way and a wrong way to do this, as well as "resources" that most people should avoid tapping.

The most important rule in keeping things afloat is to avoid strategies that create problems later even though they solve problems now. This would include creating high-interest-rate debt or withdrawing money from retirement plans without accounting for the eventual taxes due.

Retirement plans are often the go-to asset for many people in financial hardship. That's no surprise, considering that it's a pile of money with your name on it, and it's easy to get access to whether it is through a loan or a hardship withdrawal. But before you just start pulling money out, consider this list of where (and how) to pull it from, prioritized from most desirable to least:

♦ **Roth IRA contributions.** While the earnings on your invest-ments are taxable and subject to a 10 percent IRS penalty if used for the wrong thing or at the wrong time, your actual contribu-tions can be withdrawn at any time without penalty or taxation. So if you've stuck $20,000 into your Roth IRA over the last few years and it's now worth $30,000, you could take out the original $20,000 without penalty or tax.

♦ **Penalty-free IRA distributions.** If you incur certain expenses during a year in which you're experiencing a hardship, you can withdraw an amount equal to those expenses without being slapped with the 10 percent IRS penalty (traditional IRA owners would still pay taxes on the withdrawn amounts). These situations include unreimbursed medical expenses in excess of $7\frac{1}{2}$ percent of your adjusted gross income, college tuition for you or your family, and health insurance premiums if you got laid off. All these excep-tions have complex rules attached to them, so be sure to review IRS Publication 590 before you make your withdrawal.

♦ **401(k) and retirement plan loans.** After tapping the "free" money in your IRAs, the next best place to pull money from is your employer retirement plan by way of a loan. The fact that you are taking this money in the form of a loan has two primary benefits. First, you're being forced to repay it as long as you con-tinue your employment with that company. Second, the loan is not considered a taxable event in the eyes of the IRS, unless you later get fired or laid off.

◆ **72t distributions.** If you're within 5 to 10 years of retirement and it looks like you're going to need a substantial amount of money to tide you over, consider setting up a Section 72t withdrawal plan for your retirement account. This IRS rule allows you to take money from your retirement accounts before normal retirement age without paying the 10 percent early withdrawal penalty. However, you must take the calculated withdrawal for at least five years and until at least age 59½ if you elect this option.

◆ **Hardship withdrawals.** After you've exhausted all the other loopholes in getting money out of your retirement plans, consider taking a normal hardship withdrawal. This means that you're under age 59½ and don't meet any of the other exceptions for tax or penalty-free withdrawals. Just be sure to set aside some money for taxes and penalties (usually 30 to 40 percent) out of the distributed amount. Otherwise you may find yourself in trouble with the IRS when tax time rolls around.

Watch Your Back

While it might be tempting to use credit cards or borrow against your home to help make ends meet, this should be avoided since it will slowly increase your monthly debt payments while simultaneously putting downward pressure on your credit score. It may feel like a quick fix, but in the long run it'll only make it that much harder to get your feet back on the ground.

Day-to-Day Survival

It's hard to get your feet back on the ground when your power has been shut off, your fridge is empty, and you can't put gas in your car to get to an interview. That's why you shouldn't hesitate to access programs that make sure you and your family can function well enough to move forward with minimal disruption. Chances are, by taking advantage of these safety nets early, you'll actually avoid being more dependent on them over the long haul.

Unemployment Insurance

Although you've likely noticed that both federal and state unemployment taxes are collected from your paychecks, most Americans are really only covered by the unemployment program offered by their state. The money collected by the federal government is primarily used to help fund the state programs with which it partners.

While each state may vary slightly in how their unemployment programs work, they're all basically the same when it comes to the key components such as qualifying conditions, benefit amount, and application procedures. Here's what you need to know:

In the Know

A great starting place for all things related to unemployment benefits is the Department of Labor's website at atlas.doleta.gov/unemploy. This website includes a clickable map with links to each state's unemployment insurance website.

- **Benefit amount.** Benefits are typically based on an individual's wages earned during a base period prior to their unemployment. For most people, this translates to a weekly unemployment check ranging from $40 to $450, with variations between states with higher and lower costs of living.

- **Benefit period.** Most unemployment programs cover residents for 9 to 26 weeks out of any rolling 12-month period (not necessarily a calendar year). Additionally, many states offer extended benefits (typically 13 weeks) that are available for people who meet certain criteria.

- **Eligibility requirements.** To be eligible for unemployment benefits, you generally must be able to prove previous employment in the state you're seeking benefits from, have been laid off from your previous job, and show participation in the job-hunt process.

- **Application process.** Thankfully, the days of the humiliating lines at the unemployment office are on the decline. Many states now allow you to apply or reapply for unemployment benefits online or by phone.

◆ **Part-time work.** If you are able to secure some part-time employment or odd jobs, your state may not reduce your unemployment benefit completely. Most states use a formula that phases out the benefit you receive as you earn more than certain amounts.

◆ **Taxability.** Unemployment benefits are taxable, just like wages earned from an employer.

Watch Your Back

While it might be tempting to use pawnshops or payday loans to help make ends meet, do everything you can to avoid these options. The interest charged on borrowing at these establishments can easily run 250 to 500 percent annually, leaving desperate consumers only further behind financially.

SNAP, WIC, and Other Programs

Especially if you have a family with multiple children, putting food on the table can be one of the largest expenses aside from the roof over your head. From a psychological perspective, an empty pantry can induce as much anxiety-induced paralysis and depression as any other facet of being temporarily unemployed. Those reasons make government food programs a key stepping stone for many individuals and families in transition.

Officially called nutritional assistance programs, these programs help to ensure that basic dietary needs are met, especially for children. Considering the rising cost of food, even a small amount of financial assistance in this area can ensure that limited funds can be used for other essentials such as utilities and medical care.

Even if you are temporarily displaced or one partner is out of work, you shouldn't feel guilty or nervous about using these programs. Applying is simple and the use of benefits is discreet—there are no sirens that go off at the store when you purchase food under one of the programs:

◆ **The Supplemental Nutrition Program (SNAP).** This program, formerly known as the Food Stamps program, provides roughly $100 per month for each member of your household. To qualify, your income must be at or near the poverty line, which would calculate to roughly $1,500 to $2,000 per month. Benefits are added on a monthly basis to an EBT card, which looks and functions like a debit card.

◆ **Women, Infants, and Children (WIC).** The WIC (pronounced "wick") program ensures that pregnant women and children under five get their basic needs met through monthly allotments of things like milk, cheese, eggs, peanut butter, etc. To qualify, a family of four must currently earn less than $32,000 to $33,000 per year.

◆ **School lunch programs.** While it may only seem like a drop in the bucket, receiving a free or discounted school lunch five days a week can keep much-needed cash in a parent's pocket. There are both federal and state programs that help to ensure every child who qualifies receives a healthy lunch. Check with your local school or district for more information.

The Earned Income Credit

Many people, even those that decry welfare, have received government benefits at some point in their life in the form of the *Earned Income Credit (EIC)*. They didn't realize it, though, since they probably thought they had just lucked out and received a big tax return around April 15th. The EIC is the government's way of giving a leg up to lower-income taxpayers. For many individuals and families experiencing hard times, the EIC can feel like a gift from above.

def•i•ni•tion

The **Earned Income Credit (EIC)** is a fully refundable credit offered to lower-income taxpayers. It provides a tax refund for qualifying taxpayers, even if they haven't paid anything into the system. The size of the credit varies with the number of dependents a taxpayer claims on their return.

If you or someone you know has fallen on hard times and may qualify for the EIC, you don't necessarily have to wait until April 15th to get it. In fact, certain taxpayers can receive a portion of their EIC in each paycheck from their employer through a program called the Advanced Earned Income Credit. This can be especially helpful month to month for someone who didn't previously qualify for the EIC, but then experienced a pay cut or was forced to find a new job at a much lower wage. For more information on the Earned Income Credit, check out IRS Publication 596.

One of the go-to sources for Americans struggling with high medical costs from a disability, as well as struggling widows or widowers raising children, is the Social Security Administration. If you or a spouse has paid into the Social Security system for at least 5 to 10 years, there's a good chance that you may have hundreds, even thousands of dollars in monthly assistance available to you. For more on this, be sure to review Chapter 16 and visit www.ssa.gov.

Bankruptcy: Hitting the Reset Button

While most people in North America stay fed, clothed, and warm even in hard times, it's often at the expense of caring for their debts. That makes sense, of course, since putting food on the table is more urgent for most people than making sure their credit card company gets their minimum payment.

That means though, people experiencing even minor prolonged hardships can see their debts balloon out of control and past the point of no return. That's where bankruptcy can, for some, be like pressing a reset button. When they become too overloaded and stop functioning, they can reboot. Although they often have to start over from scratch, it's a lot better than remaining frozen and without hope.

What Bankruptcy Can Do

The ability for consumers to walk away from debts has been reeled in substantially in the last few years. But the legislation that has driven the tightening of rules wasn't so much about keeping truly desperate Americans from getting a fresh start. Rather, it was about clamping down on people who have made bankruptcy a lifestyle. These people, who would file bankruptcy every five to seven years, were costing corporate America a ridiculous amount of money which was, in part, passed on to the rest of us.

With that in mind, it's important to remember that bankruptcy is designed (or has been refined) to help get people back on their feet—something legislators have realized can be done without just erasing debts. Thus, much of what bankruptcy is likely to do for you now is to help create a barrier between you and ravenous creditors by creating a court-ordered payment plan.

In the Know

Though bankruptcy has the power to stop the collection actions of certain creditors and even wipe out certain debts, it doesn't protect you from everything. Generally speaking, IRS balances, state and government taxes, and some student loans are exempt from bankruptcy protection.

The Downside of Bankruptcy

When wrestling with the decision whether or not to file bankruptcy, many might feel that it comes down to a battle between pride and convenience. But high financial IQ individuals know that the decision to file bankruptcy is, first and foremost, a financial one. You have to balance the immediate benefits a bankruptcy brings with the reality that it may ripple throughout the rest of your financial life.

Most importantly, it's key to realize that a bankruptcy stays on your credit report for 7 years in the case of a Chapter 11 (payment plan) bankruptcy, and 10 years in the case of a Chapter 7 (total bankruptcy). That means that you're going to have an extremely hard time getting loans at reasonable rates (if at all), renting a home, and maybe even getting a job for the foreseeable future.

But even though a bankruptcy eventually drops off your record, it doesn't mean that it won't still haunt you. There's a good chance that half the applications you'll see, for everything from loans to jobs to apartments, will have a question about former bankruptcies. And while it might be tempting to omit your financial past, lying on some applications can actually be considered an imprisonable offense!

That's not to mention just the immediate costs of filing bankruptcy. Many consumers don't realize until they've already started the filing process how the bills can really stack up. Between the attorney fees, court fees, time off work, etc., you can easily spend a couple thousand dollars on bankruptcy proceedings. Of course, that's a little maddening for people who only owed $10,000 to $20,000 in debts! With all these things in mind, bankruptcy should remain an option of last resort. So before you resign yourself to bankruptcy, take a look at the resources in Appendix B, do your homework, and sleep on the decision.

The Least You Need to Know

◆ Welfare and unemployment are part of every high financial IQ individual's arsenal for making it through tough times that are beyond their control.

◆ Due to the taxes and penalties, it's important to think strategically about how you tap your retirement nest egg for emergencies.

◆ Using SNAP, WIC, and free lunch programs can free up hundreds of dollars each month that can be used to keep you afloat.

◆ Consider bankruptcy only as a last resort, since the present and future costs are often far more than most people bargain for.

Chapter 18

Keep Growing Your Financial IQ

In This Chapter

- The 1-2-3-4 plan for growing your financial IQ
- Key questions to ask
- Finding a financial mentor
- Passing your financial IQ on to your kids

One of my college professors said something to me once that has stuck with me and shaped all my future learning endeavors. He said, "All I ever learned in college was how little I really know." That's a great picture for what you've accomplished in this book. While you now know more than 99 percent of consumers, you also hopefully have a sense of just how much there really is left to learn. We've just scratched the surface in 16 different areas of personal finance and money management. In reality, I could write an entire book covering all the nuances and need-to-know information on each one of these topics.

So like any good graduation speaker, I'm now going to call on you to press on, to expand your knowledge and experiences, and to pass on your knowledge to those who don't have it. I want you to use this book as a springboard into the other areas you need to study and grow your financial IQ in.

But don't just expect it to happen by osmosis or chance; you've got to be deliberate in your acquisition of a greater financial IQ. You've got to put yourself in the path of people smarter than yourself, whether they are authors, educators, or professionals willing to share their knowledge.

If you stop here and don't keep expanding your financial IQ, you'll slowly slip behind. Because the financial world is constantly evolving, including the ways that professionals seek to make a living off of your financial goals, you'll become more and more vulnerable if you don't invest the time to stay sharp. To continue to learn is to remain the master of your own financial destiny. To stop learning is to turn over your financial destiny to someone else with the hopes that they'll look out for you more than themselves.

The 1-2-3-4 Financial IQ Study Plan

Another saying that has stuck with me over the years is that failure to plan is planning to fail. In other words, if you don't come up with a deliberate plan to grow your financial IQ, if you hope it just happens by chance, you probably won't. But if you layout a framework of the things you're going to do regularly, just like how you'd train for a marathon, chances are you'll make it to the financial finish line.

So I want to suggest for you an annual 1-2-3-4 financial IQ study plan that, if followed, should keep you at the top of your game and ahead of the curve. It's an annual cycle that involves some reading, some conversations, and even a class or two. It shouldn't take you more than an hour or two per week, which is a small price to pay for the results I can guarantee it will yield.

One Class Per Year

As much as I appreciate a good financial book, there are few things that can replace the live learning experience. The expertise, the discussions, even the environment, help many of us to learn in different ways than when we just read. With that in mind, look into taking one class per year, whether it is a weekend conference, a weekly class at your junior college, or even an online class.

Watch Your Back

Do your homework before attending any seminar or workshops. Many financial advisors and other people marketing financial services offer free workshops as a way to attract new clients. Even workshops held at local libraries and community centers, with generic-sounding names, are often cleverly disguised marketing gimmicks.

Many people are surprised to learn that most local community colleges offer extension and emeritus classes for adults who simply want to expand their knowledge on certain subjects, without necessarily getting a degree. One of my local community colleges offers short-term classes in everything from investing in real estate, to tax preparation, to reading stock charts. Best of all, the classes are usually taught by local professionals and are, by the school's demand, free from any type of sales pitch. It's simply a sharing of knowledge between adults.

If you don't have a community college in your area, or the idea of sitting in a room full of strangers gives you uncomfortable flashbacks to high school homeroom, there's good news. The Internet has changed everything when it comes to expanding your financial IQ and learning from some of the most brilliant minds on the face of the planet.

Many colleges, including elite schools like Yale, Stanford, Berkeley, Duke, and MIT, now offer the public the ability to audit courses online for free. In other words, you can watch via webcam or prerecorded video as financial and economic gurus teach classes on every financial subject imaginable. Many of the classes have online chat rooms to go along with them, where people like you and me can discuss what is being taught.

Here's an example of some recent classes offered online for free:

- Yale: Financial Markets
- Rutgers: Investing in Your Future
- Purdue: Planning for a Secure Retirement

- MIT: Entrepreneurial Finance
- Utah State: Family Finances

Check out Appendix B for information on online classes.

Two Magazine Subscriptions

While I've emphasized the financial media's tendency to make often contradictory investment recommendations on a regular basis, that doesn't mean you should abandon the financial press. While I would strongly advise against building your portfolio around the recommendations you find in personal finance magazines, these same publications are often a treasure trove of great financial IQ–type articles. They regularly include tips and stories on avoiding getting scammed, getting the best deals, new government programs, changes in the tax laws, etc.

By investing just $20 to $30 and subscribing to a couple of the more popular personal finance magazines (see Appendix B for a full list of my recommendations), you'll be peppered with bite-size and easy-to-read nuggets of useable information. Be careful to not let your quest for knowledge overwhelm you, though. It's not uncommon for people to subscribe to too many magazines, become overwhelmed, and not read any of them. Stick with a couple of magazines initially, and then add more as you find you have the time and interest.

Three Books

Whether they are more of the *Complete Idiot's Guide* series (there's one that expands on almost every chapter in this book) or books by other authors and publishers, you should set the goal of reading three personal finance books per year. If you give yourself three months to slowly read each book, it fits perfectly with the goal of also taking one class per year. That means that every three months, you're either sitting in on a good class, or sitting down with a good book.

I'd strongly suggest that you mix up the topics and the authors to keep it interesting and keep your knowledge from becoming lopsided. In addition to the recommendations you'll find in Appendix B, search for user-created lists of personal finance book recommendations on the major online book retailers.

In the Know

Before you shell out $10 to $20 three times per year for personal finance books, be sure to check out the growing trend of book swapping. Websites like www.paperbackswap.com and www.bookmooch.com let you exchange previously read books with other readers for just the cost of shipping.

Four Quarterly Reviews

Above all else, your quest for boosting your financial IQ should be driven by your financial situation, not what classes, magazines, or books are most popular at the time. To ensure that you're both applying the knowledge that you've acquired, as well as identifying areas where you need to grow your knowledge, you should sit down and review your own financial situation once every three months.

You don't need to spend multiple days giving yourself a complete "financial physical" (that probably only needs to happen once per year), but you should be asking yourself some basic questions on a regular basis. These questions will both keep your finances out of trouble, as well as shape the types of books, magazines, and classes you utilize.

Here are some key questions to ask yourself:

◆ What has been my most significant financial frustration in the last six months?

◆ What is the biggest financial event or challenge I'll face in the coming six months, year, and five years?

◆ Am I on track for my various savings goals (retirement, children's college, emergency fund, etc.)?

◆ How are my investments doing? Are there aspects that I don't understand as well as I should?

◆ Have there been any major changes recently to the economy, investment markets, or laws that I don't understand?

Smart People Ask Questions

Everyone's probably heard a teacher, at least once in their life, say there are no stupid questions. Nowhere is this truer than with financial IQ. While it might be tempting to pretend, especially after you've read a few books or attended a few classes, that you know everything about everything, don't give in to that pressure.

In reality, the smartest people I know in any subject are the ones who incessantly ask questions. It's no different for those with a high financial IQ. Whether it is about their investments, about their advisors, or about broad financial concepts, they keep asking these critical questions:

◆ **Will this help achieve my goals?** When it comes to personal finances, the question that underlies all others is whether or not a decision moves you toward your goals or away from them.

◆ **What's in it for me?** High financial IQ individuals, while they might believe in the overall goodness of mankind, also recognize that much of the financial world has a hidden agenda. They're always keeping an eye out for how conflicts of interest are shaping the other guy's recommendations.

◆ **What does it cost?** Since the number one conflict of interest is profit, savvy consumers are always looking at the costs. They recognize that nothing is free, even if you're not paying fees that you can see. While they're not opposed to paying for good help and advice, they want to know exactly what it costs them so they can make an informed decision.

◆ **What's the risk?** Virtually every financial decision, investment, strategy, and purchase has a risk associated with it. Sometimes there is a direct risk of loss, other times there is an opportunity cost of making one decision and foregoing another. Either way, they are always looking for the downside.

◆ **What am I missing?** High financial IQ individuals know that they live in a world dominated by the fine print. They take the time to read it, clarify it, and even renegotiate it to ensure that they aren't caught off-guard by what someone failed to mention.

In your quest to boost your financial IQ, it's important to realize that the most important people to ask are your advisors. It's also important to realize that the best way to get honest answers, and even a free education, is to make them understand that you're not trying to be adversarial, but responsible. Explain to them that you value and want to develop long-term relationships with professionals who take the time to explain and educate you as to what's going on. Chances are, you'll learn as much from a willing professional as you will anywhere else.

Find a Financial Mentor

Mark Twain once said of his father, "When I was a boy of 14, my father was so ignorant I could barely stand to have the old fool around. But when I got to be 21, I was astonished by how much he had learned in seven years." Mr. Twain makes a great point about the wisdom that comes with age and the foolishness of youth, which applies as much to our financial IQ as it does to any other subject. If we could just be wise enough to listen to those with a few more years under their belt, we'd probably save ourselves a lot of financial heartache.

I know it has been true for me, especially as a newly minted financial planner over a decade ago. If it weren't for a wise and battle-scarred mentor (my father), I would have likely been making the same mistakes for my clients that many of my peers were. Instead, thanks to someone being willing to share both his time-tested strategies, as well as his mistakes and missteps, I was able to accelerate my learning curve and reach my goals faster.

Watch Your Back

One of the worst places to find financial advice is in online chat rooms, message boards, and websites that rely on user-generated answers. While you may occasionally find a nugget of good advice, it is usually intermingled with incorrect advice provided by people with no professional experience in the topics being discussed.

I don't know who that person can or should be in your life, but I do know beyond a shadow of a doubt that you should have one. Whether you call them a mentor, a sage, or just a really smart friend, it's ideal that you can regularly bounce your newly acquired knowledge and the subsequent decisions off someone else. Even better, they should feel the freedom to speak freely, telling you when they believe you're putting yourself in harm's way or drawing the wrong conclusions.

Since no one's yet developed a "dating service" for people searching for financial mentors, your best bet is going to be to look around your own world for some candidates. Here are some guidelines on what to ask for:

- **Choose stability over swanky.** In choosing a financial mentor, you want to choose someone who's been successful at navigating his or her own finances. But it's important to realize that many of the people who drive fancy cars, live in big houses, and take fancy vacations don't possess financial wisdom. In fact, many of them are one paycheck away from losing it all. In choosing a mentor, make sure it is a person who truly has accumulated wealth, is not drowning in debt, and believes that net worth is created through hard work and planning, not get-rich-quick schemes.

- **Think twice before asking family.** While some of the easiest success stories to identify might be your own family members, think carefully before you open up your finances to them. Whether it is them giving you a bad piece of advice or you not taking their good advice, the potential is there for some awkward holiday dinners.

In the Know

Sometimes talking about debt problems can be too uncomfortable with even the closest of friends and family. To receive individualized advice and mentoring in debt problems for a relatively low cost, visit the website for the National Foundation for Credit Counseling at www. nfcc.org.

- **Ask to meet once per month.** The best relationships, mentoring and otherwise, have very clear and defined expectations. Asking successful people to take out time to share their wisdom with you is a big commitment, so help them know what to expect. Ideally, you should ask them to meet with you once per month for a year, after which you can both reevaluate. Also consider asking them to read the same books you're reading, so that you can bounce your new ideas off them.

Passing Along Your Financial IQ

Just as it is a huge gift to you when someone takes the time to share their hard-earned wisdom, it is also a gift for you to do it with others. This is especially true with children if you have them, considering that so many young adults nowadays are financially illiterate.

But don't just look at it as another parental obligation. Increasing your children or grandchildren's financial IQ has a couple of bonuses that pay wonderful dividends. First and foremost, you'll help to ensure that your children become financially independent and do not continue to drain large amounts of money from your financial goals during their adulthood. Second, you'll go a long way toward guaranteeing that the wealth you eventually pass on to them, the wealth that you worked so hard to accumulate, will not evaporate.

Getting kids interested in investing doesn't have to be hard if you use the right resources. In fact, there are a number of mutual funds out there that are designed to help educate children about investing, including the Stein Roe Young Investors Fund and the Monetta Young Investor Fund.

Helping your children develop their financial IQ isn't rocket science. You don't have to set up a classroom or get them to read this book. You simply have to share your own financial journey with them. Talk to them about the financial decisions they're making and how you successfully or unsuccessfully made similar decisions at the same age. Whether it is a young child trying to decide how to spend their allowance, or a college graduate trying to decide which job offer to accept, sharing your experiences without providing the answers may be one of the smartest things you ever do.

The Least You Need to Know

◆ If you don't continue to challenge your financial IQ, it'll be a matter of time before your knowledge is outdated and you're at greater risk.

◆ Utilize the 1-2-3-4 plan to keep your financial IQ growing throughout the year.

◆ Some of the best educational opportunities are available for free online through some of the most respected colleges in the United States.

◆ There's no reason to repeat the same mistakes that a financial mentor can help you avoid.

◆ Passing your financial IQ on to your kids will help protect their money—and yours!

Appendix A

Glossary

12b-1 fees A fee charged by a mutual fund meant to cover its marketing expenses; part of this fee is passed on to the broker who sold it.

adjustable rate mortgage (ARM) A mortgage or loan whose interest rate changes at some preset intervals (monthly, yearly, etc.) based on a preset formula.

alternative minimum tax (AMT) Tax system designed specifically to generate revenue from high-income taxpayers who have otherwise legally avoided taxation.

annual percentage rate (APR) A method of calculating the interest rate you're being charged on an account that enables you to make a side-by-side comparison with other rates.

automated clearing house The ACH system is a financial network that includes most major banks and brokerage houses, which allows free or low-cost transfers of client assets, taking two to three days.

average daily balance A mathematical formula used by banks and credit card companies to calculate eligibility for free services or interest due, that sums the total of all the month's daily ending balances then divides them by the total number of days in the month.

bait and switch A dishonest sales tactic where the consumer is shown or promised one item and which is then replaced with another item or term right before the sale is completed.

bankruptcy The legal process in which a borrower asks for court protection and assistance in dealing with their creditors.

bid-ask spread The slight difference between what a buyer of a stock, ETF, or closed-end mutual fund will pay, and what a seller would charge, at any given moment.

biweekly mortgage payment A payment plan in which you pay half of your mortgage every two weeks, resulting in an extra month's payment being made every year.

blue-chip stocks Stocks of the biggest and strongest companies in an economy, considered less risky by many investors.

cash value insurance Life insurance that has enhanced premium and savings features in addition to the standard death benefit it provides.

cease and desist A letter sent to a collection agency ordering it to stop all contact with a consumer.

certified pre-owned Used cars that have been thoroughly inspected and repaired according to a manufacturer's standards.

Chapter 7 Refers to bankruptcy proceedings in which an individual's assets are sold and used to pay off debts. Most of the remaining debts after all assets are sold are discharged or erased.

Chapter 11 Refers to bankruptcy proceedings in which an individual is allowed to propose a payment plan to help eliminate debt.

churning Excessive trading or trading recommendations by a stockbroker in order to generate additional commissions and fees.

class-action lawsuit A lawsuit filed on behalf of a large group of people with identical claims and complaints. It's often used when the cost of filing individually would be more than the possible damages recovered.

co-branded product A financial product offered by one company that a second company puts its name on and resells to its own customers.

COBRA Short for Consolidated Omnibus Budget Reconciliation Act, a government act that protects certain financial rights relating to someone's employment, including the ability to continue health-care coverage after termination.

coinsurance The portion of health-care costs that you and your insurance company share on a percentage basis.

combined income Formula used by the IRS to determine if someone's Social Security benefits are taxable.

compound interest Interest that is calculated on both the remaining principal of the loan, as well as the interest that has been added to the loan since the last payment.

comps Also known as *comparable sales* or as a *competitive market analysis (CMA)*, an analysis of what other similar homes in an area have recently sold for.

Coverdell Education Savings Account (ESA) A specialized individual account (as opposed to state-run Section 529 plans) that allows a parent to save for a child's college education. All earnings and growth are permitted to be withdrawn tax-free if used for qualified education expenses.

credit report An individual's history of borrowing money, consistency of repayment, employment, and residences.

credit score An estimate of an individual's likelihood of not repaying a loan. The higher the score, the better.

credit union A financial institution that operates very similar to a bank with the major exception that it is owned by the members who bank there, as opposed to corporate shareholders.

CSS PROFILE Form used by many private colleges to determine if a student qualifies for financial aid.

Department of Housing and Urban Development (HUD) A nonprofit government agency that works to protect the interests of home owners.

discount brokerage firm Lower-cost investment firm that provides the tools for clients who wish to invest on their own.

diversification   The process of spreading your investments across multiple types of assets to lower your portfolio's overall risk.

double-cycle billing   A credit card company practice of calculating your interest on the previous 60 days' average balance instead of 30 days, ensuring a higher interest calculation.

earned income credit (EIC)   A fully refundable tax credit offered to lower-income taxpayers that varies with the number of dependents a taxpayer claims on their return.

ERISA   Short for Employee Retirement Income Security Act, this federal legislative act protects certain employee benefits, namely retirement and pension accounts, as well as retirement health-care coverage.

federal funds wire   A system for transferring money that utilizes the Federal Reserve System, resulting in transfers generally being completed the same day they're started.

Federal Trade Commission (FTC)   Helps protect consumers from unfair business practices.

FICO score   The most widely used credit score, calculated by the Fair Isaac Corporation.

financial aid office   On-campus department that acts as the gateway for all types of financial aid information and applications.

financial IQ   Intelligence of financial issues that goes beyond simple memorization of facts, but also demonstrates the ability to make sense of new situations and protect oneself from being taken advantage of.

financial literacy   Demonstrating knowledge of basic financial concepts and computations.

foreclosure   The process of a bank or lender taking back a house that is collateral for an unpaid mortgage.

Form 1099   An IRS form used to show the amount of the previous year's capital gains, dividend, and interest income that must be reported on a taxpayer's return.

FSBO   Short for "for sale by owner," when a home owner chooses to sell his or her home without the help of a real estate agent.

gap insurance Type of insurance policy that is meant to protect you in the event your car is totaled and your insurance payout is less than what you owe the bank.

good faith estimate (GFE) Form provided by lender to a borrower within three days of completing an application, showing all estimated costs associated with the loan.

HIPAA Short for Health Information Portability and Accountability Act, this act creates federal legislation that protects consumers' private health information from misuse and accidental or intentional disclosure, as well as additional guidelines for how and when a consumer may be denied health coverage.

home-equity line of credit (HELOC) This loan allows a consumer to borrow money against the value of their home, above and beyond their current mortgage.

illustration A sales tool used by life insurance companies to show what the potential premium, cash value, and death benefits would be at each year throughout a policy's existence.

index fund A mutual fund that attempts to replicate the performance of one of the most widely followed stock market indices.

individual retirement account (IRA) Used by individuals to save for retirement. There are two main versions of IRAs, the Roth and Traditional IRA. *See also* Roth IRA *and* Traditional IRA.

inflation The rate at which the cost of our goods and services increase as each year passes.

installment agreement An agreement between a consumer and a business or government agency, usually the IRS, to pay outstanding balances.

long-term care Special insurance policies bought to help cover expenses of having to be placed in a nursing home or similar facility.

modification A process where a mortgage lender changes the term or interest rate of an existing loan without making you go through the entire refinancing process.

mutual fund   An investment in which a group of investors pool their money together to buy stocks, bonds, or other investment assets.

mutual fund family   Term used within the investment industry to refer to a mutual fund management company and all the different funds they offer.

negative amortization mortgage (NegAm)   These loans actually allow you to add your unpaid interest to the loan principal, which causes you to owe more at the end of the month than at the beginning.

net asset value   The raw value of a mutual fund share, before a sales load is added, or a premium or discount has had an effect.

NSF   Abbreviation for nonsufficient funds fee, which is charged when a transaction or withdrawal is placed against an account with less funds present than needed to cover it. *See also* overdraft fee.

Offer in Compromise   An offer made to the IRS to pay a portion of an outstanding debt in exchange for the remaining debt being erased, similar to a debt settlement.

opportunity costs   The opportunity missed when one choice is made over another.

origination fee   Essentially a commission, paid in part to the person who handles setting up your loan.

overdraft fee   Charged when a transaction or withdrawal is placed against an account with less funds than needed to cover the transaction. *See also* NSF.

payday loan   A very high interest loan or advance made against your next paycheck.

payment allocation   The practice of banks applying funds you send above and beyond your minimum payment to the lowest interest rate portion of your balance.

points   A fee, usually expressed in 1 percent increments of a loan's total value, paid at the time of lending to obtain a lower interest rate.

powertrain warranty   Auto warranty that covers the engine itself, some parts of the transmission, and occasionally the drivetrain and the axles.

principal   The remaining portion of a loan's original balance that was borrowed.

prospectus   A document required by the Securities and Exchange Commission which describes the risks, costs, and other details for any newly issued investment security.

reordering   An abusive banking practice where a bank changes the order in which transactions on the same day are processed, to account for the maximum number of overdraft fees.

required minimum balance   A requirement that a bank customer maintain a certain balance each day, week, or month, in order to earn a preferential interest rate or have account fees waived.

retail brokerage firm   Full-service investment firm that focuses on individual client-professional relationships.

Roth IRA   IRA that offers individuals the ability to contribute to their account out of their after-tax income. The proceeds from a Roth IRA may then be withdrawn completely tax-free in retirement.

Section 529 plan   A state-run plan that allows parents to either save money or prepay tuition for their child's college education. When the money is later used for college, the IRS waives all taxation on the growth of the investments.

short sale   When a home owner experiencing financial trouble gets permission from the bank to sell his or her home for less than what is owed on the mortgage.

subprime lending   Loans made to borrowers with below-average credit who consequently pay higher rates and fees for their loans.

term   The length of time, usually expressed in months or years, until a loan with a fixed payment amount is fully repaid.

term life insurance   The most simple and affordable form of life insurance, which provides a cash payment only if the insured party dies within a certain window of time. Term life insurance policies have no cash value or savings component, unlike whole life or cash value insurance.

Traditional IRA   Created in 1986, these accounts allow individuals to receive a tax deduction and tax-protected growth on their retirement savings. Money is taxed when it is finally withdrawn, with a penalty applied if the owner is younger than 59½.

trailer   The ongoing fee paid by a mutual fund to an investment professional whose clients are invested with that fund.

Appendix B

Resources

Here is a list of the resources, organizations, and websites that might be useful to you in your journey to eliminate debt.

Additional Resources from Ken Clark

collegesavings.about.com

www.TheMoneyTherapist.com

The Complete Idiot's Guide to Getting Out of Debt. Alpha Books, 2009.

The Pocket Idiot's Guide to the FairTax. Alpha Books, 2010.

Banking Resources

Find the best interest rates: Bankrate.com; bankdeals.blogspot.com

Learn more about banking: banking.about.com

Safety of your bank deposits: Banks—www.myfdicinsurance.gov; Credit unions—www.ncua.gov

Credit Cards

Find the best deals on credit cards: www.epinions.com/credit_cards; www.creditcards.com; www.cardratings.com

For info about the Credit Cardholders' Bill of Rights: www.creditcardrights.net

Learn more about credit cards: credit.about.com

Epstein, Lita. *The Complete Idiot's Guide to Improving Your Credit Score*. Alpha Books, 2007.

Your credit card rights: www.FTC.gov/credit

Credit agencies and scoring:

Free Annual Credit Report
Annual Credit Report Request Service
PO Box 105281
Atlanta, GA 30348
1-877-322-8228
www.annualcreditreport.com

Stop credit card junk mail:

OptOutPreScreen.com
PO Box 600344
Jacksonville, FL 32260
1-888-567-8688
www.optoutprescreen.com

Direct Marketing Association (stops junk mail): www.dmachoice.org/consumerassistance.php

FTC's Do Not Call List (stops telephone solicitations): 1-888-382-1222; www.donotcall.gov

Credit counseling:

National Foundation for Credit Counseling
801 Roeder Rd., Suite 900
Silver Spring, MD 20910
301-589-5600
www.nfcc.org

Investing and Financial Advice

Websites

bonds.about.com

financialplan.about.com

www.investopedia.com

www.morningstar.com

The Motley Fool (www.fool.com)

mutualfunds.about.com

stocks.about.com

Books

Arnold, Curtis E., and Beverly Blair Harzog. *The Complete Idiot's Guide to Person-to-Person Lending*. Alpha Books, 2009.

Buffet, Warren, and Lawrence A. Cunningham. *The Essays of Warren Buffet: Lessons for Corporate America*. The Cunningham Group, 2008.

Epstein, Lita. *The Complete Idiot's Guide to Value Investing*. Alpha Books, 2009.

————. *The Pocket Idiot's Guide to Investing in Mutual Funds*. Alpha Books, 2007.

Fisher, Phillip A. *Common Stocks and Uncommon Profits*. Wiley Investment Classics, 2003.

Gorman, Tom. *The Complete Idiot's Guide to Economics, Second Edition*. Alpha Books, 2010.

Graham, Benjamin. *Securities Analysis*. McGraw-Hill, 2008.

————. *The Intelligent Investor*. Collins Business, 2003.

Kennon, Joshua, Debra DeSalvo, and Edward T. Koch. *The Complete Idiot's Guide to Investing*. Alpha Books, 2006.

Little, Ken. *The Complete Idiot's Guide to Socially Responsible Investing*. Alpha Books, 2008.

————. *The Pocket Idiot's Guide to Investing in Bonds.* Alpha Books, 2007.

Lynch, Peter, and John Rothchild. *One Up On Wall Street.* Simon & Schuster, 2000.

McKay, Charles. *Extraordinary Popular Delusions and the Madness of Crowds.* Wilder Publications, 2009.

Stanley, Thomas, and William Danko. *The Millionaire Next Door.* Pocket Books, 1998.

Magazines and Newspapers

Barron's: www.barrons.com

Consumer Reports & Consumer Reports Money Advisor: www.consumerreports.com

Kiplinger's Personal Finance: www.kiplinger.com

Money: www.money.com

SmartMoney: www.smartmoney.com

The Wall Street Journal: www.wsj.com

Financial Professionals

Certified Financial Planner Boards of Standards
1425 K St. NW, Suite 500
Washington, DC 20005
1-800-487-1497

Financial Planning Association
1600 K St. NW, Suite 201
Washington, DC 20006
1-800-322-4237
www.fpanet.org

Free Financial Advisor Background Checks

For commissioned stockbrokers: finra.org/brokercheck

For fee-based investment advisors: adviserinfo.sec.gov

For insurance agents: www.naic.org/state_web_map.htm

Brokerage Account Safety

Securities Investor Protection Corp (SIPC)
805 15th St. NW, Suite 800
Washington, DC 20005-2215
202-371-8300
www.sipc.org

Owning and Renting a Home

Learn more about real estate: homebuying.about.com

Find an agent: National Association of Realtors—www.realtor.org

For sale by owner resources: www.forsalebyowner.com; www.fsbo.com;
www.owners.com

O'Hara, Shelley, and Nancy D. Lewis. *The Complete Idiot's Guide to Buying and Selling a Home, Fifth Edition*. Alpha Books, 2006.

Sutton, James, and Edie Milligan Driskill. *The Complete Idiot's Guide to Mortgages*. Alpha Books, 2006.

Real estate research tools: www.realestateabc.com; www.realtor.org/research; www.zillow.com

Mortgage calculators: finance.yahoo.com; www.eloan.com;
www.ginniemae.gov

Government and professional organizations:

Department of Housing and Urban Development (HUD): 1-800-333-4636; www.hud.gov

Mortgage Bankers Association
1331 L St. NW
Washington, DC 20005
www.mbaa.org

Tenants rights: www.hud.gov/renting/tenantrights.cfm

Health-Care Costs

Learn more about health care: healthinsurance.about.com

Driscoll, Marilee. *The Complete Idiot's Guide to Long-Term Care Planning*. Alpha Books, 2002.

Driskill, Edie Milligan. *The Pocket Idiot's Guide to Health Savings Accounts*. Alpha Books, 2006.

Freidman, Mark L., and Donna Raskin. *The Complete Idiot's Guide to Medical Care for the Uninsured*. Alpha Books, 2008.

Health insurance company ratings and rankings: www.jdpower.com/insurance; reportcard.ncqa.org

Health insurance consumers' rights: www.dol.gov/ebsa; www.naic.org/consumer_health_rights.htm

College Planning Resources

Learn more about college planning: collegesavings.about.com; www.finaid.org

Rye, David. *The Complete Idiot's Guide to Financial Aid*. Alpha Books, 2008.

Student loan resources:

Department of Education
1-800-4FED-AID—General
1-800-621-3115—Defaulted student loans
www.studentaid.ed.gov

SallieMae
PO Box 3800
Wilkes-Barre, PA 18773
1-888-272-5543
www.salliemae.com

IRS and Tax Resources

Learn more about taxes: taxes.about.com

Bernstein, Peter W. *Ernst & Young Tax Guide*. PublishNow 2009.

JK Lasser's Your Income Tax. Wiley, 2008.

Internal Revenue Service contacts:

IRS Help Line for individuals: 1-800-829-1040

IRS Help Line for businesses: 1-800-829-4933

National taxpayer advocates: 1-877-777-4778

Important IRS publications (available at www.irs.gov):

Publication 1—*Your Rights as a Taxpayer*

Publication 3—*Armed Forces' Tax Guide*

Publication 17—*Your Federal Income Tax*

Publication 334—*Tax Guide for Small Businesses*

Publication 554—*Tax Guide for Seniors*

Publication 590—*Individual Retirement Accounts (IRAs)*

Publication 594—*The IRS Collection Process*

Publication 596—*The Earned Income Credit*

Publication 908—*Bankruptcy Tax Guide*

Publication 915—*Social Security Benefits*

Publication 950—*Introduction to Estate and Gift Taxes*

Publication 970—*Tax Benefits for Education*

Publication 971—*Innocent Spouse Relief*

Finding a tax professional:

National Association of Enrolled Agents (NAEA)
1120 Connecticut Ave. NW, Suite 460
Washington, DC 20036-3953
202-822-6232
www.naea.org

American Institute of Certified Public Accounts (AICPA)
1211 Avenue of the Americas
New York, NY 10036
1-888-777-7077
www.aicpa.org

Social Security and Medicare Resources

Learn more about Social Security and Medicare: ssa.gov/pgm/
links_survivor.htm; www.aarp.org/socialsecurity; www.ssa.gov/
retirement; www.ssa.gov/disability

Epstein, Lita. *The Complete Idiot's Guide to Social Security and Medicare,
Second Edition*. Alpha Books, 2006.

Social Security retirement planning page: www.socialsecurity.gov/
retire2

Resources for Hard Times

Bankruptcy resources: U.S. Court System—www.uscourts.gov/
bankruptcycourts/resources.html; National Association of Consumer
Bankruptcy Attorneys—www.nacba.org

U.S. Department of Labor—unemployment insurance links: www.ows.
doleta.gov/unemploy

Food and nutrition services—food stamps and other assistance: 1-800-
221-5689; www.fns.usda.gov

Medicaid: 1-800-633-4227; www.cms.hhs.gov

GovBenefits.Gov—links to thousands of government programs: www.
govbenefits.gov

Directories of Online Classes

Open Courseware Consortium: www.ocwconsortium.com

Open Courseware Finder: www.ocwfinder.com

Open Culture: www.oculture.com

Free-Ed.net: www.free-ed.net

Index

W-X-Y-Z